ReR Megacorp/November Books

First published in Great Britain by ReR:
79 Beulah Rd
Thornton Heath
Surrey CR78JG. UK

General Editor for ReR/November Books: **Chris Cutler**
Design and Layout: **Tim Schwartz** | OnionProductions.com
Cover Photo: **Ray Stevenson**

We have done our best to trace and contact the owners of all the images.

ISBN: 978-0-9560184-6-5

GLEN SWEENEY'S

BOOK OF ALCHEMIES

The life and times of
the **Third Ear Band,** 1967-1973
with prologue and epilogue.

Luca Chino Ferrari

General Editor's note:

Many references are made in passing that I'm afraid may not be self-explanatory, especially to readers too far away in space or time from the original events. I was there in the thick of it, so I have taken the liberty of adding a few explanatory footnotes to Luca's text. Any errors and opinions in the footnotes therefore, are mine, not his.

Chris Cutler
London. 2020

In memoriam:
Paul Minns, Mel Davis, Ben Cartland, Mike Marchant, Ron Cort, Roger Bunn, John Hopkins, John Peel, Paul Buckmaster, Glen Sweeney.

The Giant Sun Trolley is coming
League transversing it globally encircuits
Beneath the eversun
Where lances of pain
Become rays of warmth
Emanating mindwards and on
Till, reaching the epiphany
Of space and time
Flash in ozonic splendour
For Cosmic Man.

CONTENTS

I

An Introduction to Glen Sweeney's Alchemies

Glen Sweeney (1924-2005) was an alien. Maybe. Or a prankster. Or a visionary innovator. Probably a mystic of the underground. He was older than the rock & pop generation of the Sixties, more advanced in musical ideas than most. He had intuitions and knowledge of ancient religions, symbols and philosophies. He grasped the drift of Western culture. He was hungry too, and honest enough to admit that he was playing just to get food: one day in 1996 I asked him: "Why did you form the Third Ear Band?" He replied: "Because I was starving and the only thing I wanted to do was to play drums".

Anyway, he was a witty, clever, deep and irresistibly funny chap.

He had boundless memories of roots in Fifties Skiffle and the prehistoric jazz scene, but never filled with nostalgia or pathetic feelings about the 'good old days'; instead, a huge sense of self-irony. Also he made a lot up; it was part of his character. There was always a fine line between reality and imagination...

Reading the interviews selected for this tribute, you can feel his absolute consciousness of his time, the clear contrast between a strong idealism and an awareness of the limit of the Sixties' dream of an 'open society' - a free, libertarian world.

His main band – the Third Ear Band – played for Druids; its music was the soundtrack of many live happenings and events. The choice to play music without words in the *Age of Cheap Philosophies and Empty Babble* was a revolution in itself, the strongest way to celebrate the power of a music able to shake not only the easy areas of the heart (e.g. the Beatles) but the deepest viscera of humanity.

Esoteric, organic, magic, alchemical; these were the tags music journalists applied to Third Ear Band music - a music, as Glen said, that was impossible to classify; a syncretism made by countless references to the British pagan tradition, Alchemy, Druidism, the Egyptian book of dead, pre-Socratic

1

philosophical theories, suggestions from the Sixties Underground (John Mitchel's books, Ufology, the I-Ching, avant-garde art...) and so on.

In this book you will find all the main things written by Glen through the years: a paradox, in a sense, because even if an unrivalled talker, he was always silent behind his hand drums.

You can read his funny and clever interviews with some of the main magazines of the time, rare manifestos – and the lyrics and poems he intended to publish in the last years of his life. Also some very pretty drawings he made for flyers, posters, ads and press releases.

The last section, with some stunning aphorisms, doesn't at all render the true, witty, spirit of the man, but for those who didn't have the privilege of knowing him, it may perhaps offer a vague idea of the extraordinary person he was.

An alchemist of sounds who didn't take the music scene too seriously... his Third Ear Band's recordings are, I think, among the best outputs of the popular music of the time.

Luca Chino Ferrari
November 2019

I was with Glen when he "went cosmic"; the window was open for his spirit to fly, a shaft of sunlight and a peaceful raga playing. Glen convinced me when we first met that he was an Alien, and at this point in time I believed him, once again. We met when we were both working in Liberty's, the iconic Regent Street store. At that time (the early 1960s) around 50% of the staff were "resting" actors or artists. In Glen's case, musicians. His job was in the store's display of modern furniture, which gave him the opportunity to keep his drum-kit in the stockroom, hidden away in the labyrinth beneath the store. A couple of times a week it was packed up and taken to a very bohemian Soho club, *The Cave de France,* where Glen played *avant garde* jazz.

Swinging London began. We got a flat together in Notting Hill. A jazz and poetry group was formed called *Sounds Nova*. Steve Pank appeared on the scene at that time and joined playing trumpet. A few pub gigs materialised before it collapsed.

Tune in turn on drop out. The hippy scene began.

Jobs were abandoned and we existed on dole money, but had time to be very creative. Dave Tomlin and the *Free School,* an audition and another musical adventure: *The Giant Sun Trolley* playing each week at UFO, the all night happening club. Anything was accepted. One night it was Dave, Glen and a tuneful howling dog. We attended many 'far out' happenings and sometimes we were part of them.

Dave waved goodbye and went off to India. *Hydrogen Jukebox* was formed. Glen got the name from *"Howl"*, Ginsberg's epic poem... *'the crack of doom on the Hydrogen Jukebox'*. Indeed it was doomed!

TEB followed, and much of this has been recorded so I need say no more. Always inventive, a creator of wonderful fantasies, Glen was my magical soul mate.

Carolyn Looker
London, October 2019

*"Most memorable image...? Glen dancing the tango with Polanski
in a local pub in Northumbria where they were on location for Macbeth..."*
(Paul Minns, 1996-2018)

II

Glen Sweeney, a Necromancer of the Drifting West

Luca Ferrari

In 1996, when I decided to write a book on the Third Ear Band, I got the kind collaboration of all the members of the group except Richard Coff (apparently no-one knew where he was) and Ursula Smith (I failed to get her address). And I didn't know her husband was Steve Pank, former promoter and driver of the band.

The first title for the book was Tickling the Third Ear and my idea was just to write a chronological and historical reconstruction of the TEB's story, to free the band from that aura of mystery that surrounded it. But just when the essay for the introduction was completed, I decided instead on Necromancers of the drifting West. For me, the Band has advanced the cause of so-called 'World Music', and the multicultural/intercultural dimension of the relations between the West and the rest of the world. At the same time, I think their music was a sort of sign, a premonition of musical and cultural decline in Old Europe (it's for that reason I had the idea of 'necromancers'). They were a strongly political group too, because silence - acoustic (natural) - sounds (no words) – minimalism – aesthetics are all really 'political' in this age of an excess of experiences.

I have to admit now that it was imprudent to write an interpretation of the TEB's music and that probably, read today - even as slightly adjusted for this book – the following short essay is quite outdated, or at least debatable.

I remember I asked Glen and Paul to excuse me for this gamble and they were kind and indulgent enough to do so..

Anyway, here's the old text because, apart from some rather rare attempts, even now there are very few substantial contributions that treat exclusively of the experience of the TEB - and the absolute relevance of Glen Sweeney to the history of popular music.

Music for the 'third ear'

1. For a conscious listening

I'm not persuaded that the sound of a certain historical period in a certain society forecasts the times and social models to come, as the French writer Jacques Attali claimed in his landmark essay *Noise: the political economy of music* in 1977 (English translation 1985).

The immersion in sounds or noises we are subjected to these days seems to reflect the times - of triviality and superficiality - we live in; actually it seems to describe them perfectly - speaking of the deep social and cultural crisis into which Western countries have fallen, and the strong negative impact technology and the Record Industry have had on the music created and used by people.

The anonymous *non-places* (this suggestive expression was coined by the ethnology researcher Marc Augè) in which music is casually used as a simple sound upholstery - keeping company with consumption - suggests the idea that the re-production of sounds and the hidden possibilities of listening to music *everywhere*, have made the listening experience less the *product* of an active and conscious process and more the *result* of passive and unconscious *behavior*.

Advertisers have understood this process and use music to persuade us "in a pleasant way" to buy, revealing our presumed needs to us.

The music that goes deep into our daily life has turned into a *non-place* itself; deprived of any identity, history or relation with the time and place of living, it becomes a sort of undefined and virtual phenomenon.

Music surrounds us, and the chaos it determines (just try to tune into any 'free' radio station...) is a melting pot of commodities that remind us of something "already heard"; the symbolic images it evokes and its strongly iconic aggression fatally betray us and mark the failure of any creative or stimulating ideal of a society in which people listen with open minds...

To oppose chaos with silence, which we only experience from time to time, seems like a quick and naive utopia, since it proposes an escape (a happy island, a pure oasis, an ivory tower) in which some kind of "creative resistance" (an alternative voyage through personal, coherent inner trajectories) might equip us to avoid the risk of being dazed and submerged.

There can be antidotes to this, of course, but they are hard to achieve; a listener has to research deep inside the past and present of popular music, and consider specific phenomena such as:
- the relation between the record market and artistic creation:
 product /commodities *versus* product / art
- the influential role technology plays in the creative process:
 what is the effect of technological innovation and the use of increasingly sophisticated sound-machines?
- the relation between the space and time of listening
- musical *authenticity*, and its effects on listeners' imaginations.

These criteria may help us to achieve a detached approach to the music we are exposed to - and inevitably immersed *in* - every day of our lives. We could at least accept, as an exclusive dimension of experience (not less right than the others, of course) *random listening* - as simple background music.

2. The music of the Third Ear Band

Born and bred in the golden age of European popular music - when the record industry thought it could sell so-called 'alternative' products (*Harvest Records* was one of the first underground labels), the Third Ear Band, between 1969 and 1972, recorded only three albums, as well as playing wherever they could, from free open-air concerts to huge crowds (250,000 at Hyde Park, in 1969) to classical London venues (the Royal Albert Hall, the Purcell Rooms, the Queen Elizabeth Hall, &c.); and from social centres spread across the island and the continent, to 'holy' places like Glastonbury Tor, Stonehenge and Primrose Hill, where they accompanied Druid rituals.

The sound of the band was defined by music critics as 'organic', 'natural', 'mantric' - and the effects produced on listeners as 'relaxing', 'cathartic', 'hypnotic'...

In the life of the band the live dimension was privileged, through its leader and percussionist, Glen Sweeney; it evolved a theory that music has to live through the direct interaction between musician and listener, and thus exist as a *happening event*, unique and unrepeatable.

Sweeney intuited the end of the musical genres of his age (especially jazz), freeing them from their historical and cultural bounds and expanding the sound horizon to 360° - anticipating by almost ten years the phenomenon of so-called *world music.*

It's the mixture of musical genres and subgenres that takes the central role: Indian classical music with its raga forms, acoustic British folk music, free jazz, John Cage's avant-garde sound/silence/noise provocations and Zen randomness: every concert different from every other; every studio session different too, with the clear effect that the few albums recorded in a studio cannot reveal the essential core of the Third Ear Band's music.

Their compositions, sometimes 15-20 minutes long on stage, were composed of elementary and invariable drum patterns, a cello (or later, electric guitar) played mostly to approximate Indian tanpura drones, a violin and an oboe (or later, a flute and a soprano/alto sax), whose fundamental task was to improvise scales related to folk, Indian raga or avant-garde music - or to work with material borrowed from modal free jazz.

3. File under...?

Also, consider TEB's experience as a parable of the political connections existing between Art and the record industry: as soon as the sixties ideal came to an end, the industry closed ranks and cut off all those who couldn't guarantee a minimum profitability. Even after their great work for Roman Polanski's *Macbeth*, which was well-reviewed everywhere, the Third Ear Band was compelled by circumstance to look elsewhere for success. It was these ups and downs that led to the break-up of the band after a short but intense career in which the only compromise they made was to have tried - in a questionable pop-rock turn - to be more accessible to imaginary listeners: these disastrous recordings came to light in 2004, when they were released as *The Magus.*

The band's fate had in any case already been decided on the release of *Alchemy* in 1969, its first album for EMI-Harvest, which was boycotted by the label's managers because the cover and title referred to esoteric practices, the track titles alluded to Eastern religions and the band name was a clear reference to expansion of the mind through music...

British youth culture on the other hand, had by then assimilated the progressive introduction of Eastern philosophies, the I-Ching, LSD, sitars, hashish... and it was logical to them that a group such as TEB should have its own space.

On many occasions Glen Sweeney went along with the religious mandate of his band: "*We can offer a complete dream. The old Celtic Bards used to have the same ability*" he said to *Melody Maker* in July 1969.

But the contradictions exploded on impact when EMI tried, against its commercial instincts, to sell a product that, compared with most British music of the period - which was broadly based on song structures - wasn't at all easy to sell. As TEB's manager, Peter Jenner, said to me, in 1996, "Their sound was unique. The problem was that for classical musicians they were pop, but for pop people their music was too abstract."

Sweeney was perfectly aware of the risks of misunderstanding when he admitted: "The trouble is, you can't be mystical without being called pseudo-mystical. (...) I'm at Glastonbury most of the time, but we're all completely honest about it. We'll even use it honestly to make money, because the ancient Egyptians who were into it all said that you had to be rich because only then could you resist temptation" ("Melody Maker", June 1970).

This attempt failed too because of the unbelievable ingenuousness of Blackhill's management, whose "fame rested as much on the bands they lost as those they retained" the oboist Paul Minns said in 1996) and who believed that a market existed that would be able to 'catch' the good faith of a music that couldn't be wedged into a 45-minute record because, basically, it was born to be played live.

A music that, without pretence, was intended to embody the needs of spirituality and mysticism in the younger generation, proposing a sort of recuperation of the pagan pre-Christian tradition that was already established in Celtic popular culture and that was characterized by pantheistic elements taken from ancient philosophies (TEB's second album "Third Ear Band" was inspired by Empedocles' four elements theory...).

Once the underground youth culture was buried and the record business had triumphed, the seventies of the last century put the final seal on the scene, with technological powerplay coming from 'Progressive' bands, who were inspired, paradoxically, by the only musical form that didn't interest the Third Ear Band: the nineteenth century classical symphony.

In 1988 Sweeney unexpectedly tried to re-propose a technologically updated project of his music with new and controversial results, just when a new music fashion was spreading everywhere, the so-called New Age – a music characterised by elements of sound expansion and looseness.

It was a formula exploited in a hasty way by *Materiali Sonori*, the Italian record company behind the TEB reunion in their spasmodic search for a new audience: the main ambiguity of this experience - due to the evident irrelevance of the Third Ear Band, compared to the emptiness of most New Agers - made the return of the TEB questionable, since it was offered to an audience of professional collectors and nostalgic hippies.

4. Fates.

The Third Ear Band, as a pole star of popular music, showed the way to possible salvation from the aggression and violence of contemporary society, as characterized by an excess of information, images and individualism (again Marc Augè). One could tell it was an unavoidable sacrifice to fight the logic of profit and the stupidity of society: Glen Sweeney, founder and leader of the band, a necromancer of the drifting West, was able to read the viscera of the past and the present, forecasting dark times ahead. *"Music out of time"*, someone wrote - probably too deep and emotional to be tolerable for most listeners - too abrasive to the ears, because shocking to the mind and unbearably poignant to the soul.

III

Poems and Lyrics by Glen Sweeney

Here is the text of *Eternity in D*, a love song written by Glen Sweeney to Carolyn, at the time his muse and inamorata. Originally played by *Giant Sun Trolley* – the band formed by Dave Tomlin and Sweeney in London in 1967, an acoustic duo consisting of guitar, percussion and vocals, and sometimes a trio with bass player Roger Bunn. That year they played a number of gigs, many at the UFO Club, but the most important of which was at the legendary *14-Hour Technicolor Dream* at the old Alexandra Palace, on April 29th, 1967. Years later, on January 17th, 1971, the Third Ear Band reprised the track in instrumental form for a radio session on BBC's "Top Gear".

Eternity in D
Song to Carolyn
She walks in beauty like the night and
Tells me not to get uptight
Her eyes they watch me all the time
One little blink would be a crime.

Her jeans they fit her like a skin
My head is full of mortal sin
The sphinx it winks when she appears
And whispers mysteries in her ears...

Her name is written in the sand
I see the pen and then the hand
The ocean sings a song of love and
Noah is searching for his dove.

The clouds are crying for the moon

Just turn the page to find the rune
A Beatle hides beneath the Stones
And in the distance Dylan moans...
There must be some way out of here
Why does our Jesus not appear

And then her voice says: "Calm your fear:
The womb is not the tomb, my dear".

Poem to Maggie And Ron
This poem was inspired by Ronald Reagan
and Margaret Thatcher. Glen Sweeney, London 1987.

This witch sits spiderwise inside
Her web of lies and cries
'Only he loves me who dies'
And the room filled up with laughter

Ha ha ha ha ha ha

Her master with his
Million sins
His sawn off mind
His seven chins
Sings of
Blood
And death
And slaughter

Tiger
Thanks to Willy Blake

Tiger, Tiger
Burning bright

Soon you'll be
An unknown sight
No more forests
Of the night
Something that
You cannot fight has replaced thy
Fearful symmetry; felled
The soaring jungle tree and
Left a Symbol of our culture:
A Coca Cola tin on which
Stands
A vulture.

The Future Star Wars

There is war in the stars
Venus fights Mars
And earth is ripe for the kill
The prophets of doom
Prepare for the boom
And they teach their kids to kill
It is plain to see
That our destiny
Is to fight till the end of time
And love will become a crime
For the future of man
Is a cosmic plan
By the architects of fear
And the Gods they await
Will arrive too late
With a nod a wink
And a leer.

Animals know best

An unrealised lyrics intended for the Hydrogen Jukebox album written in 1978.

Five portals hath the caverned man
The wise men know it's true
But they spend their lives in academies
Learning who is who

The five colours they do blind the eye
The seven sounds will numb the ear
And learning names and other games
Will lead a man to fear

Telepathy is a portal the wise men all refute
For love is the key
They cannot see
As they argue and dispute

Another portal is the door we're taught to lock and bolt
But fear gets in
Through the pores of the skin
And grips us by the throat

The animals all build their nets
And live their lives for free
And in a way the price they pay
Is a lack of security

But animals don't cling to life
Adventure is their game
And as they die they wink their eye
And say what's in a name?

《 》

What if the Sun stopped shining
All the World turned black
Do you think that with our technology
We would ever put it back – Sun shine -
Moon glow – wind blow – river flow -

Supposing the birds started talking
And they told us all they know
Do you think we all would listen
Do you think it would make us know -
Moon glow – rivers flow – tree glow -
Winds blow

And what if the stars were friendly
And flying saucers were real
Do you think it would make us happy
Do you think it would help us feel
Winds blow – Moon glow – rivers flow

Do you think if we're all immortal
And none of us ever felt dead
Do you think that we would find the time
To watch a spider spin his web
Winds blow – Moon glow – river flow

Don't you think that we should
Worship this sun that gives us life
Instead of these human (other) idols
That cause all our trouble and strife
Winds blow – Moon glow – river flow – tree glow.

« »

Science is wonderful don't you agree
Just press the switch on your colour TV

Children who watch five murders each night
Lose touch with reality
But the parents just hiss
Cause they don't want to miss
The tales of banality

Science is wonderful don't you agree
Just press the switch on your colour TV

Glittering prizes are given away
On shows where people perform
Acts so outrageous
That even God who made us
Would turn his back in scorn

Science is wonderful don't you agree
Just press the switch on your colour TV

Advertisers cast spells
And invent new hells
That only their products can cure
But each magic name
Has the same silly claim
It's gonna make you as young as before

Science is wonderful don't you agree
Just press the switch on your colour TV

Politicians all dream
Of the nightmare screen
Where the cameras pan to and fro
And every pore on the skin
Gives away a sin
That the make-up man said wouldn't show

Science is wonderful don't you agree
Just press the switch on your colour TV

Now pigs they don't fly
And the cameras don't lie
What you see is what you get
And if it don't taste the same
You should have used your brain
Instead you got ripped off again

Science is wonderful don't you agree
Just press the switch on your colour TV.

« »

Have you heard the sound of one hand clapping
have you heard the sound of one man rapping
tired of sleeping in the street
want somewhere to rest your feet
Have you heard the sound of one hand clapping
have you heard the sound of one man rapping
tired of politicians lies
don't listen with your ears
listen with your eyes.

« »

Who has locked the doors we opened
Who has folded up the afternoon
Who has stolen from waters
Our reflection of the Moon
The automobile had become the altar
The priests are all wearing
Overalls white and in the darkness
Of our future the sacrifices

Scream all night

The sacred oil is running low now
Already it is more precious than blood
And forty thousand Noahs are watching
For the first signs of the flood
The farmers' field are lying empty
The chemical sprays have stripped them bare
No mice or birds or rabbits inhabit them
The polythene trees bloom everywhere
As I sit before my mirror
Snakes and lizards invade my room
Who has taught them this song they are hissing
Who could have penned this bizarre tune
Who has taught the birds to hate us
Made the trees go deaf and blind
Who controls our thoughts from Sirius
Placed machinery in our minds
Will we see one day above us in the dynamo of night
A silver machine shaped like a saucer
Glowing with a holy light
Will it land its portals open
Will our Jesus then appear.

Man

Man is what he is not
And is not what he is
So take my advice don't whistle while you piss
All the world is a stage
And I want to be a star
But the cameraman yells cut
Every time I reach the bar

On the screen I'd be a scene
But something seems to come between

And I'm just a might have been
In a technicolor dream
And I have to sit and scream
As the music starts to play
And the crowds all melt away

I need a girl to love
Sincerely that's the rub
But she just prefers good grub
So I sit down in the tub
And go rub a dub dub
Turn those taps full on
And sing the old swan song
In the town it's bustle bustle
In the country rustle rustle
Go to sea it's lap lap lap
Go to war it's rat tat tat
All this trouble all this strife
I must be getting' tired of life
Think I'll have to take a wife

When you gotta go you go
Cause you mustn't brake the flow
In the grave is no disgrace
It awaits the human race
None I think do there embrace
So wipe that smile off your face
Clap your hands and shout hooray
You gonna live another day

Nymphs and shepherds we should be
Though I'd rather you than me
That's the reason we can't see
God is smaller than a flea
He said shepherd shear your flock

Come on baby let's rock around the clock.

Reptiles ruled this planet Earth
Reptiles ruled this planet Earth
Until the aliens came
And found us sitting in a tree
Monkey was our name
Monkey was mutated
Human was his name
It didn't take this creature long
To learn the aliens game

The aliens thought that they'd create
A creature with a soul
But man was still part animal
And ego was his goal
The aliens had created man
The human race was born
It didn't take them long to learn
That man was the devils spaw

Now each of the five had left behind
A religion for his tribe
Entrusted for safe keeping
To a man they called a scribe
He told them what to sing
For he knew that in the land of the blind
The one eyed man is king.

This age of greed passed slowly
War was everywhere
The human race lived blindly
In darkness and despair
One day a giant mushroom
above a desert bloomed

It's a shock wave triggered a sonic alarm
To which the aliens tuned
Their saucers headed straight for Earth
Their mission to save man's soul
They left a secret weapon
That man called rock and roll.

Chorus:
Old Darwin's theory was a joke
God is just a nice old bloke
The body snatchers came to steal
Think about it!
Are you real?
The human race was blasted
With weapons of awful power
Such was their technology
It didn't take an hour
Not all the human perished
And those that did survive
Formed a holy priesthood
In number they were five

They built the great stone pyramids
And practised a magic art
That gave them fantastic powers
In each and every part
Legion grew their numbers
Mighty were their arms
But high in the sky
The alien eye
Filled them with alarm

Chorus:
Old Darwin's theory was a joke
God is just a nice old bloke

The body snatchers came to steal
Think about it!
Are you real?

Now each of the five had left behind
A religion for his tribe
Entrusted for safe keeping
To a man they called a scribe
He told them what to sing
For he knew that in the land of the blind
The one eyed man is king.
This age of greed passed slowly
War was everywhere
The human race lived blindly
In darkness and despair
One day a giant mushroom
above a desert bloomed
It's a shock wave triggered a sonic alarm
To which the aliens tuned
Their saucers headed straight for Earth
Their mission to save man's soul
They left a secret weapon
That man called rock and roll.

Chorus:
Old Darwin's theory was a joke
God is just a nice old bloke
The body snatchers came to steal
Think about it!
Are you real.

Fear was on their faces
As they stared up at their doom
There they screamed fingers pointing
There beyond the Moon

A star had moved, had changed its place
In this universe of man
And was rushing now towards the Earth
Part of aliens plan

This planet name was Venus
Moved by the aliens skill
Its orbit aimed to close to Earth
The human race to kill
Fire and flood engulfed the Earth
The Sun and Moon stood still
The alien ship departed
Of Earth they'd had their fill
Chorus:
Old Darwin's theory was a joke
God is just a nice old bloke
The body snatchers came to steal
Think about it!
Are you real?

Kingdom of the brave

Composed in 1974-1975 when he was living with Carolyn on a houseboat on a river in Kent, the following three poems later appeared on the Hydrogen Jukebox's album Apocalyptic Anthem, *recorded in 1978 but only released y in 1991 by* Materiali Sonori *as "Prophecies". The texts differ a little from the song lyrics.*

1

Drake is in his hammock
An oil slick marks his grave
The pigeons shit on Nelson's hat
In the kingdom of the brave
The tax collectors are howling
Like jackals in the night

The angels gun their motors
They're spoiling for a fight
Then the lookout shouts his warning
He sees a ghostly light
Is it Atlantis rising
Is Utopia in sight?

2

The stars have lost their meaning
The compasses point east
But the Captain's busy inviting
Everybody to a feast
The ship is listing badly
The crew don't seem to care
They are all too busy discussing
Which uniform to wear
Then the lookout shouts is warning
He sees a ghostly light
Reflection of the water
Rescue is in sight

3

A gale then starts a blowing
Panic sweeps the ship
The Captain yells Hard a Starboard
The Bosun says bullshit
The crew are manning the lifeboats
Time is running short
But to the voice of reason
No one gives a thought
Then the lookout shouts is warning
He sees a ghostly light
They seem to hit a timewarp

And disappear from sight

4

There are some who say
You can see her still
When the Moon is high
And the beauty of her sails
Would make a strong man cry
Her crew are mustered on the deck
Their mouths are open wide
And they say you can hear
Rule Britannia
Over the roaring tide

To be continued
A whale in the sea
Sang his song to me
he said I'd love to be
On the BBC
But the whalers
Hate music
And they shoot at me
So I guess
I'd better be going
I've searched every wave
On the ocean's shore
I've turned every leaf
On the forest floor
But I can't find the words
That I'm looking for
It should say
To be continued

In a paper boat

I sailed away
I was gone for a year
And a day
But I knew that all
The papers would say
was something like
Hello Sailor
I've searched every wave
On the ocean's shore
On the forest floor
But I can't find the words
That I'm looking for
It should say
To be continued

In the eastern isle
I saw Buddha smile
I asked him why
And after a while
He held out his hands
And with great style
He said
I've got a lot of money
I've searched every wave
On the ocean's shore
On the forest floor
But I can't find the words
That I'm looking for
It should say
To be continued.

Abrakadabra
I've heard the works of Eliphus Levi
Kafka and Verlaine
I've been astral travelling nightly

with commuters of the brain
but the sign posts of the occult
all seem to read the same
I'm heading for the palace
of pain... singing
ABRAKADABRA now!

I've seen the demons of the drug stores
cast their pearls before swine
I've seen the pedlars of madness
down on Hollywood and vine
but the second hand of oblivion
sweeps the corridors of time
and I'm frozen in a catatonic mime... singing
ABRAKADABRA now!

I've seen the captains of confusion
order millions of their doom
heard the horseman of the apocalypse
like thunder on the tomb
heard the children of innocence
screaming in the womb
and I'm hiding in a crater on the moon... singing
ABRAKADABRA now!

I've heard the pious popes of pornography
preaching to the poor
heard the flood tide of humanity
crying out for more
I saw the soothsayers of war
that left me screaming in terror
on the floor... singing
ABRAKADABRA now!

I've heard the bibles of bullshit

preached the sermons of hate
I've seen the sign that says no niggers
above the pearly gate
I've sung the hymns of hypocrisy
and before it gets too late
I'm joining the fairies of fate... singing
ABRAKADABRA now!

VI

Writings

Although Sweeney himself admitted his disclosures were unreliable, devoted to trivial amusement, gratuitous inventions and sensational quips, like other incomparable mythmakers, Sun Ra, Frank Zappa, Captain Beefheart - he tried nonetheless on a few occasions to tell the story of his groups. What follows, goes back to September 1987 when I asked him by letter to reply to some questions I had sent him...

The facts

The group was electric and was called *The Hydrogen Jukebox*. The name came from the poem *Howl* by Alan Ginsberg. Ginsberg himself came to see the group at the *Roundhouse*.[1] We recorded one album *Apocalyptic Anthems* - all songs by Glen Sweeney. The line-up was Glen on drums, Mick Carter on guitar, Brian Diprose on bass guitar and Jim James on vocals and guitar. The group disbanded when all the instruments and gear were stolen.

The acoustic Third Ear Band was formed as resident band at the *Arts Lab*[2] in Drury Lane and consisted of Glen on hand drums, Richard Coff on violin, Mel Davis

---

[1]   As the name suggests it is a circular building; originally built in 1847 as a locomotive turntable (or wheelhouse) and then used as an engine shed by the *London and North Western Railway*. It fell into disrepair and closed in the 1930s, after which it slowly decayed. In 1964 it was reopened when the playwright Arnold Wesker moved *Centre 42* there. The opening concert, on 15 October, 1966, was the *All Night Rave* to launch the the the underground newspaper *International Times* (IT) with Soft Machine and Pink Floyd. Leaking, cold, derelict and with terrible acoustics, it went on to host a long series of underground events and concerts. One of the iconic memories of 1967 for those who were there is the sound of *Sam Gopal Dream* echoing around its massive dome. As a theatre space it hosted Peter Brook productions, *Living Theatre* and notoriously, *Oh Calcutta*, as well as the legendary *Evening of British Rubbish* with Bruce Lacey and the Alberts and The *Dialectics of Liberation* Conference, arguably the intellectual pivot of 1967. It closed in the 1980s, after years of failure, eventually to reopen, renewed and refurbished with private money, in June 2006.

[2]   Founded by Jim Haynes, an American - born in Louisiana - who was stationed in Scotland with the US army in 1956 and stayed on when his military service ended. After his studies at the University of Edinburgh, he ran a bookshop and helped set up the experimental *Traverse Theatre* and the *Edinburgh Festival Fringe*. In 1966 he moved to London where he co-founded the *International Times* and, in 1967, opened the *Arts Lab* in Drury Lane. It had a Cinema, a theatre and a restaurant, and hosted experimental mixed-media work. John Lennon and Yoko

on cello. At first the band was just a street band; we would play in park events, "be ins" and "love ins", etc. From there we began to play colleges and joined *Blackhill Enterprises*. They signed us to the *Harvest* label and we recorded our first LP *Alchemy*. They also got us to play the Hyde Park free concerts with such stars as the *Rolling Stones, Blind Faith* and *Pink Floyd*.

Because of this we became well known and did many tours of England and Europe. Two more albums were recorded.

To understand the mood that the band made is to understand the sixties. The fans were into many esoteric studies, such as Zen, cosmic consciousness, meditation, Yoga, etc., so the music of the Third Ear Band was an invitation to the audience to take a trip without using LSD.

Our music was improvised inasmuch as it was not written, but the basic structure was always the same – a minimalist rhythm track overlaid with hypnotic riffs from the violin; the cello would provide a basic drone - this was the only eastern influence - leaving the oboe to provide the melody. When you listened to this music live (it was not the same on record) with repetitions lasting sometimes 20 or 30 minutes, the mind would go into free fall and you would find yourself daydreaming.

That is how it has been described to me by audiences.

The relationship between the music biz and the band was simple – as long as we sold records: O.K. And with the press - as long as I could provide mystic articles, that was O.K. too. Finally *Macbeth* ended it. *Macbeth* was bad news for all involved; the play has some kind of curse on it and it put nearly all the people involved in it out of business.

Tax problems drove me to Greece, but I was not there all the time and I picked up no influences. At present I am learning to play the mridangam. This is a double ended drum from Southern India. The music is "carnatic" and is reputed to have been handed down to man from the gods in order that we may reach spiritual fulfillment. It is totally improvised - once you have learned the basic patterns of the 72 ragas. It is not commercial music, so we have our own recording studio and distribute the tapes by post to our fans.

Ono exhibited there and participated in the *Alchemical Wedding* at the Albert Hall to raise money for the Lab. The Arts Council refused to fund it and it closed two years later with Haynes £8000 in debt. Though short-lived, the Arts Lab was the model and inspiration for many similar initiatives.

The following piece was written in June 1988 just before the first Italian tour when I needed a thing to use for the press.

The Giant Sun Trolley and Third Ear Band's biographies
by Glen Sweeney

The Sun Trolley fought a musical guerrilla war against the authorities in Hyde Park. Music was banned, so The Sun Trolley would capture the small bandstand and play until the park police arrived, then the fun would begin: one policeman would be sent to find the keys to the bandstand gate while the others demanded we stop playing. "No music in the park!, they would shout. "What about the birds?" we would say. Eventually, to our delight, the local newspaper headlines read "Police ban Birdsong in the park". We felt we had won a victory.

Another event, in Oxford, staged for German TV. The Sun Trolley had taken over a small public garden. We began to play; around us hippies had climbed the trees and were flapping their hands and making bird whistles. The police approached, gazed solemnly at the chaos; one produced a notebook, looking at my bass drum. He wrote: "The Giant Sun Trolley", asked my name and then said "I'm sorry, sir, but you cannot park here!".

Luckily the U.F.O. Club opened in time to save us. At U.F.O. we had to play at dawn as the club closed, so we invented songs like *Eternity in D*, where everybody played one note as long as possible, or until the club was empty – which did not take long!

The final gig for The Sun Trolley was at the Alexandra Palace: the 14th-Hour Technicolor Dream. Then Dave Tomlin went to India to study and I discovered *The Hydrogen Jukebox*.

Hydrogen Jukebox was a name looking for a band. I found the band at the Roundhouse (an old engine shed taken over by the underground). They were a free/avant-garde group, and we began to do gigs: one night at the U.F.O. I wired a large pair of scissors up to the P.A. with a contact mike and then, as the band began to play, Dick Dadem (trombone) began slowly to cut the dress off his girlfriend. The effect was sensational: we were famous for one whole night. The next morning we found the van and all the instruments had been stolen.

The band slowly drifted apart. It reunited in the late '70s to make one album, *Apocalyptic Anthems*, never released. I now had to try this experiment, which had been in my head for years. What if I selected some musicians and we just sat down and played? We had no amplification, so it would have to be acoustic. The musicians would have to be free spirits!

I selected Paul Minns, oboe, Richard Coff, violin, Mel Davis, cello, and myself on hand drums. I chose those instruments because whatever mixture of sounds we played – rock, jazz, folk - it would sound avant-garde...

That same weekend we went to the London *Arts Lab*. We played for one hour and at the end we had come up with three very strange tunes!

That same night we went to the *Folk Cellar* in Soho, where we played for two hours. *Third Ear Band* was born.

I called the music "alchemical" because it was produced by *repetition*. Each tune would change every time we played it. On the drums, the beat reduced itself to minimalism to the point almost of microtonality; it was listening to each beat as if it was a symphony.

Third Ear Band finally met the famed *Blackhill Enterprises*, an underground agency. They had discovered *Pink Floyd, Deep Purple* etc., so I made sure they discovered Third Ear. They had a project cooking with E.M.I., a label called *Harvest Records* – it was to be "underground". So we signed and completed the first album, *Alchemy,* in one weekend. It sold well, but a lot of the people from E.M.I. disliked the cover, so the distribution of the record was very bad.

Meanwhile *Blackhill* had started doing free gigs in Hyde Park and asked us if we would like to open for them. We started with *Blind Faith*: it was magic playing to 150.000 people; the energy was fantastic!

We went on the Isle of Wight, but we met bad vibes. Bob Dylan's appearance was full of hassles and Bob had not fully recovered from his motorbike crash.

Back in the studios for the second album, we found negative vibes everywhere. *Harvest* had tired of the underground and the engineer refused to mix the *Fire* track, so we muddled through as best we could. The album was doomed.

The band gigged on. Occult forces now seemed to manifest themselves. A club in Manchester we played regularly was located in an old crypt – the seats were in fact old stone coffins. As we played late one night a ghost appeared and no one could believe their eyes. The gig was cancelled. "Bad for business", said the manager.

We went to the druids to seek their protection and played with them at their holy places and solstices. Things got better but the band needed a rest.

We were in the *Blackhill* office one day when the phone rang. Andrew King picked it up, I couldn't hear the conversation, but Andrew began to give me strange looks. He put the phone down. "Do you know who that was, Glen?" "No" "A guy called Stanley Kubrick... He wants to use the *Air* track from the second album for a film titled *Clockwork Orange*". "You must be kidding", I said. Andrew gave me a funny look: "Own up Glen, it's some friend of yours, right?" "No. What did you tell him?" Andrew grinned "I told him to piss off!". "Why?", I said.

Then the phone rang again. "Hallo, Blackhill Enterprises". Something was happening... I could tell by Andrew's face. "Roman who?", he bellowed: "Polanski!" I panicked and grabbed the phone from Andrew's nervous fingers (as they say)...

It turned out to be the *Macbeth* film, which we recorded at George Martin's *Air Studios*... Of course, you know what they say about Macbeth and bad luck! They are probably right!

© 1988-2020 Estate of Glen Sweeney

Another of Glen Sweeney's interesting reconstruction of the Third Ear Band parable was published in Harvest Festival *(EMI-Harvest Records 521, 1982), "a 120 page 4-colour 5-CD musical celebration of the Harvest label, covering its output from 1969 to 1979."*

Between contributions from various artists like Pink Floyd, Kevin Ayers, Edgar Broughton, Roy Harper *and others, on this very limited edition album, Sweeney offers his personal memories, taken from an interview probably made at the beginning of the '80's, about the origins of the band.*

The Third Ear Band track on Harvest Festival is Stone Circle *from* Alchemy: *it also shows some photos of the Thirds, with posters and record covers. Glen was very proud of it, particularly the portrait with his hand drums, on the album cover...*

Dave Tomlin and I practically invented the whole hippy scene (!!!). We were the first into Hyde Park and Glastonbury with the Druids. Peter Jenner picked up the idea and started to get the whole thing together. The Third Ear Band started opening the shows at Hyde Park.

Originally I had an electric group, standard rock'n'roll, but we were all on something or other and one night we forgot about our instruments and by the morning they and the van had disappeared. I took my advice from the *Mothers of Invention* and 'necessity' and thought I'd better do something because I was a lazy bastard. I knew two or three guys and put them together and went down to a place called the *Arts Lab*, which was very well known, and did a concert where I met a guitarist called Davy Graham who was famous for eating any kind of flowers you left around. The gig was an all-nighter and it gave us the opportunity to learn how to play.

We started to do gigs with *Blackhill* at about £25 a show and it went on from there. We penetrated the continent doing clubs like the *Paradiso*, where we were so stoned we couldn't play and just looked at the audience who thought we were an ace group and so underground.

One day, to my utter astonishment, Pete Jenner said that we had a record deal. This again caused ultimate paranoia and half the band collapsed on the spot. My philosophy was always to get stoned and then you could play everything. To my astonishment this worked perfectly. At this time EMI was run by a lot of old ladies who were in love with Cliff Richard. I met them once but we were all on acid so it was a bit of a strange one.

We did a gig at Alley Palley (Alexandra Palace) called the *14-Hour Technicolor Dream*. 'Hoppy' [3] who ran the gig thought that banana skins were a turn-on, so everyone was smoking banana skins, which didn't work and made you ill.

I remember Polanski, who we worked with for the *Macbeth* soundtrack. They had rented him this really flash flat in Chelsea. Moving to drums was a mad moment. For some reason I came into a large sum of money and Coff (who now runs an infant violin school in Miami) suggested I buy a full set. I couldn't play them and went back to hand drums.

After *Macbeth* it collapsed. Paul Buckmaster joined the band briefly but left shortly after stating that his reputation was in danger.

---

[3]   John Hopkins, a British photographer, journalist, and political activist (b 1937), who helped set up the *London Free School* in Notting Hill, the *International Times* and *The UFO Club*, all of which figure heavily in the coming pages. He was famously arrested in 1967 for possession of cannabis and sentenced to nine months in prison, less to do with the drugs and more with trying to throw a spanner in the underground works. It failed, There were simply protests, benefit concerts and louder calls for legalisation.

On a very rare occasion, Glen wrote a piece about the Third Ear Band for Zig Zag *magazine (published in August 1969). He considered* Zig Zag *to be just a 'straight paper', not really involved with the underground and he didn't like to give interviews to it.*

The Third Ear Band

Some people are confused about their music; some relate it to the manifestation of strange occult forces, but most just groove to it unaware of any religious or mystical connotations. Glen Sweeney, their drummer, talks about the inception, development, and music of the Third Ear Band.

I was kind of outcast, first from the straight jazz scene - because wherever I played I found this set of rules you had to obey, even in the free jazz scene. I found that if you tried to play 8 bars of straight rhythm, they all pointed to the door and you were out. Finally, I sussed that even the idea of free had become a kind of fixed idea. So I gave up music altogether for a while and just became what was popularly known at the time as a beatnik.

It wasn't until I met Dave Tomlin that I found a kind of a kindred spirit – somebody else who had sussed out what I had – and he got a group called The Sun Trolley together at UFO, which was a tremendously fertile place for ideas. And together, Dave and I and various other guys who sat in with us, we tried everything, and it was during that time that I got the germ of the idea for what is now the Third Ear Band. Dave got busted, and at the time I was really interested in eating – you know, staying alive – and there was this sort of free jazz group passing through UFO at the time, so I immediately leapt aboard.

This group, the Hydrogen Jukebox, was run by one of those mad tenor players, you know, who had an incredible Black Power ego thing, and he eventually wound up accusing about 5000 people at the Roundhouse of having killed Coltrane – I think that's where the Jukebox collapsed.

The prototype Third Ear was electric and we were doing what we called 'electric acid raga' – which was terribly pretentious, and in fact was the most diabolical thing you ever heard in your life. This cat on guitar, he had the most powerful amp and he was on acid about nearly every day; in the end, you just couldn't stop him playing. Until he eventually flipped.

After that, most of our equipment was stolen and we found ourselves with just oboe, violin and hand drums – and we were really depressed, we thought it was the end, really. But we had such extraordinary feedback from the underground, everyone kept ringing up asking if we would like to play and our eventual 'saviour' was Jim Haynes of the *Arts Lab*. He got us in there, gave us the best of his rooms, put us on three times a week – and that was the start of the present band.

I've found some very good guys now and I think they're all really into it, but in anything you find you have hang-ups and blocks, and until you can resolve these, I don't think you can get through to the music you are looking for. Now and again you hit it – we hit it once at the *Arts Lab* and that gave us the incentive to go on. We lost it there too because this guy came up with a tremendous ego hang-up and split – so nothing ever remains constant really in this kind of group; I suppose we're the horror of managers and agents who want something to crystallise and solidify so they can handle it.

I think the media can kill your music stone dead. At the moment we are attracting a lot of people because, basically, we have managed to cover up the rationalisation of the music so they actually hear the sound. They actually make the trip of the music; they get the tensions in it, the climaxes, and also, I feel it really gets through to them - partly because the sound is not defined by any particular bag, like blues or rock, etc. We refer to our numbers as ragas, though they're obviously not, and the alchemical thing, though it may seem to be, is not - in the way we use it - a fantasy. The alchemists, far from just trying to make gold from other things, had this idea of doing the same experiment over and over for years, and somewhere, something would change. We do this in music, and sometimes weird things happen.

We're all interested in music – the other three guys are out of classical music colleges – and we do a lot of listening and a lot of talking about it; and we've got a basic theory that music, or sound or whatever you like to call it, came a long time before music notation... and working through that theory we found that Western notation is a kind of symbolism that has evolved in order to be a kind of measure of the music. It's a very authoritarian sort of thing really because it's all around the idea that one guy can write it down so that other guys will be able to play it more or less exactly as he wrote it. So we did a lot of research into music which was way back before the time of that kind of notation and this led us into what they call the magic area – and we found that in those times the music was viewed from a more cosmopolitan point of view; you got the *seven* notes, which were related to the seven planets, or the *twelve* thing, which was related to the zodiac. And this is why the Third Ear Band is still out there. Because all of us are into research – and some of the stuff we try out is based on these principles; like the thing we do called *Druid*. I don't say all of us, but three of us firmly believe that with music you can do a lot more than just titillate peoples' feelings... in some of those books there are mind blowing theories - like music actually built the Great Pyramid... things like that.

Our musical structures came by accident really, and by sheer necessity, because we had fixed tunes with the original Third Ear but the guy who wrote them was the one on acid, and he ended up in a nut-house. That left the three of us and no-one had any real idea in that direction, so we found ourselves in the Arts Lab without a tune between us. But Jim said not to worry, just get in there and see what happens. And that was what we did... I suppose, if you listen to enough music, it's inside you somewhere – and the sheer necessity of the situation brings it out, and what came out was what we call *structures*. We still use, and improvise on these structures. Sometimes we play them almost the same – it depends how each member is feeling. If you're feeling beat, you tend to repeat more or less what you played on your last trip... but if you're feeling really good and something new crops up, you put it in, and everybody changes their thing to fit.

We are now getting into a very strange scene regarding audiences. We're beginning to attract teenyboppers for Christ's sake, and at the last thing we did at Norwich we had, I suppose, about 8 very thick mods – real hardnuts – and they were digging it like mad... one of them stripped off. So I don't know how big the audience is really.

©1969 "Zig Zag"

Liner notes from Glen Sweeney's Hydrogen Juke Box Prophecies *written by Glen for the* Materiali Sonori *CD published in 1991.*

The Hydrogen Jukebox

Hydrogen Jukebox, when I first met them in 1967, was a band without a name or a drummer. I took over the drums and gave them a name - Hydrogen Jukebox - which I got from Ginsberg's poem *Howl*.

The group was famous for, I think, about three months. Then I formed Third Ear Band and for the next three years I was busy with instrumental music.

By 1972, after recording the film score for *Macbeth*, I went to live on a big old boat on a river in Kent hoping to get some rest. To my amazement my head was full of songs and poems, I put them on paper as fast as I could write.

Mick Carter, who had worked with me on Hydrogen Jukebox, lived in Kent and was building a small studio, so we had the idea for an album using the Hydrogen Juke-Box name. It came together like a dream, but by then – 1976 – the music scene was into "punk" and our album sat on Mick's studio shelf until I sent it *to Materiali Sonori*.

I hope you like it!

I should have called it *Alchemical Archeology* since that's what it is; a relic of the past – time-warped into the present...

Three manifestos

Next is the well-known manifesto written by Glen, printed on the cover of Alchemy, Third Ear Band's first album, published in May 1969. Through the years it has been quoted in a lot of articles dedicated to the band.

Third Ear Band music is a reflection of the universe as magic play illusion simply because it could not possibly be anything else. Words cannot describe this ecstatic dance of sound, or explain the alchemical repetition, seeking and sometimes finding, archetypal forms, elements, and rhythms. Contradictions are their energy force, dualities are discarded in favour of the Tao; each piece is as alike or unalike as trees, grass or crickets. This is natural, magical, alchemical music that doesn't preach but just urges you to take your own trip.

If you can make it into the music you're adrift in fantastic Bosch-like landscapes, a strange acoustical perfume fills the mind; on rare occasions a vast door seems to open; band and audience appear to float in a new dimension transcending time and space where nothing exists except this very strange and beautiful music.

Note this is just how one person felt on hearing the group live, because ultimately sound, like the wind, does not exist in a concrete form, it is magic, alchemy - and anyway someone said they would like something about the group on this L.P.

Another manifesto published on a flyer written and drawn by Sweeney in 1968.

The music of the Third Ear Band music is a reflection of the universe as magic play illusion. At first hearing it may seem a naive meaningless dance of sound, but dig deeper, get your head into it, you'll hear alchemical repetition seeking the actual archetypal forms, and rhythms that can change consciousness. Labels, even melodies, are left far behind; each piece is as alike or unalike as blades of grass or clouds. Under hypnotic repetition the listener's rational mind loses control; he is adrift in a strange Bosch-like musical landscape that changes endlessly.

On very rare occasions a vast door seems to open and band and audience find themselves in a new dimension transcending time and space. It is the music of the Druids, released from the unconscious by the alchemical process, orgasmic in its otherness, religious in its oneness. Communicating beauty and magic via abstract sound whilst playing without ego enables the musicians to reach a trance-like state, a 'high' in which the music produces itself.

This is the aim of the Third Ear Band; to act as carriers of consciousness, and to play a music that being non-conscious is an organic synthesis of all musics.

For Magic Music, published by Materiali Sonori in 1990, Glen wrote a new brief manifesto with a more clearly pantheistic vision of reality.

Third Ear Band's new album *Magic Music* is about music as pure vibrations; as such it can be linked with colour because colour is vibration. It can even be linked to the music of the spheres, which state that the vibrations of the planets can be heard with the third ear (silence).

The free ragas that we play are modal, each note can be heard as a sound-colour that produces its own mood. Our rhythms come from all over the world, and we use these ideas and many others to try to make a new world music.

A letter to I.T. (August 1968)

Sweeney wrote this short letter to IT (International Times)[4] *which was published on page 18 in the August 23rd, 1968 issue (no.38), provoked by an article by Raymond Durgnat titled* Why I kicked my underground habits, *published in the previous issue, in which he had strongly criticized the anti-Vietnam aid festival in Trafalgar Square as a way for high society to take* 'a deserving cause as a pretext for its smartest clothes and congratulates itself on its high-mindedness'.

In his letter Glen also alluded to another article by Durgnat entitled Fading Freedoms/Latent Fascisms & Hippie Highest Hope. A paranoid guide by

---

4   Founded in London in 1966, *IT* ran fortnightly until October 1973. Editors in the early years included John (Hoppy) Hopkins, David Mairowitz, Barry Miles, Jim Haynes and the playwright Tom McGrath. Paul McCartney and Allen Ginsberg were amongst those who supported the paper financially. Its launch - at the Roundhouse - in 1966 also launched the London underground. *Soft Machine* guitarist and poet Daevid Allen called it "one of the two most revolutionary events in the history of English alternative music and thinking". On several occasions in 1967, the police raided their offices in an attempt to force the closure of the paper – eventually they arrested John Hopkins on an opportunistic drug charge. The legendary 14-Hour *Technicolour Dream at the Alexander Palace* was organised (by Barry Miles, John Hopkins, David Howson, Mike McInnerney and Jack Henry Moore) to try to keep the paper solvent. *Pink Floyd*, *Soft Machine*, *Pete Townsend*, *Graham Bond*, *Tomorrow*, *Jon's Children*, *The Pretty Things*, *Savoy Brown*, *Denny Laine*, *Alexis Corner*, *Ron Geesin*, *Gary Farr*, *The Move*, *Mike Horowitz*, *Christopher Logue*, *Suzy Creamcheese*, *Simon Vinkenoog*, *Dick Gregory*, *Yoko Ono*, *Sam Gopal Dream* and the *Giant Sun Trolley* were among many who appeared. Everyone seriously engaged in the London scene read *IT* – at its height it had a circulation of 40,000 copies. It's worth thinking about that for a moment. Its roots lay in Beat culture - and early contributors included Alexander Trocchi, William Burroughs and Allen Ginsberg.

Raymond Durgnat, *published in four parts in OZ magazine, Nos 12, 13, 14 and 15 (May- August 1968)*.

Dear IT,

Please, please no more of Mr. Durgnat's articles on what is happening inside his head; three pages in *OZ* and now two pages in *IT*. Is it our fault that these confused critics and D.J.'s can't stop thinking and dig the life? The scene needs less negative criticism, more positive alternatives.

Glen Sweeney, Third Ear Band [a sound has no legs to stand on].

V

Interviews with Glen Sweeney

*Muz Murray was one of the protagonists of the London underground
scene and founder of* Gandalf's Garden, *a mystical psychedelic magazine that
published 6 issues between 1968 and 1969, "offering hope and a positive
lifestyle to the lost and lonely". Here's an interview with Glen from the
beginning of 1969 that appeared in issue 4, probably the first interview with
Glen ever published.*

The Third Ear Band

The THIRD EAR BAND is the first mystical OVERGROUND (celestially-
orientated) musical group to hit the Scene. Glen Sweeney, Drummer and group
Unifier, tells of the group's origins and future plans to play at psychic power
centres throughout Britain this summer.

"What we're into now with the Third Ear Band really began when we were on
a gig, and some kind person, or mysterious force, or whatever it was, stole all
our amplification equipment and just left us our instruments. This seemed so
significant that we took it as a sign. Apparently we had been going in the wrong
direction by going electric, and that event caused a tremendous change in our
whole approach. And that's how it has always happened with the Third Ear.
We've never exactly known what we were doing or what we were meant to do.
Things just seemed to occur naturally. I was originally on the jazz scene and in
a terrible state, you know, doing the whole bit; being on the phony junkie trip -
which nearly every jazz musician was on - trapped in a ridiculous pad in
suburbia; hire purchase scenes on my drums and everything else, which they
came and took back; no rent money, no job and no food – so I was gradually
starving.

"I began to withdraw into myself, and the lack of food brought on a kind of
mental trip in which I was able to review my life with great clarity and become
aware of all these hang-ups I'd had in my subconscious. When all that was over
I had become a completely different person. It was about this time I turned on

to Zen and this was the thing that got me together again. In my own way I became a very religious person.

"Soon after this, I met Dave Tomlin, a multi-instrumentalist who, it seemed to me, had become a kind of musical guru. And he turned me on to an aspect of music that I had long been searching for. He was the first guy I had ever met who used his music to influence people, to turn them on, or freak them out. When I used to play with Dave's group, the Sun Trolley, at UFO club, just two or three of us would take on up to two thousand people, with no amplifiers or anything – and Dave could get them all with him and do incredible things to their heads. I had never seen music used that way before.

So when he split from London to take up gypsy caravaning on the Mark Palmer scene, the Third Ear seemed a logical extension of what Dave had been doing. But I had a hard time finding people who had any idea of this particular area of music, and I had to find ways to turn even musicians on to thinking like that. And then, eventually, when we did form the acoustic group, we had all the gear stolen. In a way it was fortunate, because we started to get it together at great speed from then on.

The basic Eastern sound had always been there, and now it had the opportunity to develop in the right way. If you go into it really deeply, playing Eastern-style music entails a completely different way of thinking. Western music is sort of 'put together in pieces', whereas the Eastern style seems to be more 'organic'. And as you play, you soon discover that it is not even coming from you, and that your job as a musician is just to get yourself out of the way. This is the state we have got into now, where everyone realises themselves as a channel – and the music just comes.

We are beginning to move into some strange musical areas, doing a piece we call *Druid*. Once or twice when we've played this thing, we've gone into a weird sort of experience we call a 'time-shift'. Nobody really knows what it is. The whole *Druid* piece is repetitive and extremely hypnotic and yet you have some of the instruments doing far out things so that a fantastic tension is built up. It's like alchemy. The alchemical emphasis is on the endless repetition of experiments, doing the same thing over and over again, and waiting for some sort of X-factor to appear. This is more or less what we do when we play. And our X-factor is this time-shift thing.

It happened once at the London *Arts Lab* and as we played it seemed as if time had slowed down and we had drifted into a completely different dimension. When we finished, nobody moved at all. They were kind of stuck there. So I felt that perhaps it had happened to them too. So that's the thing we are trying to get into. Although it can be quite a strain during public performance, like living on the edge of a cliff, since nobody knows what might happen. To be on stage and feel it happening can be quite frightening. You go out of yourself, and when you come to, you discover yourself on stage with hundreds of people staring at you. You get this split-second thought: 'Have I been playing? Have I ruined the whole thing?' In a way, it's very similar to meditation and mantra chanting, which is why I feel what we are doing has a very religious depth.

I'm just hoping we come across on record. We've just cut our first disc called ALCHEMY, with Richard, who plays violin and viola, Paul on oboe, myself on hand drums and Mel on cello (that makes the deep magical drone), and if we can make it with records and the Straight Scene, playing all over the country, we want to do a lot of free scenes in the summer, playing at power centres like Glastonbury Tor or Silbury Hill, Avebury Ring, or Merlin's rock-tomb which is supposed to be near Manchester. Flying saucers appear to travel between these places on definite routes, and anything could happen where the 'energy lines' cross.

"There is also a point where Eastern and Western mysticism meet and I hope we have captured this on record. We cut the whole L.P. in only six hours – and every one a first take, although we had a bit of a hassle trying to get it made the way we wanted it. They wanted to put in echo and phasing and all sorts of commercial rubbish, but we held firm to what we felt it should be.

There are no lyrics on any of the tracks. I've always felt that music should be pure. If you have lyrics, you are preaching in a way. Somehow words are a block to communication. It's almost impossible for me to explain exactly how I feel about this, that's why I'm a musician. The only way to really understand what I mean, is to first listen to a pop group and then listen to us, then I hope you will know what we're trying to say."

©1969 Muz Murray "Gandalf's Garden"

An article on the Third Ear Band by journalist and publisher Chris Welch, printed in Melody Maker,[5] *July 12th, 1969, investigates the first steps of the group... Glen had a high opinion of Welch, especially because of his great sense of humour.*

Third Ear Make You Listen.

In the day of The Big Bash, when groups sent their audiences mad with noise, there seemed a strong likelihood of complaints from races dwelling on neighbouring galaxies, about the racket we Earthmen were creating.

"Hello, this is the planet Blotto here, just north of Andromeda", crackles the message in the ears of a startled radio telescope operator.

"I say, can you do something about the noise old chap? Much as we enjoy *The Who* and *Pink Floyd* out here on dull Blotto (three suns, high methane content, several two star hotels), the racket tends to upset our highly delicate nervous systems. Can you hear me? No – I can't hear you either!"

PEACE

But now groups are cooling down all over the globe. Cream became Blind Faith and took a step down from sheer volume. John Mayall dispensed with drums in search of peace.

The ultimate are the Third Ear Band who proudly claim they can actually lull their audience into a trance if not a deep, refreshing sleep.

Merely cocking one ear to the sound of Glen Sweeney, Richard Coff, Paul Minns and Mel Davies, however, is enough to convince one of human intelligence at work.

---

5   In the 1960s MM was Britain's main - and possibly the world's earliest - weekly music magazine, first published in 1926 to cater to dance band musicians. Founded in 1952, its rival, The *New Musical Express* caught on to *Rock and Roll* much sooner but, by the mid 1960s, *MM* was back in the leading position with a new and young readership and writers like Chris Welch, Richard Williams, Michael Watts and Steve Lake – among the first to write seriously about popular music. In the back of the paper there was an extensive small-ads section where musicians could look for bands and bands for musicians; and many now famous names made their first connections through these pages. *MM* lost its leading role to a new generation of university graduates - big on semiotics and the *New Wave* – who were taken on to revive the fortunes of the *NME* in the late 1970s. *MM* staggered on, changing formats, until 2000 when it finally shut down.

Their music is demanding, intriguing and unique. A non-electric band, they feature Richard on violin, Paul on oboe, Mel on cello and Glen on tabla and hand drums. They have only been operating a few months and are quickly gaining recognition for blending Eastern and European influences.

A recent highlight for them was an appearance on the Blind Faith free concert.

They are managed by the old firm of Blackhill Enterprises, and have their first album "Alchemy" released on EMI's "okay" label, Harvest.

Although they are (gulp) Underground, they are also cheerfully (burp) pop.

Ex-bebop and free drummer, Glen Sweeney told me this week that his current favourite sound is "Dizzy" by Tommy Roe.

"I got some great rhythms off that one. It was groovy", said Glen sounding mildly surprised, as we drank taste-proof coffee in a plastic egg palace.

I complimented Mr Sweeney on their Hyde Park performance. "Yes, we sound good in the open air. That's how it started really. Me and Dave Tomlin, a jazz tenor player, used to play in the park as the Sun Trolley.

"We got busted by an incredible amount of park fuzz. This was before the official free concerts started, in the summer before last. Somebody recorded a lunatic conversation between us and the fuzz, on tape.

"I really don't know what music we were playing then. It was all under the influence of the big turn on of UFO. I used to play a full kit of drums until they got stolen. Then I got hold of some hand drums. There are always a lot of drums hanging around Notting Hill Gate.

"We started the Third Ear Band proper at the end of last summer. Before that it was half electric. But the electric lead guitarist wasn't too successful, and when he left, we found we had an all acoustic group.

WEIRD

"Then Blackhill signed us up for what reason I don't know. It was on the strength of one church hall audition.

"We'd rather people called us a pop group. We do ragas that aren't really ragas at all, and unless we get a turned on promoter, we get into some weird scenes. At Norwich once, when the promoter saw the audience sitting down and closing their eyes to our music, he accused us of putting them to sleep! Complete paranoia. So I imagine we wouldn't do too well on the Pop Proms.

"It's just a question of advertising. We've stayed very much Underground – no photos – and I think this was necessary so people wouldn't put us in a bag. We'd rather they just came up and heard us without ANY preconceived ideas. I suppose it is a bit shattering to see violins and cellos.

"I'd say ninety per cent of our music is improvisation. It's not really Indian music, although we use a drone instead of the usual bass line riffs. The music draws from everywhere.

"I think our appeal is that audiences can draw their own thing from us. We make no announcements and none of the numbers have titles. People in colleges we play come up after and say they can get fantastic images in their mind when they listen. We can offer a complete dream. The old Celtic bards used to have the same ability".

"At Hyde Park we had a beautiful audience, but if you get a bad audience there is not much you can do about it.

"We once had eight drunk rugby players yelling dirty songs at us. We played quieter and quieter. In the end they seemed ashamed and shut up. But I still don't think they dug the music!".

One of the more extensive interviews with Glen was published by IT in issue 63 (August 29th, 1969), just as the band was going to record the second album. Mark Williams was the attentive interviewer.

3rd Ear Glen...

The Third Ear Band, in its various forms, has been with us for over a year and will hopefully exist for many moons to come. They happily regard themselves as a commercially oriented underground pop group and have therefore suffered ridicule and misinterpretation from every level of the music business. Luckily this doesn't appear to bother them too much, as is apparent from this interview with group leader and drummer, Glen Sweeney.

Mark: Could you tell me something about the Sun Trolley.

Glen: That story's been told so many times. The music of the Sun Trolley, I never did figure it out. It was mainly Dave Tomlin, I just played drums really, and followed what he did. He had a group which toured with Ornette Coleman and was reputed to be one of the best jazz groups on the scene, so I always figured that musically he always knew what he was doing and by just working with him at UFO it taught me a lot about music, which I used later to get this going. It was the kind of group that was totally ignored by the underground and yet made Vogue magazine on the straight scene. It was always a happening thing you know – you never knew what would happen from one week to the next.

M: Musically, or personnel-wise?

G: In every way, I mean at one time there were as many as 15 musicians on stage, including *Soft Machine* and I think about five traditional musicians; there were often poets reading too. I remember UFO flipped – went out of their minds, I think, not being able to understand it – they thought it was mind blowing and they all went potty.

M: You played there quite a few times though, didn't you?

G: We used to do the Graveyard Shift. Go on about 4am and the idea I think in Hoppy's mind was that we would clear the club! Once we went on at 3am and played two notes until 7am. It was absolutely mind blowing. You'd see these cats wake up & hear these two notes going and then go back to sleep - and then wake up and these two notes would still be blowing.

M: Didn't you get bored?

G: Well in those times I was always out of my mind or something so...

M: Did you consciously prepare for the change in the group's music?

G: Well it came out of jazz and I was working at UFO and I suppose if I was honest I was basically anti-rock, but that was because I'd never got my head in tow, so working at UFO I was listening constantly to *Soft Machine* or *Procol*

47

Harum and everything and I very quickly realised that all these young lads were miles ahead of jazz... so I then became a rocker I suppose. I was into pot and I was alarmed (sic) - and they were, so it was a bit paradoxical really. I couldn't just buy myself a guitar and leap out on the stage with them, they would have kicked me off. Wanting to stay alive and also being very ambitious, I just did what was happening and waited for things to happen, and then these violin players started coming at me, I couldn't get rid of them, so I thought maybe violins would work. That was the original Third Ear Band, which was incredibly pretentious and diabolically evil to listen to – I mean, nobody really knew what they were doing and we had this lead guitarist who had this powerful amplifier and used to have it full up. Once he got started we couldn't really stop him. He was good, he had his own thing going, but he had no awareness at the time of any group thing. That was Clive Kingsley, who is now down in Brighton with a group called *Sun Dragon,* who are apparently quite good. We couldn't really get it together because we would be doing things at the back of a hall and although we could hear what we were doing, the audience couldn't and I think that's how the thing we have now got itself together. Then we went away somewhere and collapsed temporarily. We were called 3rd Ear Band then. We last played at UFO when the gear got nicked. Then we collapsed and we had all this beautiful thing from the underground, people would ring up and say 'would you like to do this, would you like to do that?' The only guys I could I get hold of were the violin, oboe and me, Ben Cartland, Paul Minns, who is still with me. So I got an old head off a banjo from the Portobello Road, and we made a drum by stretching it over a vase. We wandered into the Arts Lab late one day and Jim Haynes said 'Are you going to play?' So we played and he said, 'Why don't you work here regularly' and he put us on three nights a week. At the time we didn't have any idea of what we were doing but we got in there and played and that's when it happened.

M: I've dutifully read all the publicity about your mystic influence – how strong are they?

G: When I say we – it's very difficult really, I suppose I am the prime mover in the group. I suppose I try and influence everybody to accept the fact that we are into magic. That's a terrible word but we are into that area, because if you take the underground as a whole, a large area is into that. These are the kind of ultimate rules of reality and if you learn how to manipulate them.... it has kind of manifested itself into our music really, but only so long as we stay right out of the way of it. As long as we don't pretend that we are the authors of it. And I think the way it manifests itself is that we work a lot out of town, we hardly ever work in town; and out of town, it seems to me, is where the underground is; everywhere you go there's like, 100 heads compared to what there is in the Grove.[6]

M: These are the kind of people *IT* are trying to reach a lot more; at the moment we are reassessing our position. *IT* and things like the 3rd Ear Band going out to the Provinces are very much a life-line; they are the only contact with what's going on for many people and I think we should respect that and develop accordingly.
G: That's where we are at out there and all the cats think it's magic and I don't think we should interfere with what they think.

M: I think there is already quite a lot of misunderstanding and cynicism amongst certain elements of the pop business about your type of music and the aura you emanate.

G: Oh, certainly, I mean we are the most underground of all because nobody will write about us. The only people at the moment who will write about us are the straight press, it's reached the point at the moment where, you know the hand-out that *Blackhill* did, got first place in *Pseuds Corner* in *Private Eye.*[7] Well

---

6   The Ladbroke Grove and Notting Hill area of London was the centre of the Beat/Hippy/underground, blessed with the Electric Cinema (the oldest in London) and the Mangrove restaurant — a constant centre of political and racial struggles - the *Grove* was the place to be then. It was also the home of the *London Free School* - founded in March 1966 by John (Hoppy) Hopkins and Rhaune Laslett - which drew in, amongst many other major players in the London underground, Michael X, Pete Jenner, Joe Boyd, Andrew King, Michael Horowitz, Jeff Nuttall, Dave Tomlin, Nigel Waymouth, Alexander Trocci, R.D. Laing, Harvey Matusow and the proto Pink Floyd. LFS effectively gave birth to *International Times*, The Notting Hill Carnival and, through fundraising concerts at *All Saints Church Hall*, in Notting Hill, UFO and the alternative club scene in London.

7 A British fortnightly satirical and current affairs magazine founded in 1961, relentlessly anti-establishment and often skirting the boundaries of legality. *Pseuds Corner* was a small column in which they reprinted quotes from

there you are man, I mean *Private Eye* is so pseudo... Every time I go for an interview with these straight cats, you haven't got a prayer you know, the guy is basically putting you on. The only one I've met so far who was at all decent about it was Chris Welch; well he played it for laughs since he plays everything for laughs – even the big groups... I have always known that with a group like we've got, we can't possibly win. I mean, you know, you got things like *OZ*, with a serpent on the album cover; they printed that 15 times and then gave us a mention which you had to use a microscope to find. *Time Out* will never touch us. If they use our name everybody in the group leaps up and down in surprise. The only thing we really bother about is our audience and our audience is growing to fantastic size, I mean that last tour we did we pulled 200 people more than Marsha Hunt and White Trash. So we have got these promoters leaping about with joy and I mean we don't charge that much; they are scoring a tremendous profit and we are just content to go along.

M: How do you see it continuing?

G: I think we are quite popular, *Musicland* says that we are now number three in the charts, Imhoffs is 15 - straight charts you see, and that was a pretty dodgy record, I mean everybody was kind of sitting on the floor crying when it was being made. You know when they made *Sergeant Pepper*, he wanted to play harpsichord, he didn't just want to play a violin, so we had to get rid of him, he couldn't play the harpsichord really. That left us with a trio, one guy sitting on the floor crying, that was Richard. I phoned all around to the cats I thought might be able to help us and we got this guy called Mel, who is a free jazz cello player. When he turned up all the others walked out. And the record was the result of that. It must be quite freaky compared to what we can do now.

M: How tight is the band now?

G: It's just beginning to get itself together, because we have got a permanent group now. There is Minns, who has been with us all the time, Richard Coff, from

----

the most pretentious pronouncements of celebrities, politicians and the press. It still flourishes today, a whistleblower and bane of the establishment that takes no prisoners and doesn't suffer fools gladly.

the States, whose been with us eight months, and this new chick on cello, Ursula. She's very good, because she's got no sort of ego thing going, she's just content to back everything. That's what we want.

M: *What kind of background has she got musically?*

G: They are all classical except me (I am the only guy who knows everything about music), that's probably why I have used the magic bit really, you see it makes me level with them; I mean they know the music thing and I know the magic thing. But another thing which is really hurled at us everywhere, is being acoustic, that's not our fault, I mean somebody stole our gear. People tend to classify all the time and I have got the idea that everybody is looking for a little bag to stick us in to get us out of the way. We don't want to be got out of the way and we will go electric as soon as we have got the bread. Same as *T. Rex* did.

M: *Not very successfully. I don't think that record is in any way successful. I mean the single is a joke, the production is abysmal.*

G: Well, I don't know about production, those studio engineers they all know about the electric groups, but they didn't know anything about acoustic ones. So they came out and kind a stuck of mike in front of each of us, and we would try and say, well they weren't getting the right sound and they would say, well there isn't anything else we can do. So this time we hope to make a record of what we are doing now. We go back into the studio in the next two or three weeks.

M: *Good. When will the next album released?*

G: I don't know. You know the *Harvest* scene, what is happening there. They have apparently abandoned us. I think they would rather stick to Lulu and Cliff Richard really. I mean, do you know how much advance we got – £150. They really cut the price down. I mean, when I read about *King Crimson* being offered £ 150,000.... we can't win whichever way you look at it. But we are determined to stay in there, because if the people dig you, why not?

M: Is the music changing at all do you think?

G: Well yes, it's a kind of original music really.

M: There are obviously some elements of other music in it, or are there?

G: I don't know, I guess if you looked you could possibly find a lot of classical things and a lot of Indian things but they are all changed in the process of playing. They are changed mainly by the fact that not many people play the tambura on a violin. And they also change by the fact that if you play Indian drums you usually have tabla, which is two drums. You see I only use one drum. I played the tabla at one time, but I don't know how long it would take me to be original on it. It takes these cats something like 15 years to play classical Indian music – you would have to go right past that, and I can't really see me doing that, so what I do is I play those themes I have got. If I want to play a rock and roll theme, you can use a theme that is in the *Melody Maker* like Tommy Roe's *Dizzy,* which works out beautifully really. I think Chris Welch thought that was a put on.

M: People are bound to view you incongruously, I mean a group that does your sort of music going around the country just like an electric pop group with the same outlook to success as an electric group, I think it strikes people that way.

G: Well that's their problem. I mean, the underground started out, I always thought, in respect of the artists, encouraging a kind of creativity. I mean, UFO was the biggest club that ever happened, they never knew what would come on next you see. Then when Hoppy got busted, Joe Boyd took over and you had this kind of endless promotion of pop groups and then UFO went down the drain. When we used to play there, you could expect anything. There used to be a group called *Charlie Brown's Clowns* who would come on and do these incredible mime things, or you could get *The Purple Gang*, who were basically a sort of Skiffle group. In fact you had everything, jazz, pop, drama... Well now you see, the pop thing is become almost an establishment on its own, you're allowed a little deviation, you're allowed tenor sax or can play a little bit of classical music but you mustn't be radically different and that's why the

Blackhill Agency gets so much feedback by backing us. They constitute a threat to the whole kind of pop promotion scene, because we're one odd group and that is dangerous. I mean, what the system needs is groups that can be replaced instantly by each other. I suppose the longer we go around the scene, the more feedback we are going to get.

M: *But unfortunately, any group of any type, yourself included, has to use the machinery that exists in order to develop their careers.*

G: Exactly. This is where you have to be very clever, either clever or naïve. I mean, we were very naïve when we started. We used to stagger into these clubs with no amplification, no microphones, carrying little candles, and we would go on after people like *The Who*. We would light our candles and these 500 teeny-boppers were out there. I mean I should think only the first seven heard us. I think we kind of hooked them just on the curiosity bit. And it's taken nearly a year before we were in a position so that people could actually hear the music. Then we got a record made. Much more together. So that takes care of that bit.

M: *It does sound a lot tighter I must admit. You can hear what is going on. The audience are digging it because they can hear a lot more.*

G: Yes, well that's right, I mean when we were playing with candles, we were all very nervous and hung up because we knew basically they didn't want us on the scene, but now we are pulling crowds. It gives you a lot of energy and that also enables you to be a lot more creative and take a lot more chances, and do the Parks. I mean that really turned us on. Whatever you say about it being nicer last year, well maybe it was, but it was also much bigger this year, I mean basically I don't see what I can do for the underground unless I have got bread. If you have got bread you can do a lot.

M: *I think that is a fine ethos to have but you have always got to make sure and be seen to be making sure that you retain your integrity.*

G: Well you see bread never bothered me for a long time, I mean my thing was kind of beat and jazz and I always got by, having friends rather than bread – it might possibly effect members of the group; they might go on an ego trip if we scored a lot of bread but you know, I mean I am there to blow them out. If they really want to make that trip, they are out of the group; anyway I don't think they would. I think they are really in it for the music. The more money we make the more we can afford to do. I mean at the moment we are working with Tina[8] who is one of the best light shows, but who is really going down the drain financially because nobody will take her because her gear won't pass fire regulations. So I figure she's underground, so we take her. And we use Dave Loxley, who is for my money the best magic artist on the scene. So what we want to do is build a great triumph so that it won't matter if they blow us out. I mean, they might get it together, the agency scene is very tight, I mean if somebody starts to block you off, if they don't push your cheques through, you can be blown out of the whole scene, so I figure if we get a triumph together, we can manage ourselves even if they do, because as long as we build the audience it will be okay.

M: Do you think the Grove has still got the atmosphere it had, say, 18 months ago?

G: No, I can't recognise anybody there any more. You meet the odd cat whose been out of the country and has come back to the Grove to find out what is happening but the place seems full of trendy people... they have probably got groovy jobs, you know, they come home and change and put on their headbands and go to Finches and start talking about paintings things on the wall.

M: I think possibly that's a new generation coming along, I mean someone said to me at Implosion[9] the other week that the atmosphere was similar in some ways to UFO but the people were completely foreign to them.

---

8   Born in 1940, Tina Keane studied fine art and film-making and in the '60s moved from painting to producing light shows. In the 1970s she became active in the Women Artists' Group, and is now considered a forerunner of multimedia art, working with film, video, digital media, neon sculpture, installation and performance.

9   Between 1969-1973, a rock club that used the Roundhouse for its operations.

G: You find this everywhere, because scenes like the straight scene have bought the UFO trip on a lower level, I mean everybody is wearing headbands and talking about 'the scene'.

M: *But I think some of it is quite genuine, I don't think it's all pretentious.*

G: Well yes, I think it's good in any case, because if they are going to dress like that and talk like that, they might end up thinking like that. I don't think the Grove is a place for anybody who was actually around the old days, because you can't talk to the old people, you would be for ever saying 'Well, in the old days, it wasn't like that'. So you see you as a kind of witness they have got to get rid of. Besides nobody I know lives there any more. I mean when I went to see Tina, she'd just lost her pad, Dave Loxley is talking about going up to Scotland, he's moving basically because everybody is after him now. Apparently the *Rolling Stones* wanted him to do a cover; he doesn't want to do it. He's just painted the Floyd's drums though.

M: *Why doesn't he want to do it?*

G: Well you see he thinks like I think and a few people think, what is the good of doing a magic cover for the Stones when they are not into that? He can't see how that could be done, because if you are into it on a reality level then some cat comes along on a commercial art level and says 'Could you do a real freaky cover?'. Then you can't because you want to do it for real.

M: *This touches on something I mentioned before, in that it's fine for the underground to promote itself, but it has to retain its integrity whilst doing so and I think that there are so many cases where it has not, and a lot of people who have come from the underground have been very eager to grab hold of the readies at the expense of any ideas. The more that happens, the harder it is for people like yourselves to been taken seriously.*

G: Well there is only one way we can get that out, and that is by having people like you interviewing us. I can't tell straight papers that those serpents on the cover are completely magic – they are in a protect-circle, they protect the whole album and the music on it. I mean how much are EMI trying to promote their logo, it's very strange that they want to stick it right between the circle where it would break the magic ring. Well I mean that's the kind of thing *we* can talk about. But in a straight interview like *Beat Instrumental* or *Zig Zag*, you can't talk about trips like that because they immediately suspect you of putting them on; they get uncomfortable and then very likely turn the story round after you have gone, into a putdown. I have to make all this chat about improvisation or I have, to resort to kind of talking about the Sun Trolley or emphasizing how Clive is a mad tripper. If you want to make it, I mean, you have got to stay in the media, I mean you have got to be the kind of guy they say, 'oh give him a ring, he's always good for a story', and we are playing all these games because we want to get in there. We have got advantages because with all these violins and cellos we look harmless; they are all going to buy it; I mean we play to bowler-hatted straights and they are buying it. So we get right in there and once we get in there, then that kind of magic thing is going to unfold and once you have got that in the media, as Steve Pank would say, it reads, I mean it actually drives, into their subconscious and God knows what will happen then, we will have a nation of mad freakers.

M: *That's why I was interested in your associations with the Grove and also I was interested to hear your feelings about the Provinces.*

G: Well we dig the provinces the most and I mean I'm not just saying that, we are out there all the time.

M: *Fresh energy there?*

G: Yeah, places like the *Magic Village*,[10] and those scenes are like where the future is.

---

[10]   Roger Eagle, who promoted Blues and R & B at the *Twisted Wheel* in Manchester, started *The Magic Village* in March 1968 as a psychedelic – often all-night - club that quickly became the heart of Manchester's late sixties counterculture. Everyone played there. Eagle fairly quickly moved on to bigger things.

Among the few articles on the original Third Ear Band, the one written by Richard Williams for Melody Maker *(published on June 6th, 1970) is one of the best ever. Here, Sweeney explains the musical form of the group and the relation with the audience.*

A very precious group at one time.

Glen Sweeney, percussionist of the Third Ear Band, thinks that the media have done a great deal of harm to popular music.

"The methods employed by various critics to write about the music have stopped our communication, not with the audience, but with the media", he says. "Those people have just turned on teeneybop. They went through the pretentious bit early on and they have seen *Satori,*[11] which to them is an acne-faced pop star doing his thing. Our kind of music would take them back to what they've left, so they reject us. But they can't stop it, because the audience knows about music this time round".

The Third Ear Band are one of the few genuinely unique bands on the scene, using almost total improvisation to produce a consistently fascinating tapestry of sound. Besides Glen they include Paul Minns (oboe), Richard Coff (violin, viola) and Ursula Smith (cello), and their second Harvest album, which depicts musically the four elements of the universe (Air, Water, Fire and Earth), is on the point of release.

"It was conceived at about the same time as our first album", says Glen, "when we found that some of our pieces were beginning to represent the elements, which is something we'd wanted to do for a long time".

They are currently going through their biggest set of changes since the early days when Jim Haynes helped them with gigs at the Arts lab. Glen, after a year banging hand-drums, has decided to revert a conventional drum kit, and they are in the throes of purchasing a magnificent British version of the Moog Synthesiser.

---

[11] In the Buddhist tradition Satori means awakening or understanding. In Zen, something like *enlightenment.* The word became popular, as did Zen, by way of the Beat generation.

"We work out a basic drone which I always equate with OM, the sound of the universe, as opposed to most groups who work with riff patterns which I suppose are derived somehow from jazz. The synthesiser will enable us to use varied multi-toned drones, plus attack and decay effects, which will alter the notes over periods of time. We're going to be much more exciting – we really were a very precious little group at one time".

Like, say, Indian classical music (which also uses drones), the Third Ear's output has always seemed to me to be essentially a functional music, extremely useful for clearing your head. What kind of reaction do they get from audiences?

"We've never had any audience hang-ups. We've played to 150.000 people in Hyde Park, with the Stones, and 200.000 people on the Isle of Wight, plus several other festivals, and no one has ever asked us what the music is about. In fact I always get the impression that they know more about it than we do. We never intellectualize, or even discuss, the music between ourselves.

"When we started we had one piece of music, and out of that the nine or ten items of our repertoire have evolved. What emerges from the improvisations are simple structures which everybody enjoys, but playing to big audiences on the pop scene does tend to change your attitudes, and you tend to produce a certain formula so that when you find yourself in a difficult position you have something to fall back on".

"(...) Anyway the roots of our music are jazz, pop and folk, so I don't see how anyone could find it difficult.

"At the moment, because we're working on the Continent and making decent bread, things are rather easy and the creative ability has sunk, so that we've played a few bummers lately. We prefer to work with no preconceived ideas: it's much more exciting that way. For instance, we're doing a concert in June at the *Festival Hall* with a group of French avant-garde musicians, and we'll just go on and play without thinking about what we're going to do up front. Anyway, I can never see the separation between the artist and the audience. To me it's all communion, entertainment, and communication – all these things can happen while you're playing, depending entirely on the audience's heads. By the first or second number you've discovered that the audience's heads are maybe into entertainment, which means that they've been working in a factory all day and they want to be taken out of themselves. But on a normal trip I think we tend to push them back into themselves, to make them more aware of what

58

they are. However we're beginning to play a lot more rave-up things, which I suppose are entertainment.

"The ideal thing is communication, with no separation between audience and band. I admire what John Stevens is doing with *SME*,[12] bringing the audience into the music, but that would be difficult for us because of the invisible environmental image we have. People come up and say 'you shouldn't do that, it's not what you do'".

Glen and the Third Ear are involved in a very quiet and honest way with the kind of mysticism, which means Stonehenge and Glastonbury Tor.

"The trouble is that you can't be mystical without being called pseudo-mystical, and it's the fault of our previous education. I'm at Glastonbury most of the time, but we're all completely honest about it. We'll even use it honestly to make money, because the ancient Egyptians who were into it all said that you had to be rich because only then can you resist temptation. As long as I like it, I'll do it. And the *Hare Krishna* people are right... two records in the chart, and they're very honest. We played with the Druids sometimes. They're a bunch of fine old men, and when we played with them at the Tor there was this old chap of about 90 steaming up the hill, looking like he was about to die. I think they're the true guardians of the mystic traditions in his country.

Talking of the Old Druids got us on the intolerance shown by the so-called 'alternative society' towards member of older generations, and Glen said: "It's all very well, but you have to find a way of feeding it back into the 'straight' society.

"I can't see the point of importing the 'Kill The Pigs' scene into Britain because most of our policemen are really nice chaps – they're certainly not pigs. But I suppose it'll come, because we have to copy America. It's like pollution and ecology. We've been into that for ages, but if I say so now it's going to look like a hype because everybody and his brother are in to it; at the same time as they throw their Coke bottles into the river. But we've got to stay with it.

---

12   *The Spontaneous Music Ensemble* were an important contributor to the growth of free improvisation in the UK. Formed in 1966 by drummer John Stevens, saxophonist Trevor Watts and trombonist Paul Rutherford, all of whom met at the Royal Air Force School of Music.

What I really want to do is get to the straights on their own level, through the jazz thing, and get at the younger people through the underground aspects of the music. Then maybe we'll get the two to meet at some middle level".

Roy Hollingworth was sent by Melody Maker *to 'drive out' the band in February 1972, when the Third Ear Band was recording a new record at the Island Studios in London Basing Street. The album, never published, was printed in 2004 by Angel Air thanks to the late sound engineer and roadie Ron Cort, who had taken the original reels. This interview with Sweeney was published in* Melody Maker *on March, 18th 1972.*

Back to the Thirdies.

"The line-up now seems more viable. I got sick of saying that the old band, with violins and things had no right to be in the pop business. Now we look like a pop group, but it's still Third music". As to the title of the new record: "There are two sets – order and chaos. Order may go, but out of the chaos comes the dragon. Maybe we will kid everyone now that we are high powered and progressive".

Suddenly Third Ear Band are very fashionable. There was Glen Sweeney – one of those dying breeds of excellent underground characters – sipping tea at *Blackhill's* in W2. "We got an encore the other night, which was very strange, because Thirds aren't used to getting encores".

So what's happening?

"Well, it's all down to Shakespeare actually – he's done more for the Thirdies than anyone else, although he won't know that".

Their music for Roman Polanski's film of *Macbeth* has run into an extraordinary amount of publicity, and the roses are still arriving on T.E.B.'s desk. Thirds certainly did some good stuff, and if any band deserved a flip, it was them.

"Polanski gave us tremendous publicity – our name was actually on the screen for about five seconds. That's more than even Mancini[13] gets. The critics have also been very kind, and here we are, suddenly being bombarded with work. Thirds aren't used to that either".

But don't expect the Third Ear Band you have been used to. Don't expect just sheer *avant garde,* because they are changing – in the most remarkable fashion.

Paul Buckmaster, under the burden of personal fame, has now left; he's been replaced by Peter Pauli (bass and cello), who was formerly with *High Tide.* And there's another new member – Mike Marchant. This is where it all becomes different, because Marchant writes, and sings songs.

"Mike has been hanging around the group for some while. We heard the songs, and well, it seemed only natural that he should come in. It's a tremendous jump for us, I mean, we've never done songs before. It's right to say that Thirdies are feeling a little schizophrenic at the moment. I mean, there's that album out from Macbeth, and that's totally avant garde, and then there's us playing songs". Sweeney shakes his head, and sips his tea.

"It may sound a little conceited, but I can't think of any other band who could have worked with Polanski on *Macbeth.* He's never used much music before. We freaked him in places by using the synthesiser – when he just wanted medieval music. We told him it was valid to use electronics if something psychic was being expressed. As time went by he became more and more turned on by music. And that's strange for Polanski, as he tends to keep the level of music down in his films".

If anyone deserves singling out for special merit on *Macbeth* then it must be Paul Minns (oboe and recorder).

It was his constant stream of brilliant imagination that really caught a load of ears. Says Sweeney: "Minns can pour melody out of the air. I feel he's a remarkable player. In fact I can't think of anyone else like him. It became pretty chaotic in places with the film – and Thirdies are handsome at being chaotic – and then Paul would suddenly produce something, and we'd all be there".

---

[13]   An American composer, conductor and arranger, regarded as one of the great film composers - a winner of twenty Grammy awards and famous in particular for *Peter Gunn*, *Moon River*, *The Pink Panther* &c.

So what of these songs?

"Well, at the start, we treated them in a sort of *Velvet Underground*, Leonard Cohen type of way. But we became dissatisfied with the limitations of eight bars and 16 bars. We decided that we really wanted to open out. They certainly aren't pretentious songs, there's no pseudo rubbish about them. There's no "Lucy in the Sky with Feedback". But they are songs that fit Third Ear.

"They are all based around the Tarot, and they are purely descriptions of the cards, and their meanings. It's meant a lot of work, changing from a purely instrumental band, but it really seems to be working. And people certainly like it. We've witnessed things that Thirds have never witnessed before – and that is an audience really asking for more. That absolutely terrified us".

Glen lapsed into talking about the rock scene. "There's a strange feeling in the air. I don't know whether it's slowing down or whether the scene is taking a rest. Maybe it will come back and operate four times as fast. I don't know."

"Everyone toys with the idea to do a *T. Rex*.[14] Somebody even said to me that Thirds would have to do something like that. But I just don't think we could ever exist with 'bubblegum'. We just couldn't make it.

"I think us changing in a natural way – and not just for the sake of it is far more rewarding. I know we will be a far more rational band – giving out something that everyone can enjoy. After three months of rehearsing, we are now capable of playing a varied menu for more than two hours. You wouldn't have got more than 45 minutes a year ago.

Was there any regret at Buckmaster's departure?

"Well, it was always a strange thing with Buck. He sort of drifted into the band, and I could never work out whether he was really with us or not. I remember we

---

[14]   Marc Bolan (born Marc Feld) was a singer, songwriter, musician, poet - and another denizen of the Grove. He had some early success with *Jon's Children* and when their equipment was repossessed by *Track Records*, Bolan formed a quasi-folk band *Tyrannosaurus Rex*, which quickly settled into being a duo with himself on guitar and Steve Peregrin Took on hand drums. They were strongly supported by John Peel, released three albums and four singles and got to No.15 in the charts. Managed by *Blackhill Enterprises*, *Tyrannosaurus Rex* played at the first of the Hyde Park free concerts with *Pink Floyd*, *Roy Harper* and *Jethro Tull* (Third Ear Band didn't play Hyde Park until the fifth of the free concerts in July). In 1970 Bolan went electric, renamed the band T.Rex and turned into a teeny-bopper megastar.

were traveling on the continent at one time and Buck was sat writing music. It was *Space Oddity* – and suddenly Buck was famous. He drifted away, and we struggled on with Ursula Smith on cello. Then I met Buck again – he was famous by then – and before I knew it, he was back in the band. But during the period with *Macbeth* I had to tell him that we wanted him permanently, or not at all. We all know how pressured he is. In fact during *Macbeth* he should never have been working at all."

Probably the best interview ever, is this long conversation with Nigel Cross in which Glen tells the story of the TEB revealing a sharp sense of humour about life and a strong disillusionment with the Sixties-Seventies rock epic. The interview was published in Unhinged *magazine in the summer of 1990.*

The return of the acid prankster.
Glen Sweeney tells the Third Ear Band story.

It would take one of Peter Frame's family trees to accurately and aesthetically plot the convoluted twists of the Third Ear's long, illustrious career. But I guess it's not financially worthwhile for him to grapple with its intricate branches, which would pull in *High Tide, Magic Muscle, Rustic Hinge*, etc. etc. So in the meantime I would like to present for your delight and edification the Glen Sweeney story, for 'tis he who has kept the Band's inner flame aglow all the years. As far as I know, this is the first time the percussionist's fascinating past has been shoved into the British's public gaze and I'd like to see most of *Unhinged*'s current crop of musical darlings stay the long, hard course as well as Glen has. A survivor, a madcap, an acid prankster, no mere relic of the first psychedelic era, Sweeney's main strength lies in a wicked sense of humour and an unquenchable ability never to take life seriously. Whilst many pop historians regard the events of 1967 with awed reverence, Glen sees it all, as he did then, as a bit of a giggle. Sweeney is now the only surviving original member of the Ear, though both oboist Paul Minns and cellist Ursula Smith were temporarily lured back to the fold in the late '80s for

Italian tours. Spring 1990 sees a settled line up of Glen, Lyn Dobson, Neil Black and Mick Carter playing some of the most astonishing music the Ear has ever produced and there are selective U.K. Dates on the horizon.

Nigel: Let's go back to the beginning of Glen Sweeney. You once quipped that you were born either in Venus or in Croydon!

Glen (laughs): Somewhere between Venus and Croydon.

Nigel: What sort of upbringing did you have?

Glen: Quite normal, except I felt alienated because I wasn't big, strong etc. I really thought I might have been a girl, but having checked out girls, I realised I wasn't a girl. I then met somebody who was into music, in fact a clarinettist. He immediately sussed my problem and introduced me to jazz. I got into jazz and eventually wanted to be Charlie Parker but, being a complete lazy bastard, I realised that this would probably take years. So I used to hang around the clubs and pose. After a while it occurred to me that the greatest way to pose was to buy a drumkit.

Nigel: Was this the Anacondas Skiffle group you had?

Glen: This happened in between. I was totally into the scene – jazz drums - when a couple of guys I knew did an interval at a club I was hanging out at and their washboard player cracked up under the strain. I immediately leapt in, sussing how simple it must be and became moderately famous overnight because it was only local talent; it wasn't difficult to do. From there I just went back into jazz and eventually, as the years rolled by, I ended up playing the clubs around Soho - like the *Caves de France*, drinking clubs obviously, run by Cypriot mafia and they would spring up one night and disappear another – this was towards the end of the fifties. Most of the guys that I knew like Ginger Baker, Graham Bond were suddenly working, which was quite a shock in those days because there wasn't any work. What had happened was rhythm and blues – now this was more within my capability. I could lay down a backbeat and things like this, so I began to work with various failed rhythm and blues bands. Someone in the band would always have a programmed failure scene going. I remember I did a *bar mitzvah* with George Kahn – remember him? – he was a star on the saxophone; everyone was stoned so it didn't matter! He played Charlie Parker's *Lover Man* and it was so emotional, he broke down and cried (laughs). That was my scene – what would you call it? The lunatic fringe! I met many people during this period – for me it was more or less a way of life. You avoided working. You made a few quid. You got some free drinks.

Nigel: Was there a heavy drug scene at that time?

Glen: No! Only marijuana – they mostly paid you in beer so it regulated your turn on! That led into the Swinging '60s where I didn't do much at all, mostly posing! Hanging around Ronnie's.[15]

Nigel: Tell me a bit more about the Anacondas band?

Glen: It came and went. One of the high spots was a residency at the *Driftbridge Hotel* in Reigate, because it was local. We used to play there every Sunday and pull a decent crowd, because we were ethnic Skiffle – we played the actual band's numbers. This was where I met Ginger Baker – we were doing the interval when Ginger was playing with some trad band – *Charlesworth*[16] – after we'd done our set, and Ginger came up to me and threatened to do me over for doing all his band's numbers! (laughs) After that I really got to know the guy and he was great! What happened with Skiffle was – one Saturday or Sunday it ended! I've no idea what happened – I think the scene got so full of Skiffle groups that it just killed itself[17].

---

[15]   London's premier Jazz club in Frith St., Soho, co-founded by the highly regarded tenor saxophonist *Ronnie Scott*, in 1959.

[16]   That must be clarinettist *Dick Charlesworth's City Gents*, popular proponents of the trad jazz revival that animated Britain in the early 1960's and from which Skiffle emerged. *The City Gents* wore pinstriped suits and bowler hats, so I suppose Ginger was too. By 1967 Charleseworth had quit London to front dance bands on ocean liners.

[17]   There were estimated to be between 40 and 50,000 skiffle groups in the UK by the late 1950s.

Nigel: What happened next?

Glen: Well I was really into posing! (Ronnie) Scott's had become quite an in-scene.

Nigel: You're talking now of the era of the Flamingo.[18]

Glen: Yeah. All the pros and cons had taken over. *Ronnie* still used to have an evening where the Brits could have a bash, but I never got included. Then I dropped out because I couldn't buy any more kits on hire purchase – I'd been blacked by the entire scene.

Nigel: How much of a conventional drummer were you in those days?

Glen: Oh, quite conventional! Just lazy! I never bothered to keep up with drummers like Elvin Jones.

Nigel: Jumping on the beginning of the underground scene, how did you get involved?

Glen: A guy I met a long time before, a guy called Dave Tomlin, who used to play sax and was known as an ace guy – he'd taken a lot of drugs and dropped out. I found a note in my door saying 'Meet me at the club at 12 o'clock'. At the time I just had a basic bass drum, snare – so I took a chance, called a cab and went down there - and this was the opening night of the *UFO Club*. That's where I got involved in what we called "freaky scenes", because I said to Dave, "When do we go on?" and he said, "Go on?" Everything had changed – there was no such thing as going on any more with Dave. So I said, "What do we do?" and he said, "Well, why don't you wait and see". So I waited. I was getting really paranoid. There were

___

18   A major London nightclub in Soho that opened in 1952: 'A very dark and evil-smelling basement', as John Mayall described it - but it hosted the likes of Sarah Vaughan, Ella Fitzgerald and Billie Holiday. And Ronnie Scott and Tubby Hayes were in its house band. Its main clientele were gangsters, pimps, prostitutes, American servicemen, bohemians and celebrities, in part because of its speakeasy ambiance, in part because of the drugs freely available there (it had no liquor license) and in part because of its exceptional musical programme. It was also famous (as UFO would be later) for running all-night sessions at the weekends. In the 1960s it was adopted by the mod subculture and became the first to feature ska acts and Carribean sound systems; from 1962 - 1965 *Georgie Fame and the Blue Flames* were the resident band. You'd meet the Beatles, the Rolling Stones, Jimi Hendrix and anyone else who was hip there. It was also pretty much an oasis of racial tolerance. It closed in 1969.

hundreds of people down there. It was all happening. There was me, a bass player called Roger Bunn - who was another lunatic, and Dave; we marched out into the middle of the room amidst thousands of people and started playing! Dave's playing had changed completely – it consisted mainly of repetition. I thought "This is the gig I'm looking for". (laughs) "I can handle this" After the first night, we must have played for two or three hours – we actually scored a residency from around 3 am until everybody went. The idea was that we should make people leave as soon as possible. (laughter)

Nigel: This was the beginning of the Sun Trolley.

Glen: This was called the Sun Trolley and Dave was totally into guerrilla warfare music! The most famous scene Sun Trolley did was when we played in Hyde Park – we actually occupied the small bandstand by the lake and they had a lot of people there from *International Times* with tape recorders. It was going to be an event rather than a musical thing. So we started playing the most outrageous stuff we could think of and immediately the park police turned up. This was a beautiful demonstration of the establishment at work. They said, "Stop playing!" and we said, "No!" They said, "We will stop you, but at the moment we haven't got the key to the gate to get in to stop you". Apparently they couldn't step over the railings because this was illegal! So they sent a guy to get the key; meanwhile we had a philosophical conversation because they said, "There's no playing in the park". And Dave said, "What about the birds?" This was all going down on tape – they said, "The birds are not music" and Dave replied, "I don't think that's fair really, I think it's beautiful music". They said, "Birds are not people". Dave came back with, "Now you're really offending me". It went on like this 'til they managed to open the gate and eject us. They let us off for some unknown reason and then that night at the UFO club the tape was played over the P.A. And we actually got a write-up in the local press, which said something like "Park Policemen are Banning All Birds from Singing in the Park!". Around this time I run into a bunch of guys from the *People Band* and renamed them. *The Hydrogen Jukebox* came up, this idea – they were totally into theatre at UFO by then – we got this girlfriend of someone's and got her this dress made by *Melomex*, got a big pair of scissors wired up to a bug in the P.A.....at that time we were playing an incredible mad free jazz; there was a guy called Barry Pilcher, who's still around (capitalising on the

67

Jukebox's name. N.C.) – we wailed while the trombone player cut the dress in circles from the bottom, round and round, getting higher. This pulled in so many people that the band became famous overnight – got a write-up in *Melody Maker*, everything! They were all carried away by the audience, the amount of people.

Nigel: Who came up with the name Hydrogen Jukebox?

Glen: It's taken from the Ginsberg's poem *Howl*.

Nigel: Who was the guy involved in the Jukebox who was a black panther?

Glen: That was Barry, he was part of the commune in the States that produced the *MC5*[19]. The others in the Jukebox were Clive Kingsley on guitar, who once said the he knew exactly what acid was; it was like ice cream. Clive went the way of all acid-heads, he disappeared down the ice cream trail! (laughs) The *People Band* then reasserted its right over the Jukebox and took it over again. There were so many people floating around – Mel Davis, George Kahn came back into it. It reverted back to what it had been before I nicked it! I nicked it for these couple of gigs. Then Dave (Tomlin) went off to Arabia with this chick on a motorbike and I disappeared for a while, until it became vital to eat! I was crashing at somebody's pad in the Gate – I then invented the Third Ear Band.

Nigel: Do you remember playing the 14 Hour Technicolor Dream at Ally Pally?

Glen: That was with Tomlin, one of the last Sun Trolley gigs. We didn't do much. We just got stoned and moodied about.

Nigel: Wasn't it around then that you got in with Hoppy who hired you as acid pranksters to go and do these 'freak-outs'?

---

[19]   Politically active, hard-rock Detroit band formed in1964, who became notorious for their loud, high energy music (strongly influenced by Free Jazz), their live album *Kick out The Jams* (1968), drug use – and through their manager John Sinclair - close association with the Beat generation poets, the Black and White Panthers, and anti-Vietnam war protest.

Glen: Jesus Christ, yes! This was during the Sun Trolley – the Sun Trolley was like part of an 'event' and Hoppy used to hire our *Revolutions*. TV gigs from all over Europe would ring Hoppy and ask him to fix up a 'revolution' for Saturday night! Well me and Dave were always on the 'revolutions'! We did an Italian one chanting *Hare Krishna* and holding torches, which must've upset the Hare Krishnas because they later tried to attack me! Then we did a German one in Oxford. That's where I encountered the most amazing example of the British police force at work. Hoppy and all these guys knew Oxford, I didn't – we stopped in this big square where all the professors live and people climbed into trees and starting reciting poetry! Me and Dave set up in this little square and we started wailing – that's the only way I can describe it – when across the green was approaching an English bobby. He stopped in front of me and said, "What's going on here?". I couldn't believe it, it was like something on the BBC – I replied, "We're playing music". He said, "Well, I shall have to ask you to stop, there's no music allowed in this square!" So we said, "OK" since we were quite willing to move on, but he took out his notepad and said, "Just a minute". He proceeded accurately to copy out everything that was on my bass drum, which was *Giant Sun Trolley* and at the time I think I went under the name of Glen Zen – he said, "Is that your surname, sir?" And then we all buggered off. That's an example of the lunacy that was going on (laughter). We got paid quite a considerable amount of money so it was quite a good idea! That was the Hoppy version of the *Merry Pranksters*.[20]

Nigel: So, going back to the Third Ear Band.

Glen: I was crashing in Notting Hill Gate, getting very hungry and we had no equipment, so I thought we should have a go at the folk scene, more or less! I went and got Paul Minns – I'd established a relationship with him – Paul's parents were socialists and very well off – Paul was living in this room, refusing to answer the telephone, with some kind of problem. I knew he could play incredible oboe; I don't know what turned his mind that night; in fact I don't know what happened that night. I went to Paul and talked him into it. I went to see this guy Ben Cartland,

---

[20]   Followers and friends of the American author Ken Kesey, who travelled around America in the summer of 1964 in a psychedelic painted School bus (driven by Beat alumnus Neil Cassady) organizing parties and giving away LSD. They went on to oversee 'Acid Test' events across California at which they dispensed - and proselytized the virtues of – LSD. The Grateful Dead were frequent performers at these events. The state made LSD illegal in 1966, when it also became illegal in the UK.

who'd been working with *Tyrannosaurus Rex* but had bottled out at the recording or something – which I later I found out was his problem – and this American I knew, Richard Coff, on the run from the Vietnam War. So two violins, an oboe and I'd made myself a drum out of a shell I'd found in a pad! I'd managed to fix a skin on it and painted it up to look a bit Egyptian! We knew a guy, a guitarist called Davy Graham, who used to work down *Les Cousins*, really brilliant guitarist. I'd known him for a long time. We used to sit and eat daffodils together! He told us to get down to Cousins and he booked us a gig. We went down there. Davy was there. They gave us a free coca cola, which didn't help at all and Davy finished his set. He announced us as *The Third Ear Band* – Carolyn (Glen's girlfriend) thought it up. At the time we only had about one number. We all decided to play our arses off. We went through this one number, which must've lasted about 20 minutes, stood up for the applause and went to dismount at the side of the stage. The guy came up and said, "Davy told me it's an all nighter". He then gave us another coke (laughs) and we went back on and played this number over and over again, which is where the idea of 'Alchemy' came from, you see. By the time we'd actually collapsed, he took pity on us and gave us three quid, we'd now got three numbers! Then we went down Drury Lane and into the *Arts Lab*, where I knew Jim Haynes. I asked him if there was any chance of a gig and he said, "Sure". He cleared out the little hall, everybody slumped down on cushions and away we went again, playing the same stuff, by now confidently. I think we made a tenner there, food money!

Nigel: I was under the impression that there was actually an electric Third Ear Band before.

Glen: That's right. When the *People Band* reclaimed the Jukebox, I was still left with a few musicians like Clive Kingsley on guitar. What happened was after about two gigs, Clive's gear got nicked. This was at *Middle Earth* – The Electric Third Ear – electric acid ragas!

Nigel: Didn't you do a big out of town gig too?

Glen: That was the last gig with John Mayall in Portsmouth! I remember having to walk back. Well, we got lifts. One in lorry loaded with planks of wood that hadn't been planed! All the girls had to take the basket round because we didn't even get paid. After that we were so beat Clive didn't lock up his gear. He left it in some pad and it was stolen.

Nigel: You told me once about this bizarre story behind the band's name.

Glen: Carolyn thought it up. We had this groupie, the only groupie we ever had, he used to follow us around everywhere. I think he was French! He had this spectacle case with an ear in it and he reckoned it was Van Gogh's ear! During that period, everyone used to refer to it as Pierre's Third Ear! So when it came to naming the band we became the Third Ear Band.

Nigel: The Arts Lab must've been a crazy place – what's all this about the album you recorded there?

Glen: After the first gig we got at *the Arts Lab*, we began to do *Cousins* and the *Arts Lab* regular! Every week – we packed them in! I later analysed what it was – it was the excitement generated because nobody knew what we were doing! I once met a trumpet player friend of mine who played with all the top jazz-rock bands and he told me that in one of them there was a black bass-player who used to listen to *Alchemy* on a headset over and over again. My mate asked him what the attraction was and the bass player said, "You can't believe these guys. Nobody knows what they're doing. The excitement of whether they're going to make it to the end of the number is unbelievable!". And I think that was the key to it at the beginning. That was the secret – towards the end we lost it. You knew what was happening. Incredible things would happen, like Ben Cartland would often walk out – completely! We did discover that he couldn't record, because when we went into record *Alchemy* he bottled out! I had to rush out and get an old jazzer friend of mine in on cello – Mel Davis.

Nigel: This Arts Lab *gig?*

Glen: Yeah, with Christopher Logue, the poet, Rip Torn, the actor. Down the *Arts Lab* everything was happening. *The Beatles*'d walk through naked! I went down to do the gig, Torn and Logue were on stage – I'm pretty sure they had a good recorder going there. Jim Haynes said that they were doing an album for themselves and asked if we wanted to play on it. So we played and I think it's mentioned in Jim's book "Thanks for coming" – whether those people used the recordings I've no idea. There's a video-cassette of our gig at the *Albert Hall* – most people finish with the *Albert Hall*. We did the *Albert Hall, the Purcell Room* and the *Royal Festival Hall* in that order – from the top to the bottom. (laughs)

Nigel: Tell me about your involvement with Ron Geesin.[21]

Glen: That was *Blackhill*. We started to get quite a lot of publicity for such an esoteric, off-the-wall band. Eventually I realised we weren't getting paid anything – we were putting out a lot of energy! I knew *Blackhill* through DJ Pete Drummond – they'd been in on a lot of the happenings – so they knew Dave and hated him! They asked me how much I wanted a gig and I said, "25 quid" – they said, "Sounds reasonable". This was a lot of money to us. We used to get paid in hash, brown rice, anything; it was hard work. *Blackhill* wangled some package deal with *Harvest* – we'd got this demo tape which had Ben Cartland on it – the original line up of two violins, oboe and drums – it featured those first numbers we did at the early gigs. I can't remember what they sound like now. Geesin sold the tape to *Essex Music* for this library of sound effects – they must've been used on radio or TV because we got some money for them! Another thing we did, which also disappeared forever, was a tape we did for a German TV film called *Abelard and Eloise* – that was two whole reels!

Nigel: What was the Hyde Park concert that you did for Blackhill?

Glen: That was *Blind Faith* and it was bad news for them.

Nigel: Why?

Glen: Because they bombed out and we were blamed because of 'bad vibes'. A couple of heavies came around from their management company and there was

---

[21]   Scottish performer, composer and eccentric (b.1942) who released various solo projects and scored for experimental and mainstream films. His self-produced LP 'A Raise of the Eyebrows' in 1967 attracted the attention of the hip community and later that year Pink Floyd asked him in to arrange *Atom Heart Mother* for them. He also later worked with Roger Waters on the soundtrack for *The Body* (EMI-Harvest 1970).

talk of 'jumping on hands' – it came out of the blue, but then one of the guys suddenly went, "God! You're GlenSweeney!" I said "Of course I am, don't you remember *Studio 51*"[22], and the guy just went, "Man, forget it!" They went away. I think it was all down to Paul Buckmaster who was with us by then.

Nigel: How did Buckmaster come to join?

Glen: Well that was down to Coff. We were having a lot of problems with the "fourth guy" – Mel Davis had had to go, but most of the time we were without. We'd often do it as a trio and it was getting hard work. Richard kept on about this guy, Paul Buckmaster – he joined just before the Hyde Park concert. We were lined up to do *Blind Faith* in the Park with no cello. So Richard finally talked me into this Paul Buckmaster. Who was ace – *Royal Academy of Music*, you name it! He even used make up, which was a complete shock to our style. But he was good, right? After that, he
would only turn up when he felt like it. He turned up for the Stones in the Park, and he rejoined for the film, *Macbeth* – luckily for me because I was totally out of it by then.

Nigel: So it was around the Hyde Park concerts that you got this 'bad vibes' tag?

Glen: Yeah. But it was only a brief encounter because there'd been a lot of aggro around. I've got so used to aggro that I couldn't tell if there was any aggro or not. It all seemed normal to me! Guys would approach you and offer to jump on your hands! But it was very brief, whatever it was.

Nigel: But what about this business with Jagger and the Coke cans?

Glen: I knew about that. We'd spoken to Jagger at the *Blind Faith* gig. I knew they were in trouble because the band belonged to Brian Jones – Brian Jones had signed a separate contract to the Stones and the Stones were broke, down to their

---

[22]   A club in Great Newport Street, Soho, where Ken Colyer's and other Jazz clubs were located throughout the 1950s, shifting with the musical tide in the '60s to Blues and R & B. The Rolling Stones and the Yardbirds were regulars, the Downliners Sect were the house band for a while.

last ten grand or whatever. We suggested that they do the Park. Jagger suggested that everybody bring something along to bang on and drown us out – to my paranoid way of thinking the guy was worried about us! It's unbelievable, isn't it? If you get the video, you'll suss the amount of paranoia that was going down and there's no mention of the other five groups that were there – but that's show business for you.

Nigel: Where did Ursula the cellist came from?

Glen: We did a free gig at a women's prison - *Holloway*, she was playing there with a folk guitarist and I was desperate at the time – that's not putting her down, she was a great player – I nicked her from this folk guitarist. She's a Libra and they always seem to be influenced by certain people, I don't know how it works. She was influenced by Richard Coff to split up the group.

Nigel: Before she and Richard split to form Unnatural Acts, you recorded the Four Elements album, didn't you?

Glen: Yeah, that was really bad news. I was fucked-up from beginning to end! It was mainly recorded on the dreaded chemical and I don't know how it survived really. The *Fire* track started out with Richard doing a genius track – he lay down about 48 overdubs and then we joined in – then Minns laid down another 20 overdubs! Well, when we came to mix it, the engineer had one go at it and then walked out of the studio – completely! We were left with that – nobody had any idea where to start. It was basically an 8-track and there was no way there was any talent around who would touch it. I imagine now, in my maturity, that their reputations were at stake. A couple of tracks came out OK – *Air* and *Water* – the other two were just bad news, baby, but we were committed. It was going to be called *Air, Earth, Fire Water*, then another band came up with the title before us; it was going to be called *Third Ear Band in its own bag*, then Harvest nicked the idea of 'in its own bag' – they wouldn't let *us* have a bag, but they used it later on. It was bad news and we were bad news. My God!

Nigel: Didn't you get into some kind of feud situation with that other Blackhill *act, the* Edgar Broughton Band?

74

Glen: Oh yes, that was quite friendly really! It was like, wherever Edgar played we'd be on the same bill. And eventually - you know the kind of ego-tripping that goes on - it became a dispute about just who was pulling the crowds (laughter). It was obviously Edgar Broughton, right? But after you've done enough chemical you're fucked – the chemical's supposed to get rid of your ego. Don't believe it! It does the opposite. We were both OK, but let's face it, their audience wasn't our audience. But the agency's just into cash, like, "You want Edgar, you've to take the Third Ear Band, you've got to take Pete Brown". You get to the gig and you get a lot of resentment because they've had to pay for you when they wanted him.

Nigel: Did you get friendly with the other Blackhill *artists? For instance, do you remember* Formerly Fat Harry?[23]

Glen: Oh yeah. The bass player from *Country Joe and the Fish* (Bruce Barthol – N.C.). He was over here and lost – he didn't know where he was coming from or where he was going to – poor guy. He was into getting *Harvest* to sign contracts specifying free air trips to San Francisco each year. As far as Harvest were concerned he was some kind of worn-out bass player! But they thought they might be able to make some bread, but he didn't which was a shame because he was a great guy. They got a lot of people like that in the end because it was the age of 'rip off the record company' – get a great big advance and tell everybody you're on heroin!

Nigel: Did the Third Ear grind to a halt after Richard and Ursula sodded off?

Glen: Well we were committed to do another album – there was still a lot of live work going. I put another band together which became the Third Ear 'Big' Band – Denim Bridges on guitar – he had this double 'whammy' guitar, which blew everybody's mind! A couple of months later, we discovered that only one neck would play! We had quite a lot of people in there...

---

[23]   British band formed in 1971 by ex *Country Joe and the Fish* bassist Bruce Barthol, two fellow US expats Gary Peterson and Phil Greenberg, Saxophonist George Khan and Laurie Allen (who went on to work with *Gong*). They played inoffensive country rock, never made much of an impression and disbanded when the American contingent went back home.

Nigel: And that's when you got involved with Polanski… but what's the tale about getting phoned up by Kubrick?

Glen: The band had reached the pits and they didn't even want to see us in the agency! It was such bad news. I used to do what Pete Brown used to do, which was to go in there and bug 'em! So we were all sitting around smoking and the phone rang. Andrew (King) picked it up in his supercilious way; he listened for a while and said, "There's a friend of yours here on the phone, Glen!" I said, "Who's that then?" He said, "You'll never believe this, Glen, it's Stanley Kubrick – he wants a track from *Earth, Air Fire, Water* to use in a film called *Clockwork Orange* – have you ever heard of that one? I said, "No, Andrew, who's is it? What's happening?" He said, "The guy isn't going to pay any money, so it's goodbye to Stanley" and put the phone down – I nearly fainted! I thought there was a slight possibility that it could be for real. I was sitting there getting really wound up when the phone went again – he picked it up and went, "Oh Glen, this is really over the top, man guess who we've got now? Roman Polanski!" I said, "gimme that phone" and it was him asking if we'd do the soundtrack to *Macbeth*. I said, "Yeah, certainly!" I gave it back to Andrew and Andrew said, "Roman Polanski, is it?" and Roman said, "Yes, Roman Polanski." So he said, "Can we have a meet?" He really thought that would screw it up. Roman said, "Sure, I'll come around and see you tomorrow". It was the man himself. Then I was lucky. I had Bucky, Denim Bridges. I tried to get Coff back, but he immediately started to get nasty, so I got Simon House".

Nigel: How did you come to re-enlist Buckmaster?

Glen: I got rid of Buck because of all the aggro he'd cost us at gigs. He was doing Elton John, David Bowie at the same time as us. Anyway, I was sitting in Notting Hill at this pizza place and there was Bucky sitting there – so I went over and joined him. I knew the *Macbeth* was on by this time and I also knew that I was going to need somebody. I was in no fit state to put anything together and the rest of the band was terminal! So I asked him if he'd like to rejoin. He asked me what I'd got to offer. Well I know that Buck's idol was the guy who wrote the Bond title music,[24] the big screenwriter, and all Buck wanted was to score for films – he was brilliant. I mentioned casually that we were going to do something for *Macbeth* and he was there immediately! And then all these ads started turning up in the big American trade papers saying that Bucky was scoring the music for *Macbeth* and I didn't think that was fair. So I protested and they changed it, but they spelt all our names wrong. They put two Buckmasters in, but I thought that was fair enough!

Nigel: So how did you get Simon?

Glen: Simon, I'd known for a long time. He was in *High Tide*, who lived up the Grove – they had an agency there (*Clearwater*), something like *Blackhill*, only poorer. He was the only guy, who could handle it. He was great. We did the score, a lot of it was improvised, but a lot of it couldn't be improvised. And we were having a lot of bad vibes from George Martin, who ran the studio – he wanted to be on the name check: "Music by George Martin and the Third Ear Band". So when he didn't get that, we got a lot of bad vibes – but I was used to that by then! (laughter)

Nigel: You went to the Northumberland location as well, didn't you?

Glen: That was great, we went up there to synch the dance track, *The Groom's Dance*. What happened was it turned into a gigantic piss-up – it was absolutely unbelievable. Polanski hired the local band, who were experts at playing country dance band music. They had a brilliant drummer who could do press roll like he was trained in some kind of Highland band. We ended up tangoing. I was partnered with Polanski and we both had roses in our teeth. It was outrageous.

Nigel: Macbeth is known as a bad vibe play – what happened?

Glen: Well it totaled everybody, didn't it? In the end it totaled the band – only one guy survived it, that's the guy who went on to *The Professionals*, Martin Shaw.

---

[24]   John Barry, multi award winning film composer who scored eleven Bond movies. In the mid '50s he ran the John Barry Seven, who appeared often on British television and made ten hit singles.

Everybody else went down the tubes, even Polanski when they busted him in America. It took its time – the old curse – it rolled right across the board.

Nigel: What was Jon Finch like to work with?
Glen: He was great, he was pissed all the time. He couldn't act unless he was pissed. I really liked that guy.

Nigel: Did you get to meet Francesca Annis?

Glen: Yeah I met her. At the time, she said, she was a hippy – she just wanted to make enough money to go back to Kathmandu. Obviously it was all bullshit – it was the kind of chat they gave out at the time, they were all after the cash! Polanski was great – he picked all the young unknowns and taught everyone of them whilst we stood there watching. He tried to teach them to act as though they were the guy next door. It upset so many people – it was a bomb-out in America – it was financed by the *Playboy* guy, Hugh Heffner... and during the time we were making it, it was Heffner's birthday. Now in the film there are about 40 old hags with the most grotesque bodies and faces – he had them all nude singing "Happy birthday to you" at Heffner's birthday party at the *Playboy Club*! It's a wonder he didn't throw up. All in all it was a great time.

Nigel: It must have been during this period that you had the infamous run-in with Graham Bond.

Glen: My God, that came out of nowhere – I had been promoting a bit of chat about the band and its magic qualities – we played with the druids at Glastonbury Tor and I put it about that they were protecting us from the evil spirit in Manchester, because every time we went near Manchester – whenever we tried to play this scene called *The Magic Village*, it was bad news. It was an old morgue. Every time we went there the hairs stood up on the back of our heads. We started spreading this about, that we were on the side of the good with the druids and Graham Bond – he saw himself as Crowley, the 'great beast' and I had a couple of encounters with him and places started burning down. I thought it was him – *Bumpers* in Piccadilly... *The Magic Village* burnt down; eventually this ad turned up in *Melody Maker* in a box, which went something like "Glen Sweeney is Ra, an alien from

78

another planet". I couldn't believe my eyes. There it was in a big black box and I'd no idea – I thought it was some agent or gig that thought I'd ripped them off and they were trying to do me. But later I did this gig with Graham and he came over, shook hands and said, "No hard feelings, man?" I said, "No, naturally no". And he said, "Well I was out of my tree at the time I put the ad in". I thought "Jesus Christ. It's him!" A while later he topped himself. That guy was so freaky!

Nigel: Post-Macbeth, the band carried on, didn't it?

Glen: Yeah. We staggered on. We were dead!

Nigel: It must've been pretty strange – didn't Dave Tomlin come in on guitar?

Glen: That was the pits. I've got this awful thing. Whatever the trip, you must do it to the end. Dave said that the band at the time sounded like a used car and it probably did. We did it till the end until nobody wanted to know.

Nigel: Last time we were talking, you told me you were even doing things like Out Demons Out.[25]

Glen: Yeah, we were! You name, we did it. We were doing that old *Fugs* number *When the mode of the music changes, the walls of the city shake* and the walls of the city were really shaking, man! (laughter) We had whole audiences just split the gig immediately.

Nigel: I thought the band was gone more or less after Macbeth, *but you tell it differently.*

Glen: That was down to Pete Jenner – he had the *Sharks* and Pete Jenner always believed in me, basically, because he never attended a gig, he never listened to us. He thought I was in a bad state because I hadn't got a record deal – having completed the one with the *Harvest*. He bargained with Chris Blackwell at *Island*. He said, "You can have the *Sharks* if you do an album with the Third Ear Band!" At the time I was surrounded by idiots who were hoping I had a few quid! They

---

25   The Edgar Broughton Band's first hit single, a singalong.

dragged me in there – even now Simon House swears it's a masterpiece – I had this roadie Ron Cort, whose father was a hire car wallah, rolling in it – Ron really went to town on that album – he got acetates made, he got a single made. It was crap – even I didn't know what I was doing – the singer was terrible, we had vocals. All the songs were based on the tarot, but strangely enough his father was a vicar and all the songs were based on hymns.

Nigel: Whose father?

Glen: The singer! He was a little guy from Durham. I can't remember who else was there – Simon reckoned there was some ace guitarist on the gig – I've no idea though. I was on my nineteenth nervous breakdown. I was taking everything; I couldn't play!

Nigel: You once commented that it sounded like Slade!

Glen: At one point the guy – somebody said to him that he hadn't got enough aggression – you see the whole thing was being run by everyone else. I'd gone back to playing kit drums, which I was never any good at – and they got him to sing like *Slade.* You can imagine what it was like. This is when it got absolutely terrible – we'd do gigs and play the single and everybody was like "what's next!".

Nigel: So what did you do?

Glen: Well it took me three years to recover my brain. We bought this old houseboat down in Kent. There was a flood and it got washed up into a field – I didn't have anything to get it back into the water, so we just stayed there – and the council used to come and photograph it every week to see if it had moved".

Nigel: When did you record that Hydrogen Jukebox?

Glen: I came back off the boat and found this place in Shepherd's Bush. I gradually returned to normal and attempted to get back into the music. I started rehearsing with Paul, he had a house down by the Green and he had a big room upstairs. I started trying to put myself back together. We run into a few guys, Mick

Carter was one of them – and started by rehearsing with various vocalists. Eventually I came up with this guy Jimmy Jones – we had Mick on guitar and a brilliant bass player and we had an ace little band, except we were now playing almost pure rock'n'roll with a bit of freaky effect. Paul's missus chucked us out and I thought, "It's now or never" – we knew this guy down in Kent who had a 4-track, he also had a little cottage. We went down and knocked out all these numbers I'd written. And that's Hydrogen Jukebox!

Nigel: This bloke, Jim...

Glen: He disappeared. He was a gypsy – he claimed he was a gypsy. It was supposed to be Dylan, but it rapidly moved into a lot of other areas. Now quite a lot of people like it. I like it now! I buried it for years – as a memorial to Hydrogen Jukebox, I think it's worth putting out.

Nigel: How did the Third Ear Band come to reform in 1988?

Glen: That was Luca, this young Italian guy – he's a collector of sixties ephemera – the one band he'd always lusted after was the Third Ear Band. He had no idea that we existed – he expected to find me in a wheelchair! He chased me for two years – I thought it was some kind of Italian cassette rip off. "Send a tape! Send a tape!". I started sending Indian tapes, basically anything so long as it wasn't me – he got really confused and eventually came over here. I spoke to him and I must admit I wasn't very friendly. He was absolutely amazed that I was still around – he enquired about Paul – and then I received a letter offering me a gig at *Rockinumbria*, a rock big venue in Italy. He was very shrewd, he said £250 each and that put me on the road, right? I was out there. It ended up at about £50 each, but it put me back in the picture. And when I heard the people – when I saw the crowds, we're not talking about many, but one guy had flown there from somewhere and was going to fly to the next gig – I thought, "Who am I to turn all these poor bastards down?" and it put me back into work I like doing (laughs).

Nigel: Tell me about the album that's out. It's recorded live?

Glen: It was done at the first gig. The band consists of me, Paul (Minns), Mick Carter and Allen Samuel.

Nigel: *Where's Allen Samuel from?*

Glen: That's through desperation. I went to everybody – Simon hadn't played the violin for years – Ursula at the time refused because she thought it was a put on. I'm well known for my fantasies. Eventually Dave Tomlin – he wouldn't move from his embassy, said there was a guy next door who was quite a good violinist. We rehearsed with him for a while and it was brilliant. But I didn't know he couldn't play on stage. He was another Ben Cartland. – he just dried up on stage.

Nigel: *So who have you got now?*

Glen: Well he's a guy called Neil Black. He's competent. When you're gigging and recording, you need fairly professional people. You've got to put out under all kind of circumstances. It used to give me the horrors, but I've got used to it – I can survive anything on a little red or white wine. I couldn't handle anything else – I'm lucky, I don't know how I got through it.

Nigel: *How do you feel about your drumming now?*

Glen: I feel great. Dave Tomlin turned me on – I had those mridangams [pronounced m'dungas] for a long time – they're two mridangams with bongos grafted on the top and legs put on them. Those mridangam are hand carved inside – they give you the tone. By getting a smaller one, a kiddie's one actually and the two different heads, I can tune up to vaguely a mridangam sound. The problem with playing one of them is the tuning: it'd take you hours and if the weather changes, you've had it. They're built in India where the climate stays the same and they have about 8 tuners behind them with 5 mridangam. So, if anything goes out of tune, they can just chuck it behind them and guy passes them a tuned one. I was talking with Drachen Theaker[26] about this – he told me he tried all that. What

---

[26]   Original drummer with *The Crazy World of Arthur Brown* who left when their hit single *'Fire'* was released, unhappy with the low level of the drums in the mix - or because he couldn't handle touring. There are

I was aiming for isn't Indian, but a fair interpretation of it plus I would never learn their 90 ragas, I was never any good at it! I learn one day, I've forgotten it tomorrow. So I play free mridangam, free Indian playing. I went round to Dave's and he started teaching it to me and I thought about giving it up! I went round to see Drachen and he played it at top speed – and in my way, I'm really a nasty person, I sussed exactly what the basic of it was. I ripped off the basic from him and Dave, went home and released what I'd built them drums for! That's what I'm into now and I practice – unbelievable isn't it? And I'm getting reasonable at it; it sounds OK. It sounds original. Those things are tuned to some modal note that's going to carry on through the gig – if it goes out, it would sound terrible. I couldn't handle that!

Nigel: How would you describe the music the Third Ear Band is playing now?

Glen: Jesus Christ! It's now sort of Indian that's moved into the *avant garde*. With Mick's new guitar, he can now play tamboura on it and sitar – because he can tune each string on the guitar to a different sound. All that is possible plus what we now call our heavy metal repertoire – that's Mick at his most ferocious. His heart's with the *avant garde*! What I do now is, I've got good guys so I just let them get on with it – anything goes. At the last gig, the P.A. broke down, so we played Irish folk for half an hour, just me Alan and Lyn!

© 1990 Nigel Cross - "Unhinged"

different stories. He stayed in the USA and worked the Los Angeles band *Love*, Warren Zevon, Kim Fowley and the later version of *High Tide*. He died in 1992.

VI

Glen Soundbites

"About the only band we haven't done a gig with is the Beatles."

Beat Instrumental, September 1970

"The worst thing is to take the pop scene seriously."

Zig Zag, March 1970

"I like loud music, but it's got out of control now. A lot of groups just use power to hit the audience and, as it were, pin them to the wall, with the result that they now can't tell one from another."

Melody Maker, beginning 1967

"Death is part of life. It's strange to say this, but I'm totally immersed in death. I've read all the books, everything that talks about what it happens when we move to the other side. Yes, I want to be ready for this!"

Rockerilla, March 1990

"We play intuitive music. There are all sorts of elements in it, folk, classical; we draw on the entire music spectrum. But there again, our music is not made up of parts, it's whole in itself. We're a heavy band, I suppose, even though we're acoustic."

Beat Instrumental, September 1970

"We could have written it all down and faked it every night, but we didn't want to do that. It's a bit nerve-shattering to go on stage, face an audience and not know what you are going to do or how it is going to come out, but it usually works. The audience has to work as hard as we do. If they respond, then things go very well and, sometimes, even hostility is good. At least you have some kind of feeling going between you and the audience. The only battle I think we have ever lost was at *Speakeasy*."[27]

Zig Zag, March 1970

"Everything is recycled, everything; we never composed music, everything must be free. Only in this way can a new idea come forward, also by chance."

Rockerilla, March 1990

"We're into a sort of fantasy thing with music – based on the music of the druids and alchemic theories."

Melody Maker, beginning 1967

"Bad news, Baby!"

his favourite saying during the second Italian tour, January 1989

"We thrive on working to order. We find that we work very easily that way, whereas if there's nothing happening we tend to do nothing."

Beat Instrumental, October 1971

"For myself this is the only way to make an album: you never have to please the audience. The other thing is to make entertainment. Art is a deep, dark, mystery."

Rockerilla, March 1990

"It's very hard for me to get into Crosby, Stills, Nash and Young, for instance. This is because it's all vocals and I don't seem to be able to relate to it in the way I feel I should."

Beat Instrumental, October 1971

"Today's scene is one in which the best groups are ignored. The audience's whole thing seems to be to make you feel you're not there. We get these 'ignore you' vibrations. The trouble is that I always thought music was about

---

[27]   The Speakeasy Club in Margaret Street was a late-night meeting place for the music industry from 1966 to 1978. Bands played there on the cheap, hoping to be discovered and stars who could afford it also hung out there.

communication where musicians communicate to an audience who then throw it back again."

Beat Instrumental, October 1971

"The alchemical process is made out of birth, life, death, birth, life, death: the cycle repeats itself and every time it becomes more pure. So, when as a band you get to the end of the cycle you have to die to be reborn as a band. For us, the moment for dying was *Macbeth*..."

Rockerilla, March 1990

"We don't want our music to be explained. I'm sure that the minute anything like this can be explained it immediately loses its impact and people will move on to something else."

Melody Maker, beginning 1967

"Years ago I played jazz music, of course I had a normal drumkit. But I got to a point where I was bored with it, it was just a competition: the fastest, the loudest... I don't want to compete with anyone..."

Rockerilla, March 1990

"All the rest is funny hats and hoo-ha."

Glen's first joke when he met Dave Tomlin for the first time at the Notting Hill Gate London Free *School, in 1966*

TEB, outside the Roundhouse May 30th, 1969 just after Harvest Records showcase introducing its acts to the English public.
Photographer unknown

Hydrogen Jukebox 1978.
(L-R: Brian Diprose, Jim Gypsy Hayes, Mick Carter, Glen Sweeney, an unknown technician *below*)
Photographer unknown

TEB on stage at the Hyde Park free concert, July 5th, 1969.
(L-R: Glen Sweeney, Paul Buckmaster, Paul Minns *oboe*, Richard Coff *violin*)
Photo by Ray Stevenson

TEB in a London park, 1970.
Photographer unknown (courtesy Steve Pank)

TEB playing at Glastonbury Tor on May 3rd, 1970 for the Order of Bards, Ovates & Druids ceremony.
(Left photo – L-R: Paul Minns, Ursula Smith, Glen Sweeney; Right photo – L-R: Ursula Smith, Glen Sweeney, Richard Coff)
Photos by P Peacock

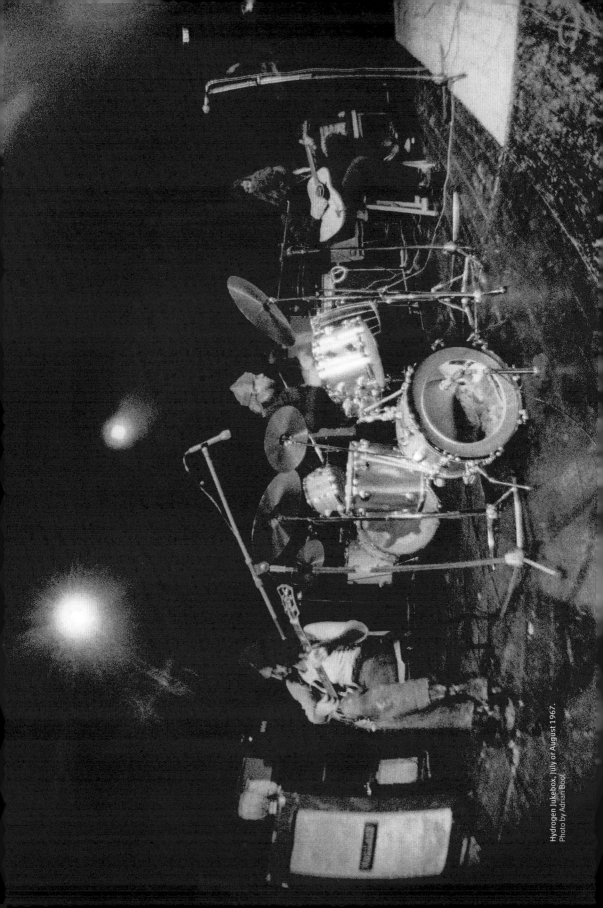

Hydrogen Jukebox, July or August 1967.
Photo by Adrian Boot.

Blackhil Enterprises promo shot, 1970.
(L-R: Glen Sweeney, Paul Minn, Richard Coff, Ursula Smith)
Photogtrapher unknown (courtesy Steve Pank)

Third Ear Band recording at EMI Studios, beginning 1970.
(L-R: Ursula Smith, Richard Coff, Glen Sweeney, Paul Minns)
Photogtrapher unknown

POSTERS L-R:
- Sun Wheel Ceremony poster. (courtesy Glen Sweeney)
- TEB poster for Purcell Rooms concert, April 21st, 1969. (courtesy Glen Sweeney)
- TEB resident band at the Crypt. Designed by David Loxley (courtesy Steve Pank)

Blackhill Enterprises ad for TEB's second album, also from *Blackhill Bullshit* # 4
Artwork by Adrian Boot

TEB concert with DADA St. John's College,
London, May 1st, 1969. (courtesy Glen Sweeney)

GLEN SWEENEY, Drums; PAUL MINNS, Oboe, Flutes; PAUL BUCKMASTER, Cello, Bass Gtr.; DENNY BRIDGES, Dble. Neck Gtr., Vocals; BEN CARTLAND, Viola, Congas. Stereo Sound System by W.E.M. Drums by GEORGE HAYMAN. Synthesiser VCS3 by ELECTRONIC SOUND STUDIOS. Management and Agency by BLACKHILL ENTERPRISES. THE DRAGON WAKES is the title of a forthcoming album by the new ELECTRIC EARBAND on Harvest Records E.M.I.

Ad for unreleased third album *The Dragon Wakes*, published in Melody Maker, August 8th, 1970. Designed by Glen Sweeney

Linda Kattan and Carolyn Looker in the Sixties. Photographer unknown (courtesy Linda Kattan)

Glen Sweeney rehearsing at the Cambodian Embassy (London), August 1988. Photo by Carolyn Looker

TEB Alchemy ad tour programme 1970. Designed by David Loxley (courtesy Steve Pank)

Poster launching the Alchemical Third Ear Band in 1990. Designed by Glen Sweeney

Glen Sweeney rehearsing at the Hydrogen Jukebox recording sessions at Dansette Studios (Kent) in 1978. Photographer unknown

Blackhill Enterprises agency ad printed in *Blackhill Bullshit* magazine # 4 (July 1970). Artwork by Adrian Boot

Poster for the *Four Dimensional Happening* at Powis Gardens' All Saints Hall. September 26th, 1968. Designed by David Loxley (courtesy Steve Pank)

Poster for *Now Is The Time!* events at the All Saints Hall (London), November 21st and 28th, 1968. Designed by David Loxley (courtesy Steve Pank)

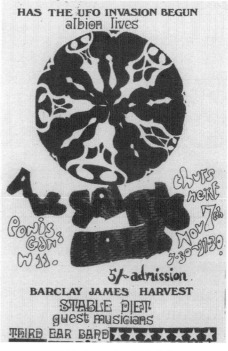

Poster for the *Albion Awakening* gig at *Middle Earth*, March 31st, 1968. Designed by David Loxley (courtesy Steve Pank)

Morgan Fisher in the early '70's.
Photo by Gary Merrin (courtesy Morgan Fisher)

Richard Coff at the Isle of Wight festival, August 31st, 1969.
Photo by Barry Plummer

Oliver Chadwick and Brian Meredith in London in 1960.
Photographer unknown (courtesy Brian Meredith)

Glen Sweeney discussing the programme for the
Alchemical Wedding with Yoko Ono, December 18th, 1968.
Photographer unknown (courtesy Glen Sweeney)

Glen Sweeney with Hydrogen Jukebox, July or August, 1967.
Photo by Adrian Boot

Blackhill Enterprises agency's artists, managers and friends at the Blackhill Headquarters in 1969.
Photo by Adrian Boot

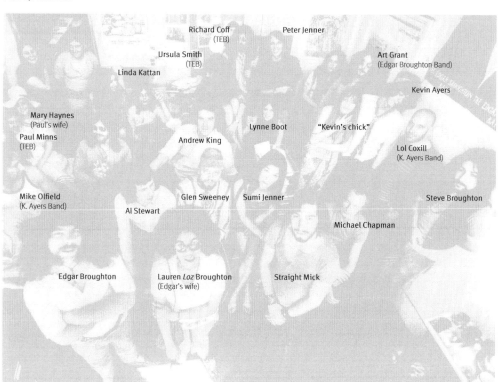

Richard Coff
(TEB)

Peter Jenner

Ursula Smith
(TEB)

Art Grant
(Edgar Broughton Band)

Linda Kattan

Kevin Ayers

Mary Haynes
(Paul's wife)

Lynne Boot

"Kevin's chick"

Paul Minns
(TEB)

Andrew King

Lol Coxill
(K. Ayers Band)

Mike Olfield
(K. Ayers Band)

Glen Sweeney

Sumi Jenner

Steve Broughton

Al Stewart

Michael Chapman

Edgar Broughton

Lauren *Loz* Broughton
(Edgar's wife)

Straight Mick

Jim Gipsy Hayes at the Hydrogen Jukebox recording sessions, Dansette Studios 1978. Photographer unknown

Mick Carter at the Hydrogen Jukebox recording sessions, Dansette Studios 1978. Photographer unknown

Brian Diprose at the Hydrogen Jukebox recording sessions, Dansette Studios, 1978. Photographer unknown

Brian Meredith and Glen Sweeney, 1968. Photographer unknown (courtesy Brian Meredith)

Blackhill office (Top L-R: Bridget St. John, Michael Chapman, Linda Bennion; Bottom L-R: Lynne Boot, Ursula Smith, Sumi Jenner, Linda Kattan). Photo by Adrian Boot

Glen Sweeney with Hydrogen Jukebox July or August, 1967.
Photo by Adrian Boot

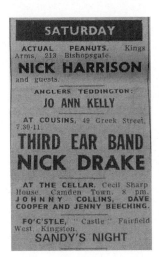

Ad for a TEB gig at Les Cousins, April 1970.

Carolyn Looker, 1968.
Photographer unknown (courtesy Carolyn Looker)

Roundhouse Poster, 1978.

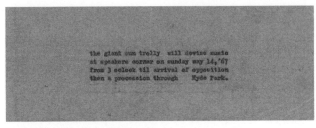

Giant Sun Trolley flyer: May 14th, 1967.

TEB ad for Windsor Free Festival.

Blackhill Enterprises promo shot for Macbeth release, 1972.
(L-R: Richard Coff, Paul Buckmaster, Denim Bridges, Glen Sweeney,
Paul Minns). Photographer unknown (courtesy Mary Hayes)

Paul Minns and Carolyn Looker, circa 1968.
Photographer unknown (courtesy Carolyn Looker)

VII

Memories and Interviews

Dave Tomlin

Poet, writer, musician, iconoclast. Author of Tales from the Embassy *(Strange Attractor, London 2017).*

Hampstead Heath, London February 25th, 2010

I first met Glen Sweeney, or Glen Zen as he was known at the time, in 1966 when he turned up at the London Free School in Notting Hill where I was teaching cacophonous music and organising chaotic and illegal processions down the Portobello Road each week-end. A remarkable feature that caught my attention immediately was that he ceaselessly tapped his fingers on whatever flat surface was within his reach. It was a strange but intriguing tattoo beaten out in a singular rhythm, which remained unchanged through all our subsequent meetings. This could be disconcerting when engaged in a conversation with him since he continued his tapping as a kind of dramatic accompaniment throughout whatever we were discussing. Only slowly did I discover his shamanistic approach to music. 'It is an Alchemical process,' he had told me, with one hand guarding his mouth lest others might hear his secret. 'If they know what I'm doing it would dilute the magic'. Gradually as the trust between us grew he revealed more depths to his practice. 'The Alchemical process is an experiment in which a single motif expressed through the subjection of material elements of matter to various mixtures and pressures, or as in my case, the arrangement of subtle rhythms beat out on a drum. However, once that motif has been chosen it must be strictly adhered to and repeated endlessly until complete boredom has been achieved. This, he had continued, is a similar dynamic to high-speed planes reaching the sound barrier, and to break through this intense strata of boredom into a new and higher dimension is the aim of the Alchemical drummer.' After delivering this profound item of Sweeney philosophy... 'So now you know', he concluded.

Glen had a similarly rebellious nature as myself and was never averse to sticking his neck out with me when provoking the establishment, when such a possibility was on offer. The London parks were the venues in that summer of 1966, when performing under the name 'Sun Trolley' we gave many free concerts of illegal guerrilla music. Mounting the bandstand - if the park boasted such a thing - or if not, any open space with a good field of view, to ensure that outraged park-keepers or the police, were unable to sneak up on us unseen, we sent our rebel music out into the far reaches of the park. If such an authority came into view our strategy was to scatter, each making for a different exit and thus, if there were a pursuit, only one of us would be nicked. We carried our instruments in bags enabling us to dispose of them quickly - before, as happened on numerous occasions, we had to do a runner. Glen took this sort of thing in his stride, being experienced in escaping retribution, since a current myth of the time had him down as an ex-burglar with two associates and a ladder. Being a little short in the leg he was unable to run as fast as his accomplices and was therefore assigned to the role of keeping watch at the bottom of the ladder and whistling if things looked dangerous. I once asked him if this story was true and... 'Yeah man. I was third man in a ladder gang,' he replied.

The music of the Sun Trolley was a kind of directed cacophony, although the directions chosen were usually deliberately provocative; an effect achieved through the displacement of the entire curriculum of the accepted laws of music, creating a completely new value system - one of which was the sounding of as many consecutive tones as possible within a specific time period. And this was of primal importance - while what these tones happened to be was totally irrelevant. Or, for instance, the musicians might each choose a different tone, which would then be played throughout an entire piece. I often chose to emulate a lone demented seagull on my tenor sax, while Dick Daden the trombonist often favoured a berserker bull elephant raging through the jungle. My screeches and squawks combined with Dick's outrageous bellows and the undercurrent of Glen's Voodoo beat, often sent any audience into a kind of collective daze, while a few, recovering from their shock, attempted to dance. This, however, was impossible owing to various psychological tensions within the Sun Trolley itself. Dick had become increasingly irritated by Glen's strict adherence to his private Alchemical rules and being unaware of their purpose raged against having to always play everything at the same speed. His boredom eventually became unbearable and, bursting its banks, overflowed into pure anarchy. He began pumping up the beat trying to force a faster tempo, causing me to slow down to drag him back. Glen of course was unmoved by this conflict and steadily pursued his course, the result being that the Sun Trolley was the first, and what's more the last, band to play at three different speeds simultaneously. This was a major break-through and we adopted this technique from then on. Thus, our music was impossible to dance to and difficult to listen to since nobody could decide whether it was even music at all.

Performing at UFO, a hippy nightclub of the time, Glen's hypnotic beat would sometimes send him into a trance-like state from which, when our set had ended, we had difficulty arousing him. Once, finding this impossible we had to walk off and leave him to it. With his eyes fast closed he did not notice the *Pink Floyd* impatiently waiting to begin their set. Realising at last that he was never going to stop they mounted the stand and went into their first number. Glen, surrounded by their wailing electric guitars at full volume came suddenly out of his trance, and such was the degree of shock that it was some time before he remembered what his legs were for.

I played bass guitar for a short while with his later creation *The Third Ear Band*, although not very successfully, since I was no bass player and was therefore forced to revert to some 'Sun Trolley' tricks. I would choose two musically acceptable tones for each piece and play them alternately, spending some time on one until, feeling like a change, I would move on to the other. Bass players are expected to play more than one note otherwise I might have considered one to be enough. Glen of course hadn't changed one iota over the intervening years and still persisted in his transcendental formula, but intriguing tales about this period I have none since, although I recorded an LP with the band, my time with them was so brief.

In later years I visited Glen and Carolyn on his launch *Alchemy* when it was moored on the Regent's Canal, hard by Maida Vale. Over a primus stove in the cabin he made tea, complaining loudly about the pleasure boats full of trippers that went swishing past - causing Glen's boat to rock in their wake and upsetting the tea cups. Discussing this problem, we devised a solution to end it once and for all. A small cannon mounted on his fore-deck would serve to blow one of them out of the water as a warning to all others to keep their distance. However, this bit of naval action never went further than words, since the days when such things could be seriously considered were by then long gone.

Glen's legacy consists of the many recordings still available that he made with The Third Ear Band. To anyone wishing to experience his hypnotic Alchemical beat, they have only to listen and hear that mystical pulse emerging from the hands of the Maestro himself.

Linda Kattan

Former secretary of Blackhill Enterprises Agency.

London, May 5th, 2017

Let me tell you about how I first heard the Third Ear Band. I had been working at the pirate radio ship Radio London's offices and was walking through Hyde Park one Saturday morning and heard the music of the *Pink Floyd* playing as I walked. I was mesmerised and happy and the following Monday made it my mission to find out who had put this gig on. A few days later, I walked into Blackhill's office and told them I wanted to work for them. Andrew King said they would love that but that they didn't have any money to pay me just then but would keep me in rolling tobacco and bus fares! I accepted on the spot. Thankfully, I was able to earn a wage soon after!

Andrew and Peter were only managing the Floyd then, but they wanted to start an agency too. That's where I would come in.

Andrew said that we would have to go to some gigs and find some artists. The first one we went to was at *All Saints Hall* in Notting Hill. When we arrived, the Third Ear Band was in full flow, and it was magical and addictive. I told Andrew, there and then, that we HAD to have them. Glen on hand drums playing new rhythms to my ear, Richard Coff playing a violin like I'd never heard before and Paul Minns on oboe - which I'd never heard before in a band, building up into crescendos that took you somewhere else. All meant that I would not be able to let go of them in a hurry. And that's how we became their management and agents. The music world was sweet then...

Years later, after I had left *Blackhill* to go and live in Cornwall, I got friendly with Glen and Carolyn again. I'd never stopped loving them. One evening we went for "a" drink with an Irish friend of mine, John. When I say "a" drink, it was many, many more. We were in an Irish pub in Stockwell and when the pubs shut we all went back to John's flat to carry on. There must have been some others from the pub who came back with us, and they were busy singing Irish rebel songs. We called taxis to take us home a couple of hours later and as we were walking downstairs to the street, Glen stopped and turned round to me and said "I think we may have inadvertently just joined the IRA."

Glen and Carolyn had three cats, Ra and Isis, (he black, she tabby) and their son, Ginge (ginger!!). If it seems odd that the parental cats were blessed with the names of Egyptian deities and their child was merely named after his colour, you need to know that Ra and Isis were also smart. Ginge, however, although beautiful, was not gifted with his parents' mental talents. Perhaps he was the dumb blonde of the cat world. On one of the many evenings I went to Glen and Carolyn's flat for dinner, music, drink, drugs and a bit of a bop, I went into the lounge and found Glen pressing his forehead against Ginge's. He signalled to me that he was unable to interrupt what he was doing, so I went into the kitchen with Carolyn. A while later, Glen emerged. I asked him what he had been doing with Ginge and Glen said, "I was trying to transfer some of my brain cells to his, to make him a bit more clever." He said this with all seriousness, and there was no question Carolyn and I both totally believed him.

Glen had this thing that he would make seemingly outrageous statements and sound so believable that I was completely taken in. And often, with the passage of time, those statements somehow became true!

Steve Pank

Third Ear Band former promoter and driver.

Norwich, February 27th, 2017

The first time I met Glen was in 1966 when I answered an ad he had put in the *Melody Maker* asking for musicians for a free jazz group. I went along and met Glen and Carolyn in their flat in Clanricarde Gardens. We sat and talked about music and philosophy, while Carolyn supplied us with bounteous amounts of tea.

At the time he was interested in playing free jazz in the style of Sun Ra, Pharaoh Sanders and other free jazz players. I played trumpet then.

We rehearsed in the upper room at the *Barons Court Arms*, playing free jazz with poetry and a basic light show. Also there was a tenor player, Jan Diakov, who later became Third Ear's road manager, and Dick Daden, a trombonist. One day Glen said the rent had gone up and we stopped rehearsing there.

Then Glen organised another rehearsal in a flat. Dave Tomlin was there with his tenor saxophone and occasionally, during the rehearsal, Dave would take the mouthpiece off his tenor and sing into the horn. Guitarist Clive Kingsley was there too. By that time I'd decided I no longer wanted to play trumpet. I wanted to focus on writing.

Around then an alternative newspaper started up, called *International Times*. They put on all night benefit events in premises in the Tottenham Court Rd. The events were called *UFO,* and they were run by John Hopkins [Hoppy] and record producer Joe Boyd. It was an amazing mix of events, a truly mixed-media happening. The *Pink Floyd* and the *Soft Machine* alternated every Friday night.

Dave and Glen formed a duo called *Giant Sun Trolley*. Glen was on percussion and Dave was on tenor. They would play at UFO in the early morning while the rest of us started clearing up.

The next thing that happened was that the band's van was broken into in Notting Hill and all the equipment was stolen, including Glen's drums and Clive's guitar and amplifier.

This was a setback for Glen and that was when he made the decision to start playing hand drums instead. He then met Paul Minns, an oboe player and Ben Cartland, a viola player and they formed a trio, which later became the Third Ear Band.

I had been doing some work on *International Times* and I was working toward publishing a newspaper myself, called *Albion*. To raise money for further issues I ran benefit events - first at *the Crypt* under a church in Lancaster road and then in *All Saints Hall*, a church hall next to All Saints Church. *All Saints Hall* was where the *Pink Floyd* played some of their first gigs.

The Third Ear Band was the house-band at all these events. At one time they turned into celebrity jam-sessions with Sam Cutler and bluesman Alexis Korner officiating. There were spots by Arthur Brown with a band that included Carl Palmer and Vincent Crane, and from the blues guitarist Davy Graham.

We also were treated to what may have been the last live performance by Syd Barrett, backed by Roger Waters on bass and Nick Mason on drums.

At around this time Glen met Richard Coff, an American classically-trained violinist. Glen invited him to join the band, and the Third Ear Band became a quartet.

The first booking the Third Ear Band did for *Blackhill* was south of London supporting John Mayall. To get to the booking, Glen hired *Motivation*: a guy called Malcolm had a van and advertised that *Motivation* would do deliveries anywhere at very reasonable rates 'very sympathetic to Hippies', however the *Motivation* van broke down on the way home from the gig and the band had to come back on the train.

Shortly after that, Glen asked me if I would drive for the band, and I accepted. Glen bought the first van, a delivery van; it had no windows. I remember a time, on the way back from the north, when the clutch went out on this vehicle and I had to slow down until the traffic lights changed to green so we could drive through them without stopping. This van was sold and after that Glen hired Ford Transits.

We worked all over the country. *The Magic Village* in Manchester; we supported the Floyd in the *Brighton Dome*, played Aberystwyth in Wales, *Fairfield Hall* in Croydon, two concerts in the *Queen Elizabeth Hall*, Manchester, the *Alchemical Wedding*, in the *Royal Albert Hall* - that was an *Arts Lab* event organised by Jim Haynes. Also on the bill were John and Yoko, hidden inside a bag. The Third Ear Band also had a residency at the *Arts Lab* on Saturday evenings. They played live on several John Peel shows and did a national tour with Al Stewart.

There was work in Europe as well, festivals and venues. I remember when the band played at the *Paradiso* in Amsterdam, two Rumanian gypsy fiddlers came up and joined in, much to the delight of Paul Minns. Meanwhile most of the audience were lying on the floor.

The Third Ear Band was the opening act at all the early concerts in Hyde Park. The first was in Kensington Gardens, on the banks of the Serpentine, and marked the return of the *Pink Floyd*, after Syd Barrett had left. The second was supporting Eric Clapton and Steve Winwood in *Blind Faith* and the third was supporting the *Rolling Stones*. The Third Ear Band opened all these events. The rumour went around that the Third Ear Band was booked to ensure that there was fair weather!

By now they had a record deal with EMI, and we were off to the recording studios in *Abbey Road* to record the album that became *Alchemy*. During the recording session I suggested to Glen that I could go and fetch Dave Tomlin, who had switched to playing the violin then. I returned with Dave, and he recorded *Lark Rise,* which is the last piece on the *Alchemy* album.

While I was working on *Albion,* and running the *All Saints Hall* events, I had a flat in Camelford road, just off Ladbroke road. It's been demolished now, but I first met the Loxley brothers there when they came into my flat looking for somewhere to stay. Dave Loxley was an artist who had been at art school up North. He did some artwork for *Albion* magazine, and posters for the *All Saints Hall*. Dave also did the cover of the *Alchemy* and *Earth Air Fire and Water* albums. He is now the Chief of The Druid Order.

One time the band had been booked to play a concert for the remand prisoners at Holloway ladies prison. It had been organised by folk singer, Bridget St John. We all met at John Peel's flat, including a folk duo - guitar and cello - called *Friends of The Poor*. At the time Paul Buckmaster was the Third Ear Band cellist, having replaced Mel Davis, but Paul had recently written the arrangement for David Bowie's *Space Oddity*. It has even been suggested that the violin climax at the end of *Space Oddity* was inspired by Richard Coff's violin flourishes at the end of the Third Ear Band *Egyptian book of the Dead*.

Paul Buckmaster had other commitments at the time and he could not do the next band booking. I suggested to Glen that he could book the lady cellist from the folk group for the next gig.

He answered, 'I already have; I've asked her to join the Band'. That was when Ursula joined.

One of the early gigs Ursula played was the Isle of Wight festival.

This was the first concert appearance of Bob Dylan after recovering from his motorcycle accident. It was also the first of the big festivals, with half a million people there over three days. Ursula said that after her cello had been miked up, she drew her bow across the strings and heard this echoing roar ring out over the crowd.

During summer 1969 the band went off for a holiday in Cornwall. Glen was fascinated by the ley lines[28] and we went there hoping to track some. The plan was to camp on the beach in Cornwall, but everywhere we stopped we got moved on. We ended up camping in the New Forest.

John Mitchell, the writer, was living in Notting Hill at the time; he had just published his book *The View Over Atlantis*, and this was an influence in bringing earth mysteries into the image of the band.

I remember Glen telling us that he had had a dream about a crab and a crescent moon - this was about the time of the first moon shot - and it seemed like a way to tie the moon in with a Third Ear Band concert. So Dave Loxley did the artwork for the poster for next *Queen Elizabeth Hall* concert, called *The Crab And The Crescent Moon*.

Glen had been in Egypt when he was doing national service with the Air Force. He was fascinated by the pyramids, the temples - and other structures he saw when he was there. Glen introduced me to the *Egyptian Book of the Dead*.

There are similarities between the *Egyptian Book of the Dead* and the better-known *Tibetan Book of the Dead*, in that both were intended to be read as funerary texts.

In the summer of 1971, Ursula was pregnant and we spent some time in a gamekeeper's cottage on the Norfolk/Suffolk Border. In September, when our son was born, we decided to stay in the Norwich area. I started to play the guitar and Ursula started playing folk fiddle. Later we formed a folk group and *ceilidh* [29]band.

---

[28]　Proposed by the British antiquarian Alfred Watkins in the 1920s, these are straight alignments that can be drawn between prominent landmarks and ancient structures (like Stonehenge), which he believed marked trade routes in the ancient world - an idea that was never accepted by the British archaeological establishment. In the 1960s various esoteric communities revived it, re-tooling Watkins' ley lines as 'dragon lines' or lines of earth-energy or prehistoric landing guides for flying saucers. John Mitchell was a prominent proponent of this last idea in his *The View Over Atlantis*, published in 1969. [Irresistible trivia: in 1976 Mitchell published *The Hip Pocket Hitler*, a collection of the Fuhrer's most witty remarks].

[29]　Pronounced kayley, to rhyme with daily. Now used to mean a traditional Scottish or Irish social gathering with dancing and traditional music.

I booked the Third Ear Band twice for Norwich gigs, once for a concert in *Norwich Arts Centre*; that was Easter Saturday 1977, and one in the *LCR* at the *University of East Anglia*.

Brian Diprose

Musician, Hydrogen Jukebox bass player.

London, February 6th, 2017

Although Glen was a mystic and follower of the occult, he was at the same time very streetwise and practical. He was very aware of the unfolding phenomena of *Punk* and the power it had over the youth of that time. He adopted their street clothes look for the band, as he knew that the flowing robes and exotic clothes of the Prog bands had passed into history and were now derided by the new generation. I believe Glen was trying to reach some of that potential audience - and that was why he decided to make the band song-based and more musically accessible. I think he had partial success with that aim, while on the other hand the diehard fans must have had severe reservations about it.

In the end I think he wound up with an album that didn't fit into any particular genre, being too different from the Third Ear Band ethos and too sophisticated for a punk audience who wanted throwaway music from young men who couldn't play their instruments. It seems to me that Britain is unique in respect of the way that music divides people into tribes who will only allow themselves to like a particular style of music to the exclusion of all other genres.

Anyway, we were carried along by Glen's enthusiasm and every Saturday we would rehearse at Paul's flat and worked at honing the lyrics that Glen brought along into songs.

Glen was the puppet-master who had a vision and an unshakeable belief in the direction he was going, and it was a pleasure to be part of the refining process as musical ideas were pulled from the jam sessions and used as the building blocks for the songs.

Occasionally we would be invited to Glen's flat where he and Carolyn would entertain us in the presence of their many cats. Here Glen would regale us with tales of life on the road with the band in its heyday. There was an aura of complete calm in that flat which was at odds with its neighborhood - a pretty gritty area of Shepherds Bush, at a time long before the gentry moved in to shove the rents through the roof.

I don't think Glen ever became an old man as most men do. He never exhibited any signs that he could be a parent or a family man and his age was hard to determine. I don't think I could have called myself a friend of his, but he enjoyed a joke and there was much laughter back in that room where we practiced. I only have kind thoughts of him and feel privileged to have spent time in his company, and I hope he was happy with the contribution I made to that strange little record we made.

Rod Goodway
Musician, Magic Muscle/Rustic Hinge electric guitarist & vocalist[30]

I ended up getting a call from Glen Sweeney. Now my whole attitude was kind of punk at that time but the thought of joining a reformed Third Ear Band was bizarre to say the least. So bizarre, what with my marriage cracking up and all, that I thought, "great, I'll go along with it"

So in the spring of 1977 I started to go up to London and down to Shepherd's Bush and rehearse with the Third Ear Band, once a week to start with. Every Saturday we'd go and rehearse - and there were tapes; we recorded them ourselves. They weren't studio tapes but they were well recorded. Glen Sweeney apparently played one of these to Pete Drummond, the Radio One DJ and he wanted us to do an *In Concert* immediately, for the BBC.

I've got a piece here that says "whilst still at rehearsal stages, members have come and gone, but with only the problem of finding a bass player left, the remaining line-up was finally settled down to Glen Sweeney (percussion), Paul Minns (oboe), Mick Carter (guitar and violin) and ex-*Magic Muscle* guitarist and vocalist Rod Goodway. Musically things have changed dramatically. The extensive use of stringed instruments has been replaced by more inventive use of conventional rock instrumentation. The new material also lends a more

---

[30]   From http://www.achingcellar.co.uk/pages/tree/third.htm

attacking quality ("a type of medieval rock'n'roll" is what Glen Sweeney calls it) – a sharp contrast with the calm floating sound of yore." I thought it was quite good because it had a lot of eastern tinges to it and that - kind of - is my dream: eastern-flavoured rock, or mantra rock: that was definitely what The Third Ear Band were into doing in 1977.

Sadly, and I take full responsibility, my marriage breakup had caused more of an impact than I'd thought and my liver (you know, with the previous problem I'd had) couldn't take the drinking and stuff that I was involved in and I had a liver failure. So I'm afraid – what with the liver and a mini nervous breakdown – I couldn't continue with the Third Ear Band and wrote many letters to Glen Sweeney and had many kind letters back. We parted amicably but sadly; I'd work with the guy again any day. Great guy.

Morgan Fisher

Electric guitarist, with the TEB in 1973

Tokyo, March 18th, 2017

My (probably record-breakingly) short stint as synth player with the Third Ear Band included just two radio shows and one concert in the spring of 1973, before I was whisked off on a USA tour, by *Mott the Hoople*. So I had little time to get to know the band personally. Paul seemed rather distant and quiet, but Mike and Glen were open, chatty and friendly from the beginning. Nobody said it, but I assumed Glen was in charge as he visited my house in Finchley (north London) a couple of times to discuss their musical approach with me; it was always a real pleasure to sit and have a cup of tea and a cozy chat with him.

I was familiar with the band's recordings and especially impressed that they had, two years before, made the music for (and even appeared in) Polanski's *Macbeth*. While chatting on that subject, I asked Glen about the London premiere of the film: who was there and how they dressed for the occasion. Were the band expected to adhere to the usual tuxedo and black tie formula?

Glen's answer: "Yeah, man – would you believe they insisted we dress like that? So naturally I had to do something freaky as some sort of protest, right?"

"Sure. What did you come up with?"

"I dyed me hair bright green!"

"Nice one, Glen! More tea?"

Andrew King

Blackhill Enterprises founder & manager

Twickenham, London, July 2nd, 1996

How did you meet TEB?

Third Ear Band played at one of the early *London Free School* gigs at *All Saints Church Hall*, Powis Square. I think the sax player Lyn Dobson was playing with them. That's how we met.

What do you remember about the first Hyde Park TEB concerts?

On the morning of the *Rolling Stones* show in Hyde Park, Paul Buckmaster phoned me to ask if he should wear a suit and tie! These shows were hard for TEB, but they just about survived!

What about the Stanley Kubrick proposal for a soundtrack?

What Stanley Kubrick proposal?

What was Blackhill's approach to the music biz? And what was TEB's?

Blackhill was only interested in Art, TEB were only interested in Money (and sex and drugs). EMI didn't know what they were interested in but felt there should be money involved. There wasn't really anyone at EMI (except perhaps Malcolm Jones) capable of having a conversation with them, so Blackhill was always the go-between; and really Blackhill had no clear plans as to what we were trying to achieve.

The TEB were so divorced from the normal sort of "act", that it was always difficult to see them as anything more than a sort of strange hobby; despite the fact that they sold a lot more records than more conventional bands (e.g. Kevin Ayers).

EMI went along with what we asked of them not because they supported us but because they were frightened of missing out on something good and thought that we had our fingers on the Big Thing.

What do you remember about your experience as a producer with TEB?

I did two albums, *Air Earth Fire Water* and Polanski's *Macbeth*. During AEFW the band were taking acid fairly regularly. I did not realize this and could not understand what they were laughing at all the time. I think it's a fine album. I saw Peter Mew, the EMI engineer, a few weeks ago, and he still remembers it as some of the weirdest sessions he ever worked on in 30 years at Abbey Road!

Macbeth was very different, and actually technically very innovative. They improvised live to the film, reel by reel, as it came up from *Shepperton Studios*. There was a time-code to synchronize to the film. I would imagine this had never been done before: we did it in *Air Studios* above Oxford Circus; Abbey Road could not handle it.

I well remember the trips down to Shepperton in Polanski's very large and old Rolls Royce, with Paul Buckmaster and Glen and Paul Minns; also a very lively meal with Polanski where he danced on the tables in a Mexican restaurant near Sloane Square. All good stuff!

Paul Buckmaster
Arranger, producer, musician, TEB 1969-1972 cellist/bassist.

Los Angeles, January 23th, 2013

When did you meet Glen and join the Third Ear Band?

Early 1969 at a music club in the Paddington/Westbourne Grove area of London. As I recall, it was David Bowie who took me there. I had my cello with me and asked if I could sit in with the trio (Glen, Paul Minns, and Richard Coff). So I jammed with them, and it was exciting; I was playing some kind of funky bass riffs in the groove with Glen. Really exciting. At the end, I was invited to join, by Glen and Paul, with Richard enthusiastic.

What was your first impression about the group?

Loved them and their music – everything about it.

I mean did you know them?

Until that evening at the club, I was only vaguely aware of them; I saw the name on posters for UFO club, Tottenham Court Road, Friday nights.

What did you think about their music at that time (I refer to the first two records)?

Loved it!

Do you remember where did you rehearsal with them?

Rehearsed (infrequently) at Glen's (or was it Paul's) place in South London, Battersea area, I think.

What was your contribution to their music? I mean, all the tracks were usually "composed by TEB", but I know that your specific contribution regarded the composition and the music orchestration...

There was no composition *per se* – i.e., nothing was written down to my knowledge; I saw no scores, sketches or any kind of notation. It was all based around Glen's drum pulse/rhythms; Paul had certain motifs or themes, that were associated with certain titles and codified as master recordings for the *Harvest* albums. Those titles would be played at concerts, but as far as I recall, we didn't have a set program. Mostly, it was Glen who started any particular piece with Richard and I – or, later, Denny – joining in a little later - then Paul, who was the actual "lead" voice in the ensemble. Richard – and later Denny – were next - accompanying with the cello – and later, bass guitar – holding the bottom end. I suppose we were all collectively "composing" with little being said beforehand – or after, for that matter! But even all that was not hard-set!

Did you have contacts with the Blackhill management (Jenner and King): what was your opinion of them?

As I recall, I had little or no opinion of them at the time: from what I could determine, they were professional and competent. I imagine that, were Glen and Paul alive today, they would be able to answer these questions far more precisely. Have you contacted Richard and Denny? Certainly Richard would be able to answer better than me!

I ask you that just because that's what Glen and Paul said (Richard didn't accept to be interviewed for the archive...)... Can you confirm that EMI didn't understand the real meaning of TEB's music and didn't give to the band the right support?

No: I cannot, but then, few people in A&R are really competent in this particular area, unless they're of the "old school" in which nearly all were competent in music; for example, the people at Columbia (CBS) records, New York – Dr George Butler – head of A&R for the whole jazz sector – comes to mind, or Jay Landers. I can't recall who was at EMI Harvest at the time, but the chances are that there were still a few people of the serious "old school" there.

Do you remember the free concert at Hyde Park ?

Yes.

What about the reactions of the audience there? And, generally, what were the reactions of people at TEB concerts?

I can't say what the reactions of the audience were since I was – along with everybody else in the band - up on the bandstand playing our gig and I could only see a small portion of them! However, from what I could sense, the audience was curious, wondering what the heck this music was we were playing. I suppose the audience were really there for the *Stones*, and "semi" couldn't care less about what we were doing. Of course they were enjoying a rare day of bright sunshine in a beautiful London park and they were open to all kinds of different stuff; maybe some of them were even fans of the TEB.

I was told, later, that they (the Stones) had chosen us to open for them because we were more likely to calm the crowd. You've got to remember that a large number of people were (stupidly) into drugs (mostly hashish and herb), me no less. So maybe that was a part of the audience ... 40 percent or more? Who knows?

All four of us had spliffed up – a large six-Rizla-skin combo of tobacco, sinsemilla[31], Moroccan kif, and heavy opiated Afghani hashish, with a concomitant thin cardboard roach – and were smoking it prior to going on stage. So you can imagine just how ripped we must have been. The music – whatever there is that remains from the gig – does not display any bravura or professionalism.

As for any other gigs, we were sometimes excellent – even transcendent to the Empyrean; that is what I, and all the members, lived for – and sometimes not quite so transcendent; the Hyde Park gig was among those. The audience didn't notice anything, though – as far as I could tell.

What do you remember about the period before Macbeth, *when the band tried to record a pop album at the London Balham Studios titled* The Dragon Wakes?

I don't recall any sessions *at Balham Studios* or the title. This may have been one of the periods I was not a member; which was one of the reasons I quit; I was an on-again-off-again member, which, as I say, was not fair on them.

I'm sure at that time you were in the band. You can listen to an unreleased take from these sessions called Raga No. 1. *Paul Minns discovered it on a reel in his attic. The line-up included you and Bridges.*

---

[31]   A highly potent form of marijuana obtained from unpollinated female plants.

Amazing! Sounds really good; and as you say, shows the potential of what kinds of directions the music might have taken ... You know, I cannot recall the session, though I'm obviously playing on it, and I cannot recall any *Balham Studios*. Paul has clearly double-tracked – or even triple-tracked – himself, and although there's no violin, I heard some brief phrases of a bowed instrument towards the end, which is probably me overdubbing some cello.

I miss the sound and texture of a violin and I have some critical thoughts about the bass guitar, which are in any event irrelevant, since nothing can be done about it. What's wrong with the bass? a) rhythmically too "on" the beat; the bassist (me!) should have being playing a regular, repeated, though slightly syncopated riff; perhaps never changing at all and perhaps staying only on one note; b) The problem here is that he (the bassist) is playing too many tonal phrases, even in the major mode! And it's a bit scattered in the ideas. I could say more, but I don't want to spoil the listening of the fans.

Everybody else is playing great, although Denny has a slight tendency to rush ... but I attribute that to us not playing together more frequently and doing lots more gigs! Who knows where it would have gone had the band stayed together and played at least four days a week ... I'm sure somewhere really special and new - and strange and other-worldly - I mean in the science-fictional sense, not "supernatural" (whatever that means). The potential was vast.

Have you ever seen that 1970 German TV broadcast, recently issued on DVD? What is your opinion of it? Are you proud of that season of your career? Do you remember who and how TEB involved the conga player Gaspar Lawal?

Is that the one with Denny's vocal? I think it's fine! Don't recall how Gaspar joined us for those TV – and some other – dates: No doubt, Glen and Paul were the deciders, and I'm glad of it: I loved the sound of the congas in the band's context at the time, with Glen on traps, Denny on electric guitars, and me on electric bass and electric cello. By the way, the roadie who drove us everywhere – whose name I can't immediately recall – and did the stage set-ups, was an expert maker of stuff - any stuff; he built a damped metal pick-up bridge with dense rubber feet for my cello, which was amplified. A few years later – in 1972 – I bought a wood Barcus-Berry bridge[32], which had a transducer buried inside it that could be plugged in ... I also had a wah–wah pedal. I was probably the first cellist to go electric! Though there was a cellist in Holland[33] I heard, a year later – maybe 1970-'71, who sounded like Hendrix – brilliant and highly skilled. I think he may have overdosed on heroin – at least that's what I heard.

How do you react to the common idea that Miles Davis' Bitches Brew *inspired 1971-1972 TEB's music?*

It's not accurate, except that – maybe – there's a bass riff for *Ecstasy in D* that recalls the bass riff under *Bitches Brew*, but it's not anywhere as brilliant as the *Bitches Brew* riff, which is one of the many touches of genius in that incredible album of fierce beauty. What's amazingly excellent about that riff is the key-modulations it goes through over the two-measure duration: 2 beats of C major, two of B major, two of E major: but here you have an even greater touch of genius, the first 8th of the E major chord is in the first inversion – E over G# – classically written by Miles with no doubling of the third – going to E major root position on the second 8th, as a syncopation, with the last two beats – anticipated in syncopation by an 8th – back to B major, with the last 8th being the perfect cadence (G-to-C) into the new two-measure cycle starting with C major!!!

Those of your readers who know a little proper classical harmony will know what I mean, but those who don't, can still enjoy the piece ... Remember, as a student at *Juilliard* - and earlier, when he received private lessons - Miles had studied classical harmony and counterpoint.

What about the Macbeth *period? What was the mood in the band? What happened in George Martin's Air studios?*

---

[32]   A violin bridge with a built-in piezo-electric transducer to convert mechanical energy (vibrations) into electrical energy, in order to amplify sound directly, without using a microphone. Barcus Berry was the company who made them.

[33]   This can only be Denis Van der Hecke, conservatory trained classical cellist who went electric in the beginning of the 1970s, very much like Hendrix and a wonder to behold. He died in 2012.

I had a little more say in the direction the music took for the movie score; Glen, Paul, Richard and Denny trusting me with my suggestions. For example, I actually wrote the dreary *Witches Song*, which we played, and sang. The singing was done by the five of us; Roman wanted it to be "kind of disgusting" ... We did a certain amount of overdubbing, to create a more dense texture in places, with me and Richard making clustery string harmonies ... I think the *End Titles* is one of the better pieces in the score; Denny contributed a lot to that, and a great driving pulse from Glen! I believe Denny composed *Fleance's Song* with Paul ... but we're all credited as co-writers, which was Glen's democratic, egalitarian virtue.

In fact in that period (January 16th, 1971) you sent a letter to Melody Maker *explaining about the rules in the band. You wrote: "... If anybody thinks differently, thinks that the band is "led" by one member (i.e. one person deciding the format, tempo, key or mode, changes etc. and imposing this on the others) then they have totally missed on the most important point, if not the most important point of the* Third Ear Band. *It's not I, it's we, and we're free"). Why did you decide to write it?*

I don't even remember writing such a letter ... wow!!! That is perfectly true.

About Fleance's song, *I know Glen and Paul didn't love it, Glen considered it "rubbish". This was confirmed by Bridges in a recent interview I had with him: what is your opinion about this track, not so orthodox in the TEB's repertoire?*

You're right: it certainly is not. Not at all typical of what one would expect from the TEB! My opinion: Roman Polanski was satisfied, and that's all that really matters in the final analysis! From a musical perspective, it's kind of "OK", but not a work of genius, for sure.

Is there something you've taken from the experience you had with the TEB that you've carried forward?

All musical experience – I suppose, all mixed in!!! But I "used" nothing specific.

David Loxley

Chief Druid of the Ancient Order of Druids and former TEB graphic designer.

London, May 26th, 2012

As every TEB fan knows you designed the beautiful Alchemy *album cover. I discovered that the picture was taken from an old book about alchemy titled* Atalanta Fugiens, *edited by German Michael Meier in 1617. Can you tell us the genesis of the cover, the reasons behind it, the real meanings?*

I didn't really design the cover, it kind of happened with parts of it coming from different people. I put all the ingredients together. The main drawing is from an illustrated book written in 1617. I think this came from Glen or Steve Pank. I thought it was a bit too medieval.

One evening in my flat a girl from California drew a doodle of some snakes and left them there as a gift. I redrew them and put them in the corners of the medieval image to make it look more celtic.

The image itself I have never interpreted for anyone before, but it has a very deep meaning, which could be the subject of a book and not just an answer, so here goes with an answer that has a book hidden in it.

The picture has a courtyard with a tunnel entrance with a man in the middle about to crack an egg on a table. This is a totally symbolic image. On a material level the courtyard is a womb; if it were the *Great Pyramid* in Egypt it would be the chamber of transformation. The tunnel is the entrance to the womb, it has an egg in it waiting for a sperm to fertilise it. The image was meant to be interpreted on the mental level according to the upper room or womb. The brain is a courtyard with an egg in it called the Pineal gland. On an abstract level this gland has the same function as the egg in the physical womb. The tunnel is the Pituitary gland or the way for light to enter into the courtyard, or brain, and fertilise the Pineal gland. Both of these eggs, abstract and material, are functionaries of the moon. The Great Pyramid at Giza has two entrances, one for the physical seeds to enter (mummies) and one for the light to enter. The physical body is the same.

The egg is the sleeping Beauty who will only wake up for the light. In the same way that the physical sperm has to give up everything or die into the egg in order to be resurrected into a new world as a baby, so the Pineal gland will only operate as an entrance to another world if the Pituitary gland, which is ruled by Mercury, gives up all of its light to the Pineal.

The Sword held by the man is not a weapon but a symbol for something that cleaves the air. Light or electrons cut through space like a sword, or a word, and represent light and the present tense. The Moon will only give itself up to the Sunlight and then reflect it onto the land. To be enlightened the man must give up everything – judgements, what he thinks he knows - and become *nothing* in order to be accepted by the egg. In return for this death he will be resurrected by the present tense, which is the womb with an egg in it.

I think I have gone on long enough, so let me finish by saying that the cover represents the real mysteries of Sex or creativity in the present tense.

What is the meaning of the snakes around the border? In an old interview Glen Sweeney said that they were there to protect the band and its music...

The serpents at the corners of the cover had no intentional meaning. Originally they would have been used to protect the four corners of the world – north, south, east and west. The serpents lift the slightly flat image of the main picture and provide some contrast to project the cover a bit more.

Do you remember when, where and how you met Glen and the other guys in the band?

I cannot guarantee my memory for some of these questions, but I think I first saw Glen at a club called the UFO in 1967 or thereabouts. At the time this was the place to be, but it was still quite a small scene with enormous potential for the future of social change. Glen was playing in a band whose name I cannot remember; it was a sort of free form spontaneous jazz group, I think.

What were you doing at the time? What was your role in the London underground?

At the time I was very young and did not see myself as having a particular role other than helping out where I could. I had just dropped out, so to speak, a concept that would sound alien today. I was into having a good time. My flat was raided by the police but, rather than arrest me for something, they just said - we will be back in 30 minutes and if I were you I would not be here; my brother and I ended up 30 minutes later walking down the road to somewhere, or nowhere. We asked in a bar if anyone knew of anywhere to stay and we were sent to Steve Pank's flat. He kindly put us up for about a week. That is how I met Steve Pank, who I have now known for forty-something years. At the time, if it was happening anywhere, it was in *Portobello Road*[34]; Steve had a magazine called *Albion,* which I did some drawings for and later on I helped him run a club in a church hall, for which I did the posters and handouts and any other menial tasks. This club never advertised who was playing, because most of the people who came to jam did not tell their managers or record companies; even Steve did not know sometimes if anybody was coming to play or not. Some of the musicians and acts were very well known, and people just turned up to see whatever happened. The council eventually closed us down for making too much noise; or that was the reason given. One of the bands that played there regularly was the Third Ear Band, and Steve introduced me to them.

Can you tell me what the real connection was between TEB and the Druids?

The real connection between TEB and druidism was, or is - well I am not sure. I was interested in druidism so I joined a group; Steve Pank was also interested so he joined too. TEB music, like a lot of freeform jazz at the time, was about being in the present tense, opening the door to another state of being. Some freeform jazz branched out into various kinds of Indian or oriental music and created fusion music. Some of this music had spiritual connotations

---

34   A main thoroughfare that connects *Ladbroke Grove* and *Notting Hill Gate*, home to the food and flea market, the Electric Cinema and the old Virgin Records offices. Now heavily gentrified and a tourist trap, but then a bohemian mixed race community.

- and meditation was also becoming popular. The TEB was a fusion between freeform jazz, Indian music, meditation and folk, played on classical instruments. It was probably the first band of its kind but it was still about getting into the present tense or another state of being. The Druid Order is about the same thing in another context, linking up with another state of being or going beyond time and space searching for reality. So I guess, although some of the connections are physical, the real connection is abstract.

What do you think about the TEB experience? Some people ask me if TEB music was devoted to black magic... What can you tell me about that?

My previous answer covers most of this question as well. TEB has nothing to do with black magic. If black magic is superstition then, no, they were not. Black magic is just going against the light; every habit and resentment we are stuck in is black magic; every desire to get revenge or hurt those whom we thought - or did - hurt us, is black magic; war is black magic if it is based on an illusion and personal pride. Primitive people need a devil to blame, otherwise they would have to take responsibility for their own actions. The devil is needed by immature people. If the devil existed he or she would be your best friend, supporting you to be in the past tense and stuck with the fantasy that you can have it all now and take it with you. It is, if we are large enough, a great honour to take the blame for the negative thoughts of others who cannot face the reality of their own failure to support the light. I'll stop there; I'm starting to sound like a born again preacher!

What are you doing now? I know you're still a Chief Druid...

At the moment, I am still a Chief Druid, which takes up some time. I have semi-retired. I still do some design work, some writing, some physical work - making things etc. It is my second dropping-out and I am looking at ways to earn some money without having to work all the time. So that ends my answers on a very practical note.

Dave Harries

Macbeth soundtrack sound engineer

London, May 1st, 2013

Describing the Macbeth soundtrack project to the press in Sounds" magazine, in 1972, Glen Sweeney said; "The way we did it, mainly, was by viewing the clip they needed music for and then maybe somebody would have a musical idea, which we would try out. And if nobody had any ideas, then we would hope for the best and try again. It worked nearly one hundred per cent. I mean, the ideal way would have been to get someone to write the whole score and hire a bunch of studio musicians to play it". Is this description correct?

Yes, they did view the clip and then compose the music on the spot to go with each scene. We did it one clip at a time so at times, to me, the music can seem a bit disjointed. Roman Polanski used to come in and review the work. We sent the music mixes to *Shepperton Studios* to lay them up with the film as we completed them. Often *Shepperton* would label them wrongly so we would sometimes show scenes with the wrong music as a result. Very confusing. Roman Polanski used to get annoyed about this! We worked in Studio 4, which was designed as a dubbing theatre with film projection facilities. Notably, this was one of the first movies to use Dolby on the soundtrack.

How did you meet the band? Did you know them before starting the recording sessions?

I first met the band because they started the project with our film-recording engineer Jack Clegg, but he didn't like working with multi-track recording, so he asked me to take over the recording along with assistant Bill Barringer.

Can you tell us about your career at that point?

I started work at EMI Studios in 1964 as a technical engineer, staying there for 6 years and working with all the famous bands of the era including *The*

Beatles, Pink Floyd, The Hollies, Beach Boys and many more. I left in 1970 to join George Martin, helping to set up the new *Air Studios* in Oxford Circus.

What was your exact role in the recording process at Air Studios?

I was the recording engineer responsible for the sound and the organisation of the sessions. I recorded the band to multi-track, locked to the picture and mixed the music down to two-track magnetic. Also I mixed and edited the soundtrack album.

Do you remember what equipment you used for recording the music?

I was speaking with Bill Barringer yesterday about the equipment. We think we used a Studer A80 8 track machine, a 50Hz pulse on track 8 to synchronise with the film. We mixed down to stereo or maybe three-track to an Albrecht film recorder. The projectors in that room were Phillips. Microphones mostly would have been Neumann U87 or U67, maybe an STC 4038 on drums. The whole track was Dolbied and we had regular visits from Elner Stetter of Dolby throughout the recordings.

What can you tell me about the condition of the band in the studio - I mean if they were competent in playing and recording, if they used drugs, if they were serious workers...?

The band worked very well in the studio and were very creative and constructive in forming the musical passages to accompany the film. I don't remember any drugs. At the time they weren't tolerated in the studios.

Was the role of Buckmaster decisive in the composing and recording process?

Paul Buckmaster was an integral part of the band, contributing particularly to the more modern sounding pieces, which were musically almost classical.

What do you remember about the recording of Fleance's Song, *probably the best-known track? I know that Glen and Paul hated it, and that was confirmed by Denim Bridges.*

Fleance's Song was recorded by Jack Clegg and Bill in Studio 2 at Oxford Circus. I mixed it with Bill in Studio 4 along with everything else. It was so good and so commercial that at the time we all agreed it should be released by EMI as a single, but the record company didn't agree.

What was George Martin's contribution to the studio work?

To my knowledge George didn't have anything to do with the recording of *Macbeth*.

Were you involved with the film premiere in London? Do you recall anything?

I didn't get an invitation to the premiere.

Brian Meredith
Former Third Ear Band cellist

Southern California, March 25th, 2014

What do you recall about your first meeting with Glen Sweeney?

I first met Glen in 1962. Glen Sweeney, Carolyn Looker and I all had jobs at *Liberty of London*, which is an old upscale department store where celebrities like to shop. Glen helped the salespeople in the furniture department move their things around. Beautiful Carolyn worked in the beauty department - she sold makeup or nylons, I forget which. I was an art school dropout at the time, who was selling suitcases in Liberty's luggage department.

The day Glen and I first talked music, I was excited to have been showing some cases to the American jazz pianist Erroll Garner. He had asked me to show him a steamer trunk and I'd hurried downstairs to blow the dust off the only one we had in storage. I doubt Glen and I even knew each other's names. To me, he was just some hip-looking little dude I'd seen lurking about in Liberty's basement. But to get that one great steamer trunk upstairs, I asked Glen if he'd please help. Well, during the huffing and puffing that followed, I seem to remember our chat rapidly shifting from Erroll Garner to Lennie Tristano and on to Cecil Taylor. Maybe Glen even name-dropped Sun Ra. Glen was big on Sun Ra.

Glen definitely let me know he was actually a professional drummer with an R&B band. Well, two nights a week he was. I remember because, being very much an amateur, I was impressed. I told Glen I played a bit of piano and cello in a 'free jazz' quartet. Well, weekends I did.

Anyway, Luca, here's where we must bid farewell to the late great Erroll Garner's special guest appearance in my answer to your interview question. No, he didn't buy that big trunk from me that day, but he did help Glen and I get acquainted.

After that, I began seeing Glen and Carolyn as a couple around town. Carolyn's sister, as it so happened, had begun dating a pal I used to hang out with named Geoff Wood. Geoff was the multi-instrumentalist leader of that amateur jazz group I was a part of back in '62, and I'm pleased to be able to add that he has remained a good friend to this day.

When did you join Geoff Wood's group?

Well, it was more like we joined each other. I mean we were just four teenage friends who each played an instrument or two. We simply hoped that playing them together as well as we could might make something akin to jazz come out. And sometimes it did. By the way, the rest of us saw Geoff as our best player, so we made him our leader in case we needed one someday. I'm thinking this was 1959...

Was the jazz you played based on 'hard bop' style? Tell me more...

'Hard bop' made a big impact on us. For example, we'd been fans of The *Jazz Couriers* in the late 1950s. Tubby Hayes and Ronnie Scott moulded that

U.K. band in the hard bop style that Art Blakey's *Jazz Messengers* had put their stamp on in the U.S.

By the time our own group started getting together, John Coltrane, Jimmy Giuffre, Steve Lacy and Eric Dolphy were all key figures whose styles had excited us. Then again, the four of us all loved the 'chamber jazz' groups that Chico Hamilton formed in the '50s. He had Fred Katz at first on cello, then Nate Gershman. They really interested me. And we quickly became immersed in Gunther Schuller's 'third stream' music with the *Modern Jazz Quartet*. The *MJQ* had always been wonderful, but this was introducing quite a new twist.

Right around the turn of that '50s decade, along came Ornette Coleman with his 'free jazz' recordings. And, a split-second later, Joe Harriott in the U.K. was showing us the brand new direction he wanted to take. I'm talking about his 'free form' jazz recordings. They were superb I thought. Still do. Not more than a year or so later, you'd have found *The Geoff Wood Quartet* absorbing Bud Shank's collaboration with Ravi Shankar. It seemed like there was simply no stopping jazz at all! That was a tremendous period, and we kept lapping it up. It all influenced us.

When did you first meet Paul?

Paul Minns and I first knew each other in the 1950s. We were both pupils at the *City of London School*, which was still located on Victoria Embankment in those days. Paul and I weren't classmates, but we were around the same age and had somehow discovered we were both Miles Davis fans. Every now and then we'd find each other in the schoolyard or lunchroom, just long enough to natter about whatever jazz had grabbed us since we'd last talked. Paul was more scholarly than I was. I know I came to associate him mostly with classical music and being very serious about everything. He would be off playing oboe with the school orchestra, I remember, while I'd be sitting in the lectures of the school's jazz society.

So when did you all start playing music together?

That wasn't until the spring of 1967. Paul and Glen and I all met up one day in Notting Hill, which is where we all rented bed-sitting rooms, and Glen explained that he was thinking of forming a new group. He said he was curious how the three of us might sound playing with a guitarist from Earls Court they both knew. I realise now that the three of them already knew how they might sound playing together. This was all about auditioning me.

None of us was working just then, so Glen just went ahead and booked us some time in a rehearsal space a day or two later. I showed up with my cello, and, along with Carolyn, Glen was there on drums, Paul on oboe, and Clive Kingsley on electric guitar.

I don't recall if Glen just played hand drums during that first session or if he used some part or all of a kit. I do remember that an hour or two later when we were packing up our instruments, there was quite a lot of satisfaction being expressed. We all felt we might be at the start of something that could work.

Then, before we had any club dates or Carolyn had come up with the name for our group or any of that, we made sure we got together and played regularly. We did that for probably close to three months. I was always surprised at how efficient Glen was at finding rehearsal spaces that cost us little or nothing during that period.

Who composed the first pieces for the band? Was it Clive Kingsley, as he claimed recently in an interview with me, or was it a collective effort?

Well, Luca, here's what I think. Without Glen or Paul being around any longer to perhaps take issue with what Clive, rightly or wrongly, believes, I think I'll leave this one alone. I know that I personally stake no claim whatsoever to any of the tracks the group ever recorded, nor to any of the compositions they continued to play after I left the group. In case it might be of interest, however, here's how I remember our music most often coming into being. We'd find a theme and then just work it and work it. Pretty much any time we re-approached a piece that was becoming part of our repertoire we'd be trying to refine its shape or perhaps soften or sharpen its mood. Sometimes these pieces were based on nothing more than a fragment of melody or a brief riff, yet we found they were enough for us to take as a motif we could improvise over. And let me get some praise into print here for those hand drums of Glen's that underscored everything. Glen's beat never faltered.

Anyway, in the course of developing what I've just been describing, one or other of us would give these musical pieces names. I shall leave this subject on that note.

Who was leading the band in the earliest days?

Glen was always the leader, and from an organisational point of view I wouldn't have wanted it otherwise. He was a hipster and he was a hustler. He made the contacts, got us the gigs, got stuff done. We looked to him in those areas. Glen was both the man with the vision and 'the man with the plan'. It would have been nice if he'd shared that vision and that plan with the rest of us, but you can't have everything. What hustler is ever really open with you? But I digress.

Another way I might answer your question about leadership is like this. Some drummers who become group leaders always provide that particular musical voice that characterises any bands they lead; the drummer Chico Hamilton, who passed away just months ago, springs to mind as that kind of leader. But for me, in the case of our group, no matter what the rest of us were contributing musically, the essential voice of TEB was Paul's. The sound of Paul's oboe was so distinctive. It was wholly, unarguably pure. So I felt from the start that if audiences were going to be responsive to what we were doing, Paul would be the primary reason. Solely in that sense, Paul was almost leading us by default. But perhaps I'm just muddying my answer here because I don't want to give the impression Paul ever directed us. He didn't. Though in retrospect, perhaps he should have.

There were times we all sounded like we desperately needed a leader of any description. In fact, to my ears, and probably to too many audiences, we too often sounded like crap.

What kind of cello did you have?

My cello was a perfectly ordinary violoncello that I'd bought at a provincial musical instrument store. I still remember exactly how much money I had to save up as a schoolboy to buy it. It cost 15 guineas.

But you're probably asking about my cello's electrification or electronic add-ons. In that regard, I give a lot of credit to Glen Sweeney. It was Glen's prompting that got me to see how I might transform the cello's sound. I'd only been around acoustic instruments previously, so I was a complete dummy. Here's what happened. Once the four of us began playing gigs, Glen quickly became concerned about the loudness of Clive Kingsley's electric guitar-playing. Part of what was bothering him, he said, was how Clive kept drowning out my bowed passages. As a counter measure, Glen hooked me up with a contact microphone to try out. Wow! I'd adhere the mic to the body of my cello at the start of each performance and, arco or pizzicato, it was now hear this! That was a major change for me right there. So then I began wondering what other possibilities needed to be explored. Glen was kind of nudging me to get curious, and I was taking the hint.

I started checking out the new guitar accessories that were showing up in the Charing Cross Road[35] music stores. I certainly don't recall anything anymore about what amp or pre-amp configuration I ended up with on stage. I couldn't even tell you now how many effects pedals I may have experimented with. But I do remember how precious to me my *phaser* and *fuzz-box* became. I absolutely do remember those little sweethearts. They enabled me to introduce sounds on the cello unlike anything else being heard. Sure, at times they let me get away with murder, but oh boy, I loved it!

Ursula Smith

TEB violin player 1969-1970.

Norwich, July 21st, 2011

What kind of musical training did you have?

I started piano lessons at the age of eight and took up the cello at 13. I had lessons on the cello at school but the teacher was never there for them, I have an idea that he didn't think girls should learn the cello. I taught myself

---

[35] In these years almost all the music shops were in Charing Cross Road and Denmark St., which is a small road off Charing Cross Road. *Macaris* was possibly the most famous, and still exists.

from what I had learned on the piano. Later I had lessons from a Polish gentleman who was a professional cellist. He helped me with the audition for the *Royal Academy of Music*.

As every serious TEB fan knows you met Glen and the other guys after a concert in a prison... What do you remember about that? Why did you decide to join the band?

I left the Royal Academy in 1966 and did a year teaching. I didn't enjoy the teaching much and left at the end of the year. Then I took a job as a cleaner in a pub. At the time I joined a folk duo with singer/songwriter/guitarist Mike Deagan. We did some bookings in a folk club called *Les Cousins* in Soho and it was there that we met folk singer Bridget St John. She was a friend of the DJ and broadcaster John Peel and one day she asked us if we would do a free concert for the remand prisoners in Holloway Prison. On the day, we arranged to meet with the other performers at John Peel's flat. John wasn't there at the time but that was where I first met the Third Ear Band. The only person I recognised was the cellist Paul Buckmaster, who I knew from the Royal Academy, since we had had the same professor.

I remember we were playing to an audience of about 90, mostly young girls, in a courtyard. Around the yard were tall concrete walls with small cell windows in them. At the end of each number all these hands came out of the cell windows and waved. One girl spoke to me in the interval and told me that she had been in the *Arts Lab* near *Covent Garden*,[36] and she was on an acid trip when the police came in and raided the Arts Lab. She was arrested and now she was on remand in Holloway. It came as a complete surprise to me at the end of the concert when Glen came up to me and asked me to join the Third Ear Band and I accepted. I learned later that the reason I was asked was that there had been several gigs that Paul Buckmaster was not able to do.

---

[36]   A district of central London but most famous in the 1960s for the huge wholesale fruit and vegetable market (est 1654) of the same name at its heart. Visitors to the Royal Opera house, one street away, rubbed shoulders with lowly costermongers at its all night pub and the street stalls that served the market's workers. The underground club *Happening 44* was located there, as was the *Arts Lab*. The market relocated in 1974 and the old buildings are now devoted to tourism and shopping.

What are your feelings about the two years you played with the original TEB?
Do you have any particular memories of concerts, events - some anecdotes...?

The band was on tour around the country. We played gigs in Scotland, in Wales, in Manchester – in a club called the *Magic Village* run by Roger Eagle – and some in a club in Birmingham called *Mothers* [37]which was rumoured to be run by gangsters.

One of the early bookings I did was the first Isle of Wight festival with Bob Dylan on the bill. We arrived on the island by ferry and then drove to the venue field. The day before had been the rock and roll night headlined by *The Who*. We were on in the afternoon with folk artists like Tom Paxton, Richie Havens and Julie Felix, and in the evening was the comeback concert of Bob Dylan backed by *The Band*.

When I walked out on the stage there were people as far as I could see. I sat down and when the amplification was set up, I drew my bow across the strings and I heard this great roaring sound through the giant sound system and the monitors.

The other band members got set up and, as we started to play, the music came together.

We did some broadcasts, mostly for John Peel, sometimes with an audience and sometimes just as recording sessions. The album *Earth Air Fire and Water* was recorded in the Abbey Road Studios.

Abroad we did the *Paradiso*[38] in Amsterdam, where most of the audience were lying on the floor; and we did several festivals in giant sports stadiums in Germany.

There was a festival in an Aircraft hangar at Le Bourget airport in Paris, where the *Pink Floyd* were playing with a whole range of other bands. I

---

[37]   Formerly the Carlton Ballroom, it was above an old furniture store in Erdington High Street. It ran from 1968 to 1971 and ran more than 400 concerts. Bits of *Pink Floyd's Ummagumma* and parts of *Soft Machine's Facelift* were recorded at concerts there. Billboard magazine voted it the number one rock venue in the world.

[38]   The *Paradiso* was a large untenanted church that was squatted by hippies in 1967 and repurposed, like the roundhouse in London, as a makeshift, echoic, ramshackle venue for events. Being Holland, it was closed by the police, tidied up and immediately opened again as a publicly subsidized youth entertainment centre – which, along with the *Melkweg* down the road, became the engine of the Dutch counterculture.

remember we stayed at the Paris Hilton and we did a TV show in Belgium. We did two concerts in the Queen Elizabeth Hall on London's South Bank – the first one was called *The Crab and the Crescent Moon*: this was shortly after the moon-landing and the title was based on a dream that Glen had had. Dave Loxley did a poster for that concert which was based on a tarot card.

The music was accompanied by a light show by Tina Keane and there was a guest appearance by sitar player Sam Hutt. Later Sam Hutt became famous as the country singer Hank Wangford.

We were booked to do a national tour with folk singer Al Stewart. Glen wanted to call the tour *Atlantis Rising*; myself and Steve [Pank, her husband and road manager of the TEB] were detailed to go and see Al to ask him if he would accept that title. He was a bit doubtful about it and said he would be just as happy if the tour was called *Ham and Eggs*. However he accepted it and during the concert we shared with him at the *Queen Elizabeth Hall* he gave a short speech about how Nostradamus had predicted the assassination of the Kennedy brothers. Then he sang a song about Nostradamus. Later when he toured America his tour was called *The Year of the Cat*.

The Third Ear Band played for two Druid ceremonies; the midsummer one on Glastonbury Tor and the Dawn Equinox ceremony on Parliament Hill in London.

We had been in Germany where we played at a couple of festivals and recorded the soundtrack for a German TV production of *Abelard and Eloise*. For that, we first watched the movie through on a TV screen and then it was played in front of us while we improvised the music.

When we arrived back in London, having had virtually no sleep, we were immediately rushed into the back of a van and driven to Glastonbury Tor. We climbed the Tor carrying our instruments. Luckily it was beautiful day. My cello was the heaviest and the biggest. But the person having the most problem was the Chief Druid, who looked like he might have a heart attack at any moment. He had to keep stopping to have a rest. When we all reached the top, I found there was nothing for me to sit on, so I sat on the side of the Hill. After the Druids performed their ceremony, we played to the people and to the Sun.

The dawn ceremony for the equinox was on Parliament Hill in Hampstead. We processed with the druids and formed a circle, and the druids started the ceremony. Paul was asked to play to announce the rising of the sun, but the

Chief Druid got the time wrong and Paul had to keep playing for ages until the correct moment of the sunrise. We were honoured to be asked to take part in these ancient ceremonies; it was a unique experience for the band.

We also did a concert in the *Royal Festival Hall,* shared with a French *avante garde* music group...

Why did you decide to leave the band with Richard Coff? What happened to the Cosmic Overdose *project?*

After Steve left the band as driver, we were doing a tour of Belgium when Richard called Paul and me together and Richard started a discussion saying he was not happy with the way the band's finances were being run - he said he had decided to leave and asked me to go with him. That was when I left the band.

Richard and I did some rehearsing and got some ideas together. Richard rang the *Melody Maker* and got an interview, but we had no equipment or management or agency.

We were busking near *Speaker's Corner* in Hyde Park, when this South African guy came up to chat to us and said he knew a guy who ran an equipment shop and he could get us some equipment there.

We went to the shop and Richard spoke to the manager who told us that this person was an intelligence agent for the South African government and that we should be very wary of him.

After that Richard rejoined the Third Ear Band and so did Paul Buckmaster. And soon after that the Third Ear Band got signed to do the music for Polanski's *Macbeth*...

What did you do after the split with Coff?

I got interested in traditional folk music and in 1970 I went to a traditional folk festival in Ireland and took up the fiddle. I used to go down to sessions at Cecil Sharp House[39] and joined in with the folk dance band there. Later I played

---

[39]   Custom-built in 1929-30 to be the headquarters of the *English Folk Dance and Song Society* and named for Cecil Sharp, the leader of the modern English folk-music revival who collected, performed, edited and wrote

with a ceilidh band called *Ginger Beer Shindig,* with some people I later formed the band *Blowzabella* with. I did a recording session for Clive Palmer on his first album. I remember the comic actor John Cleese coming into the studio.

I moved to Norwich with Steve in 1971 and our son was born there in the autumn of that year. By then Steve was playing the guitar and bass guitar and we formed a folk dance band called the *Haymakers*. We played at dances, clubs, festivals and fairs until the early 1980s.

How did Glen contact you to play with the reformed TEB?

After that period I was playing fiddle in bluegrass and country bands until I started teaching music in a school in Suffolk. Around that time Glen asked me to rejoin The Third Ear Band playing fiddle, for a tour of Italy...

What are you doing now?

More recently I have returned to playing classical music on the cello. Currently I am the principal cellist with the *Norwich Philharmonic Orchestra* and I do freelance work for local choral societies and occasional chamber concerts and string quartet concerts.

Carolyn Looker
Glen Sweeney's muse, painter.

Hammersmith, London, April 17th, 2012

When and where did you met Glen for the first time?

---

about traditional English song and dance. It houses Sharp's library and promotes concerts, workshops and educational events.

Both Glen and I were working at Liberty's in Regent Street. Glen was doing modern furniture display. He had his drumkit in the storeroom, where he would hide and practice his drumming (!) which at the time was modern jazz...

Where was Glen from?

Glen's family lived in Croydon, about ten miles south of the Thames.

What were your interests at that time?

Sartre, Kerouac and the Beat Generation, Zen Buddhism, Jazz, Occult.

Were you involved in the cultural scene in those days?

Yes, I was reading beat poetry to *avant garde* jazz to a very small audience at pub gigs.

Have you some memories of the beginning with the Giant Sun Trolley?

Many happenings at UFO with Sun Trolley! A dog howling to Dave's sax. Total 15 minutes of silence from the two, then a spaced out kid tried to bang on Glen's drum. Glen hit him with a stick – said it was Zen – kid remained far from that.

How did Glen meet Dave?

Dave was advertising for a drummer. Glen auditioned at the *Free School* - that was a cellar where Dave was squatting with a poet called Macavity. Glen was told to 'take the drum sound from here to there', Dave said, indicating directions. Glen, being good with fantasy, managed to do that and got the gig!

What was the mood at UFO?

Memories, but not clear; it was all like a scene from a Fellini movie.

And what about Sun Trolley's music?

Very *avant garde*: used happenings on stage, i.e. electric scissors cutting clothes off a dancer...

How did TEB start to play at the Drury Lane's Arts Lab?

Jim Haynes loved TEB; said they gave him orgasms. They played the Arts Lab on a regular basis: a room painted black, incense burning and the audience on the floor on cushions.

What about the legendary levitation of St. Pancras' station*? Is it true?*

Yes, we and John Peel sat outside *ohming*... Hard work but it lifted a few inches (we were on acid)...

What kind of music did the first electric TEB line-up play? Do you remember any particular tunes?

I remember Clive Kingsley's *Ronson Riff*, a marvelous thing he did by sliding his cigarette lighter along his guitar.

Do you remember something about the instruments stolen after a concert that led to the new TEB acoustic line-up?

Instruments were left in van overnight, gone in the morning. Never found out who took them. Of course they weren't insured!

How was John Peel involved in the Alchemy *recording sessions?*

A friend of Glen's took us around to Peel's flat. I remember us all discussing the existence of fairies.

Can you tell me something about that wonderful album cover?

Glen was very much into Alchemy, the illustration was in a book he had.

Any memories of the second album recording sessions?

Sorry, we were all stoned. Glen would suggest a feel or a vision for each track and the guys played it.

Is it true that EMI engineers left the studio during the sessions?

I don't think the engineers liked or understood the music, so mixing it they weren't into.

And what do you think about EMI? Why they did give up the band?

EMI were fine. I think the contract ran out.

Do you remember the gig TEB played with Bernard Parmegiani in London? Can you tell me something about it?

The Parmegiani concert was at the Festival Hall. It didn't work too well in my opinion. TEB's music was organic, the French were *music concrete*; it didn't go.

How did it go with Polanski?

Lots of memories of Polanski. He and Glen were the same height, so got on really well. Recordings were made improvising to pieces of the film that were projected in the recording studio.

What is your opinion about Blackhill? *Do you think the agency was really involved with the TEB's music?*

Blackhill never really understood the music. If they had been more supportive, made more of film music - i.e. Polanski and Kubrick admiring TEB -

and involved them more in the arts as with *Pink Floyd*.... Steered the right way the band could have been big.

One of the most obscure periods of your life together is when you lived on a boat on the river during the Seventies...

We had an idyllic summer on that boat. Glen was writing poetry, I was painting. Hard work. Because the mooring wasn't residential we had to collect our water and Calor gas about 1/2 mile away. We retired to a friend's flat in the winter, as the river flooded all the time. In fact in one huge flood, *the Ark* -- our boat - floated over into a field and settled there when the floods ended. We lived that way, chocked up in the middle of a field for a year. The council complained and, at great expense, we hired a crane to put us back in the water.

What were Glen's feelings about music just before I met him in your Shepherd's Bush flat? Why was he was so suspicious of me at the beginning?

Before meeting you, I think Glen had decided to retire from the music scene. I was involved in managing a prop-hire company, and we figured it was Glen's turn to take a rest: Glen suspicious of you? I think he was suspicious of most people's intentions till proved otherwise!

Some TEB fans are interested to know if Glen was involved in black magic...

Glen was very interested in esoteric, also in black magic, but did not practice it.

And what's about TEB's relation with Druids?

Steve Pank can tell you more about the Druid meetings and the Glastonbury Tor concert, since he is now a fully fledged Druid - and Dave Loxley, the Head Druid, who created the celtic border for *Alchemy*.

Clive Kingsley

Hydrogen Jukebox and TEB former electric guitarist

Hampshire, January 27th, 2010

Usually the story of British underground in the Sixties starts on June 18th, 1966, at the Royal Albert Hall with A new moon Carnival of Poetry... *What do you remember about that? Were you involved? Sweeney told me he was involved, with* The Giant Sun Trolley... *Can you confirm that?*

I knew nothing of that event... I doubt if it was very "underground"[40] - in that year, at the Albert Hall!!! I had not long returned from living in Canada where I had been involved in underground music which, at that time, was *avant garde* jazz pioneered mostly by black American musicians: Albert Ayler, Eric Dolphy, Ornette Coleman, and others.

Yes, Glen Sweeney, Roger Bunn and Dave Tomlin were The Giant Sun Trolley... amusingly once referred to in court by a judge as *the big green jelly*.

I met Glen, Dave and Roger first at the *24th Hour Technicolor Dream* at Alexandra Palace in spring 1967.

A musician friend of mine who I had known since the early '60s, Barry Pilcher, told me about the UFO Club and so we went there and played for free with a group we'd recently formed called *The New Music Workshop*. This included Terry Day as drummer plus a bass player. Because of that we were invited to play at the 24-Hour Dream event...

On his website Terry Day writes that in 1965 you, Glen Sweeney, Barry Edgar Pilcher and Lyn Dobson were involved in The Continuous Music Ensemble...[41] *Can you confirm that? What do you remember about it?*

---

[40]   It was. And it was anarchy. There was no running order and no *compere* to control events. The poets, performers and audience harassed and heckled one another through loudhailers and a 10-gallon drum of paraffin-oil and thirty home-made torches were found in the basement. The police were called to evict the show, and after that poetry events were banned at the Albert Hall for 18 years.

[41]   http://www.terryday.co.uk

The Continuous Music Ensemble, by my recollection, was founded by the organiser of the *Starting Gate* Jazz club at a pub in Wood Green of that name. I used to go there with Barry Pilcher, initially to jam. People like John Surman and Lyn Dobson and other jazz musicians would go there – either as guests or to jam. I got on very well and always remained very good friends with Mel Davis, long past my TEB days. Mel had quite few different group-names and outlets, one of them being *Kingsley-Davis* (or Davis-Kingsley!) *Expressions -* and later, *The Continuous Music Ensemble*. The name obviously derived from John Steven's well known, *Spontaneous Music Ensemble*. I am not aware, and very much doubt, whether Glen Sweeney really played in that group... by 1967 Glen was very 'anti' jazz (verbally that is). There was an event at the *Roundhouse,* in Chalk Farm, called the *Angry Arts Festival,*[42] where lots of things came together and briefly merged. I don't remember everything that happened at that one-off event - I was certainly there, along with Glen, Barry, Mel and many others - like the playwright Harold Pinter, who I think, may have triggered the event. Barry Pilcher and I played off and on in *The Continuous Music Ensemble*... and then Barry and I found Terry Day and a bass player and formed *The New Music Workshop*.

What were your relations with the People Band project?

I played from time to time with *The People Band* both prior to TEB and then again after I had left. Mel Davis started - and was always the key figure - in *The People Band*. The personnel were changeable and varied from small group to large band. I remember a very young Mike Figgis (now a well-known film director) playing trumpet a couple of times when I was there. *The People Band,* as you may know, evolved from *The People Show* [43]and sometimes, much later,

---

[42]   Organised as a protest against the Vietnam War by Vanessa Redgrave and Jonathan Miller. Pinter participated.

[43]   Now Britain's longest running experimental theatre project, it started in 1966 with a show in the basement of *Better Books* in the Charing Cross Road. At first they worked with scripts and plans but after a year they abandoned tight organisation for improvisation – using combinations of actors, musicians, poets and visual artists working together. Their shows have been numbered, not named, from the start and by 2018 they had reached 136.

still played when *The People Show* performed their rather spontaneous theatre events. My last involvement was at Sussex University, with the combined music and theatre version. The music part was a fairly small group – with I think Mel (piano) and myself (guitar) being the main parts. Mel could also play the cello well by that time... I don't remember whether he did or not on that occasion...

Another fundamental event for the London underground was the opening of the UFO club in Tottenham Court Road. Sweeney told me in 1990 that he "found a note on my door saying 'Meet me at the club at 12'o'clock'. At the time I just had a basic bass drum, a snare – so I took a chance, called a cab and went down there, and this was the opening night at the UFO Club"... Do you know something about that and can you confirm it?

I was not there on the opening night. I went there first with *The New Music* a few days before the *24 Hour Technicolour Dream* event. I played a number of times at the original UFO Club, once with *The New Music Workshop*, then several times with *The Hydrogen Jukebox* and TEB. And later when the club moved to the *Roundhouse*.

About the Giant Sun Trolley: on various occasions Glen spoke about it as a duo (he and Dave Tomlin) at other times he talked about the bassist Roger Bunn. Can you clarify? What was the original Giant Sun Trolley line-up? Are you sure it was a trio?

Yes, the original Trolley was Dave Tomlin, Roger Bunn and Glen Sweeney. Glen dumped Dave during the *24 Hour Dream* event to join up with Barry Pilcher and myself, bringing Roger Bunn along later to play an early morning music session. Before midnight Terry Day and the bassist of the *New Music Workshop* left. They didn't like the 'charged' hippy atmosphere... until the early hours there were two stages, with music on each, and both within earshot; not to Terry's taste, I think!

Barry and I stuck it out and eventually played a rather unusual frantic duo session around midnight. The early morning session was very calm and rather beautiful. I saw the potential of something evolving, closer to eastern music, which I already had a strong interest in.

Did you listen Giant Sun Trolley playing? What kind of music was it?

In the end The Giant Sun Trolley (which was really Dave Tomlin) simply played one note. Glen told me he was fed up with it and wanted to do much more, eventually moving from underground roots to 'pop' world acceptance. To me he criticised Dave a lot...

What was the relation between Giant Sun Trolley and Hydrogen Jukebox? Sweeney told me that for a brief period (maybe from August to October 1967) he played in both bands... Can you recall the sequence of events? Do you remember the original Hydrogen Jukebox line up? Who came up with the band's name?

No, Glen never played with Dave Tomlin and the Trolley after spring 1967 (the 24 Hour Dream event), he was always outwardly friendly to him, however, when they met. Glen had a knack of putting out warm, friendly feelings, which most people fell for, mistaking it for love. Glen claimed to be a Zen master... for a time, certainly, I thought it may be so. Later I felt he was a very good hippy version of a confidence trickster. He would say one thing to a person and something quite different behind their back! Unfortunately for me, it was a long time before I could really see it all clearly. Whether Dave Tomlin ever truly saw through it I don't know. You would have to ask him, if he's still around somewhere. I could put you in touch with Barry Pilcher; I still exchange letters with him from time to time. He has no computer access however and lives on a small island off the coast of Ireland. I have his postal address. Terry Day may well have an address for Mel Davis...

What happened exactly after the Hydrogen Jukebox split and the end of The Giant Sun Trolley? How do you were you involved in the first Third Ear Band line-up?

Very soon after the start of the new Hydrogen Jukebox Glen decided to dump Roger Bunn, saying we should get someone better and more reliable. It was Glen's idea to call the new band The Hydrogen Jukebox. Barry and I were the musicians of the group apart from the drums. My influences were really more towards the east and melodic improvisation. Barry would go along with it to a certain extent, but he was really more drawn to a harder style of free jazz.

We got a gig as the Hydrogen Jukebox at the old *Ronnie Scott's Jazz Club*. Barry was very taken by the jazz atmosphere and went off on a very prolonged solo or two. After the gig, Glen told me we should get rid of Barry because he would keep us in the jazz style.

By then I was very much into the whole London hippy scene... and Barry was not, really. So in the end I agreed with Glen - and Barry went his own way. He found two other musicians and played one gig at the *Roundhouse* also as The Hydrogen Jukebox. As a poet I think maybe Barry had a stronger claim to that name than we did! It was quite some time before Barry and I became friends again. I don't think he ever liked Glen after that...

And then what happened...?

So Glen, myself and Carolyn got together to discuss where to go from there... They came round to my bedsit and I put on an Indian classical music record (sitar and tabla). In answer to the question... I turned up the volume. They saw the idea and liked it. Next I went to their bedsit and we talked about a name. I came up with *The Third Eye*, but there was already a group called that. Then Carolyn came up with TEB.

The next question was which musicians, and how many, to join. At that time Glen played drums with a small kit ... he said he could play repetitive hypnotic rhythms, mostly using the toms and sometimes cymbals. In those days I just played electric guitar (a rather classy and costly Gibson).

I said we could do with a stringed instrument like a violin or cello to more or less take the role of the drone of a tanpura, and also a wind instrument like a flute, clarinet or soprano sax to be a bit like an Indian shennai. All to be quite high powered - to stand with people like Hendrix and Clapton, but with this Indian, eastern feel. And very melodic.

Anyway, Glen said he knew a classical oboe player who never played for people but liked all sorts of music and also lived in the Noting Hill Gate area. That was Paul Minns. Paul was very shy, very cynical, sceptical and introverted when I met him. He would only play very, very quietly and would not make best use of a mike. He wasn't used to playing for an audience. I'd played in bands and groups for audiences of all types for at least ten years, and when I played with him I gave him lots of solo space and would sometimes play along with him, but then he would just get quieter and quieter and pretty much disappear. Audiences at that time liked my playing and did not want to be put to sleep any more than I did.

Glen also found someone to play cello, a chap called Graham (I don't remember his last name). He wasn't really a musician, but he was quite keen! He was also rather nervous playing for people, but he picked up the idea of being a bit like an Indian tanpura quite well.

We played a lot of gigs: *Middle Earth, UFO Club*; many other small places and a couple of concerts. There were people around very jealous of the band, and of me...

I think Paul Minns did play quite a lot better later on, when he just had a violin to duet with. I went to see them in concert at the *Queen Elizabeth Hall* on one occasion, about a year after I left. I don't know why he left the band, but I did hear, about 5-10 years ago, that he had committed suicide. The original cello player, Graham, left when his cello went, along with my guitar and amplifier.

Who composed the first tracks of TEB and who decided to play the so-called electric raga?

All the music in the first TEB was composed (and not written down) by me, so when I left the original music went with me - but they did of course keep some elements of my original idea. Some of my tunes were *Time Garden, Sun Kaleidoscope, Luna Landscape, The Song of Los*. I used some of them later on with other groups.

Can you describe the music TEB played in that first period? Do you know how many concerts you did - and where?

We did make a couple of tapes... One went to Sweden and another I lost. We were also filmed at a gig in Notting Hill Gate by a German company... I don't know what may have happened to that. We played quite often at *Middle Earth* and the *UFO*, as well as at gigs in Nothing Hill - and once a concert in

Southampton. Also a few free open air concerts in London parks. We played at least once somewhere, sometimes more often, most weeks... spring 1967 to summer 1968 was my time with TEB.

What do you remember about the Arts Lab and Jim Haynes?

I played there quite a lot. The best gigs, though very anarchic, were with Mel Davis, Barry Pilcher and other poets, like Jeff Nutall. Great fun playing. I liked the macrobiotic food there too, although I was not yet a vegetarian. Lots going on in the whole building on different floors and different rooms. I didn't know Jim Haynes personally.

Do you recall anything about the "Levitation of St. Pancras" ritual, probably organized at the beginning of 1968?

No, nothing much at all. Something vaguely rings a bell, nothing more.

In Paul Minns' diary, the date of June 9th, 1968 - after a concert at Middle Earth *- 'The Tribe of Sacred Mushroom' - was the day all your instruments were stolen... Another source (Sweeney to IT in 1969) says that the instruments were stolen after a concert at the UFO ... Do you remember this event exactly?*

Yes. The instruments were not stolen at *Middle Earth* or the *UFO*; we played a gig in a small basement club in Notting Hill Gate and we were due to play another gig within the next day or two after that. That next booking may have been for either of the clubs mentioned. Glen suggested I leave my guitar and amp in the van along with some of the other instruments to save me carrying them back to my bedsit... the one and only time I ever left my guitar anywhere. The next day Glen told me the guitar, the amp and also his drums and the cello had all been stolen...

But why didn't you play in TEB anymore? Who decided to leave you out of it, and why? Sweeney said in Gandalf's Garden, *in 1969 that "[the stolen instruments] seemed so significant that we took it as a sign." Also, in IT the same year: "The original TEB was incredibly pretentious and diabolically evil to listen to – I mean, nobody really knew what they were doing and we had this lead guitarist who had this powerful amplifier and used to have it full up. Once he got started we couldn't really stop him. He was good, he had his own thing going, but he had no awareness at the time of any group thing...". What is your personal point of view about this?*

Glen never, at any time, suggested to me that there was any problem with my playing. He and - even more so - Carolyn just praised it. I never owned any amp over 30 watts. Once at the early UFO Club with the Hydrogen Jukebox I did borrow the *Pink Floyd*'s amp (in those early days we only had absurdly amateurish low power amps, and the club was big and noisy). I was very naïve back then, perhaps, and so engrossed in music and the hippy scene... that while I saw the jealousy of some who were around us I also saw I had 'fans' of my own playing beyond the group - although I was 100% *for* the 'group'. I didn't hear the things you have mentioned until years later... and even then watered down and from another source. For a long time I would always defend Glen when others spoke against him. He'd given me the courage to drop out of my boring office job to try for music full time! Within a day or two of the instrument loss, Glen said we could go 'acoustic'. Paul Minns offered me the use of an old acoustic Spanish guitar of very poor quality that was hanging on his wall as a decoration. I tried it, and even composed two new tunes on it, but for me it was not much use for serious playing. OK, maybe for a folk singer. Nothing really seemed to be happening with the band so I went off to Ireland for a few weeks to see a woman I knew. In the end I did a fair amount of walking. I was never invited back to play in the band. In hindsight I think I was used and taken advantage of, although I have no proof, so it remains a possible 'conspiracy theory'. The instruments may well have been 'arranged' to be stolen - my guitar being the most valuable and difficult to replace (I had no insurance). Maybe Graham, who lost the cello, was suspicious, since he more or less immediately said he would call it a day while I suspected nothing. Whether or not Glen had any hand in the theft, I think he must have been very jealous of my playing and the power (not volume) it generated. Glen always had to be the one in control and pulling the strings. I think I threatened this... He may even have been

135

deluded into thinking I was a threat to his relationship with Carolyn, his long term partner

You told me you were in contact with TEB again later, watching their concerts and going to recording sessions? What do you remember about that?

Glen invited me to go to the Abbey Road studios one day, when they were making the *Alchemy* album. I don't know why he invited me, I went to try to find out why but I never did really; he certainly never asked me to play. I went to two concerts. One out of curiosity and the second because it was in Brighton near to where I had moved. He also invited me backstage to the famous *Rolling Stones* Hyde Park concert, where they played as support. The *Queen Elizabeth Hall* concert was interesting, not bad at times, but the American violinist really seemed to be on a very weird ego trip, like he was so in love with himself and his playing in his duet with Paul Minns. They had a very pretty girl called Ursula playing cello at that time! Why did the personnel of the Jukebox/TEB change so much so often?

Have you got any particular memories about the time in 1968 when TEB recorded some tracks as The National Balkan Ensemble for Ron Geesin?

I moved to Sussex in the autumn of 1968. I've heard a few tracks, and someone gave me a tape of the first two recordings. I bought a copy of *Alchemy* but later I threw it out! I do have the CD *Magic Music,* which Glen sent me a year or so before he had a stroke. I was always prepared to get together again with him; to assume the best - that we had once been close friends, as he implied... had done his best to imply. If he ever was, he must have been very paranoid... or he was simply a very clever con artist. I was certainly aware of him being a con artist with others, so it was probably just my own ego that kept me from seeing that he was the same with me. A Zen master - or just a master of using the ego of others to further his own?

What are you doing now?

I am very interested in the teachings of J. Krishnamurti and go to the centre in Hampshire for dialogue from time to time. I do *Tai Chi* and *Chi Kung* exercises regularly, and walk quite a lot. A few years ago from 1986 or 1987, after more or less stopping playing music and giving up smoking, I did a lot of running - many marathons and other races. Nowadays just walking. Creatively, photography is now my main thing. I've been into it from my teenage years, but with the advent of digital and computers it's gone to a whole new level for me. I still have a guitar I bought cheaply while I lived in Sussex when I formed the *Sun Dragon* group. It's a nice instrument: 1950's British Selmer, I think. I should really renovate it. I also have a good quality Japanese Shakuhachi flute. But I very rarely feel like playing music now; I think I may prefer the sounds of nature most of the time.

Can you tell me about your experiences in music after the TEB experience? I know you formed a band called Sun Dragon *in 1968...and then?*

I formed *Sun Dragon* and also ran a club for a while. Played quite a few gigs, also played with various musicians playing jazz-based free music. Played again with the *People Band*. Then I studied Indian classical music and the sitar for 5 or 6 years with Imrat Khan - whenever he came to England. I also taught myself various other instruments – saxes, violin, synthesisers etc. And I started making multi recordings of my own music. I moved to Cornwall in 1976 and went back to Sussex twice before finally moving to where I live now. Since living in Cornwall I played with a lot of people on and off. Also in Devon and Bristol, playing with music cooperatives, playing with some very experienced musicians and some with no experience but an ability to play good music...

Are there any available recordings of Sun Dragon?

The only recordings I have are on a cassette and of very poor quality. Also the music is not the best of *Sun Dragon*. The best was really in live club situations. Initially, Barry Pilcher, who had also moved to the Brighton area, was involved too. He had a number of poetry contacts in Brighton and the live club events there incorporated poets, folk singers - and any other musicians. Once the venue was paid for, any money left was shared evenly with all participants. Barry met his now ex-wife in Brighton and eventually they left to go to live near one of her elderly relatives... so *Sun Dragon* changed, since I had to find other musicians. For me *Sun Dragon* was a time of recovery... I was rather depressed towards the end of 1968 - after what had happened in London, Brighton was literally a breath of fresh air!

I did send a *Sun Dragon* tape (post Barry Pilcher) to John Houseman, who was the person running the *Middle Earth* club when he was trying to set up some kind of hippy recording setup. I don't think it ever got very far. I don't remember if the recordings on the tape I sent were much different from the ones I have. I also went to see John Peel but I had no tape with me... he said he was interested because he was also starting up a record label (*Dandelion*). He said he thought I should develop an image for "being" *Sun Dragon*... rather than it being the name of a group! Eventually I moved towards studying North Indian Classical music seriously... occasionally playing with other musicians, but letting the *Sun Dragon* thing go.

I really made all my best recordings - from my point of view - after *Sun Dragon*; my own multi recordings, some collaborations with others... many of them after I moved to Cornwall in the late 1970's when I used mostly other instruments and less guitar. I did get to use quite a few basic synthesisers for a time, including some duets with a person called Peter Travers. This electronic collaboration became known as *Solar Wind*...also I played quite a lot for a year or two with saxist Lou Gare, who had been involved with a very experimental group called *AMM*. A poet/writer and musician, William Pryor, was sometimes also involved."

During the writing of my book on TEB, Necromancers of the drifting West, I asked Paul Minns to write his memories about the experience of playing in the band. Here's his important, disenchanted contribution, written in December 1996, in which we can read, probably for the first time, Paul's caustic vision of things.

Paul Minns

TEB founder and oboe player.

Newton Stewart, Scotland, December 1996

The Time

For me the music died around the time of the first Hyde Park concert with *Blind Faith* in 1969. Possibly for a variety of reasons: exhaustion (Sweeney and *Blackhill* were totally unaware of protective management, I reckon we must have played on average three times a week since starting); boredom - or even personal reasons, but I believe there was an unmistakable climate change. Flowers were out – squatting was in; self-determination was in the air, and rightly so. Unfortunately it was the time of the supergroup, which sounds better than the reality - and no one seemed to be interested in Indian music or the like. After that, Third Ear Band was staffed by various personnel with an air of the walking dead, all directed by Sweeney.

I need to talk about him now because he was both the founder and destroyer of the band.

He enjoyed the 'pop' limelight, despite its obvious lie, and totally fronted the band (I couldn't care as I was only interested in playing, but Coff was sat on regularly). For Sweeney this was better than work, but it didn't prevent him from behaving like a foreman. Really, all we had done was to produce music quite unlike any other in the scene and we could be slotted in as a contrast; but we were not pop.

Much later, when we were on the slide, he brought in vocals and then we were just another band.

But to start at the beginning...

In 1968 I met Sweeney during his existential/Zen/modern jazz phase. A drummer, he had progressed through *Skiffle* to full kit with a touch of the Orient thrown in. He prided himself on "not knowing the difference between a crotchet and a hatchet" and almost insisted on mispronouncing the names of the foreign writers, composers etc. *à la* Peter Sellers. He was on the lookout for musicians and chanced on me. I lived in a garret in Notting Hill Gate where I had lived for years, trying to make sense of my life and getting nowhere.

Fed up with classical music (I had played the oboe years before and still dabbled), I was encouraged by Glen to join him at various venues. My early gig recollection is at *Middle Earth* (a prime alternative venue in Covent Garden) with a cellist called Brian Meredith, Sweeney and Clive Kingsley - an acid-head guitarist who heard no one except himself: a sheet of sound.

These gigs didn't start until after midnight, and I remember many times catching a night bus back home. Strangely these were perhaps the happiest times for me. There was a great feeling of belonging to a movement quite unlike my classical days, when the only topic of conversation was the make of one's instrument.

These gigs at *Middle Earth* were fairly hairy, with one band regularly setting fire to themselves (*Tintern Abbey,* are they still with us?), [44] *Soft Machine*'s Robert Wyatt in underpants crying with the effort of playing 11/13 on the drums and Bowie, doing mime and playing solo guitar (embarrassing). There, in the small hours, continental film crews made their way between the stages looking for confirmation of the Swingin' '60s.

Later, *Middle Earth* was closed down after *The Tribe of the Sacred Mushroom* held a purported sacrifice of a child. We were there and it was one of my funniest memories. White tuniced, with spears, the tribe had set up a dais and we were to provide the music. I think I glimpsed a young girl but before anything could start the doors burst open and in swept Covent Garden workers looking for the intended "victim", to be followed five minutes later by many police. Being pacifists the tribe offered no resistance, thank goodness, but the child vanished into thin air in the following hilarious *melée*. It was the end for *Middle Earth*...

Other places we regularly played locally were *The Crypt* (St. Luke's Church), *All Saint's Hall* and a small basement cafè in Westbourne Grove, at the Ladbroke Hotel. These gatherings amazed me in that audiences put up with such spartan surroundings — a cross between a folk music and youth club was the nearest I had ever seen. *Les Cousins* in Soho, *I.C.A.*, the *Arts Lab* and the *Roundhouse* were more

---

[44]   No, after forming in late 1966 they made one single (Vacuum Cleaner/Beeside) and a year and a half later broke up again. The single was very ordinary - but because no one bought it at the time, it is now worth a small fortune to collectors.

'salubrious' venues, and the last two brought us in contact with non-music acts like *The People Band, Will Spoor* and *The Living Theatre*.

Somehow we were invited to play for *The Alchemical Wedding* – John Lennon and Yoko Ono in a sack – at the *Royal Albert Hall*. We were the only music? I could hardly believe so.

The earliest, virtually unpaid, gigs were surprisingly with some of the biggest names – John Mayall at Southampton (it was a booking mistake; we played in the interval and a hat was passed around) and *The Who* at Bournemouth. Our amplification was minimal – what a contrast.

John Peel gave us our first broadcast interview on *Night Ride* and organised a concert with Bridget St. John for those on remand in Holloway Jail – a shocking Victorian place. This took place outside, on a square of asphalt with the inmates cheering and waving out of the cell windows. Considering the type of music it must have seemed to an outsider like a dream.

About this time *Blackhill*'s Peter Jenner wanted to manage us. He and Andrew King had a varied stable and we fitted in quite well. People like Roy Harper, Edgar Broughton, Peter Brown and Kevin Ayers. Kevin, I remember, told me that our band sounded like an oasis amongst everything else at a *Roundhouse* gig.

Back at the agency, everyone seemed to hover as if expecting something. Something promised perhaps. *Blackhill*'s fame rested as much on the bands they had lost as on those they had retained. There was something of the schoolboy in them, especially King (called supercilious by some but to me more mocking).

Parallel to this was the EMI Harvest deal and our first experience of a promotional tour with their artists. Later, to their credit, they organised the Hyde Park concerts, both of which we opened. We were politely received but the concerts as a whole were not a great success. After that followed tours with Al Stewart (who I had never heard of and then heard too much of) and John Fahey, the guitarist.

Fahey was an ordinary American kid who played pinball and the guitar well. Stewart was a stupid link-up that did nothing for us, since his audience was bedsit girls. He bordered on the saccharine and was as musically interesting as cardboard (unfortunately I never have listened to lyrics).

My best gig memories are of the *Brighton Pavillon* with the *Pretty Things* and *Pink Floyd* – we being the filling for a change; the other was outside on Primrose Hill with *Procol Harum* and *Soft Machine*. The most unlikely was a May Ball in Cambridge, where we were practically locked up. Also we visited Kid Jensen at Radio Luxembourg on one of our forays to Europe.

In Nuremburg I was chastised one morning by a female hotelier for wearing my 'pyjamas' - which I tried to explain was my Indian long shirt.

Understandably we were fairly unknown and, I must admit, we looked pretty tame compared to bands like *Amon Düül*. There was quite a bit of aggression around because it was the time of college unrest. Our roadies were so important that for years they earned more than us. Though without the anxiety-undercurrent of the band, they were a breath of fresh air with their banter. I very much liked the way one roadie, called Paul, related to the amps as if they were people – "he doesn't like that" (after blowing something). With the unexplained need for greater volume, mikes went out and bugs were in. I managed to fit one in an alternative F vent but the tone changed for the worse. I also had my own *HH* amp, which had various gadgets, but my heart wasn't in it and they were underused.

Lastly, I was very proud to have done benefits and free gigs for organisations as diverse as a Buddhist retreat, White Rabbit's *Aardvark* scene in London's East End, an LSE sit-in, the Druids and *Release*.[45]

These were the cornerstone of my life.

The Music

'Five years playing without anything being written down', 'A giant jam and it sounds like it' – some say. Fifty percent of the time it did but when it did come right, it was magic. The group was supposed to be more important than the individual but I was frequently frustrated by the lack of "go" from the others, especially Coff, and this is evident in *Alchemy* (hear *Area Three*).

About that time I drove it from the top and I could have played with anyone. The line-up could have had a trombone, acoustic guitar or even at one point

---

[45] Founded in 1967 by Caroline Coon and Rufus Harris to provide legal advice and representation for people charged with the possession of drugs. Now it's the oldest independent drugs charity in the world.

voice - with varying degrees of audience success. Why some performances were better received than others has continually baffled me. Very little was discussed about the music between the musicians except for obvious projects like *Macbeth,* which makes this all quite difficult to recall.

The best Third Ear Band music was the earliest and this, for me, has been confirmed by the emergence of a tape prior *Alchemy* made at the beginning of 1969 [Paul means the reel of *Raga in D* that he found in his attic with the *Abelard & Heloise* soundtrack - LCF]. Direct, uncompromising and strangely like a field recording despite its studio origin. One can understand this music's affinity with the outside, where we often played like itinerant beggars, crouched in the parks.

Some pieces were blatantly naive (in the best sense), *Rite of Spring* music laced with birdsong and shades of Douanier Rousseau (*Mosaic* is such a progeny). Originally acoustic (I'm not counting the manic electricity of the Kingsley era when I hid behind the stacks) the music, over the years, deteriorated in relation to the amount of new gadgetry and amplification that was taken on board. The rush, in the 1970s, for the hemi-demi-semi-quaver sheets of sound, were no substitute for the acoustic concentration of a beautiful tone. One thinks of Miles Davis whose early priority must have been his tone, which I am sure came from his classical training. In the same vein I never practised but spent a lot of time scraping my reeds. Later I felt marginalised by my background when it was proposed that Third Ear Band should become a rock'n'roll band. For me, being an oboist wasn't enough. I had to improvise and obviously I had to be adept at playing to achieve that. Having been brought up in classical music in the 1950s I quickly realised that the solo oboe repertoire was pathetic and I would have to look elsewhere. In the band's early days I couldn't really play very well and I was very much to be seen but not heard, thanks to Kingsley. He did me a service – there was much to be observed at the *Middle Earth* venue. I had come to realise that an identity had to be stamped on each piece, either by key/scale or theme - and that listening to one's fellow musicians was the only way this music would work.

Indian music provided a key to this door. To many of our circle this came from *Dr. Jog,* and his *jugalbandi* colleague, the shenai player Bismillah Kan (EMI ASD2312 in *Music from India* series, 1965). It was only a short step from this shenai/violin to our oboe/violin.

Coff was also from a classical background; still took lessons and, for fun, played Bach's *Trio Sonatas* with me. An American draft-dodger, he visited his "shrink" just in case they came back to his door. He was constantly bemused, but since he was earning a trickle of bread it was better than starving (which we were all pretty near).

There was no attempt to duplicate ragas – the "feel" was more important. The thought of replicating Indian music makes me feel ill, and the best thing we ever did was to steer clear of this and to do our own thing. We used the term "raga" to loosely describe a single theme that increased in speed, unlike the constant music of *Dragon Lines* and *Mosaic*. There was an exception to this with a killer of a piece that we called *The Groove* - with Coff comfortably strumming and increasing the speed and me trying to keep up. I can't tell you how much I resented this – *Earth*, on the second album is the same piece. I thought of it as being Greek but this is nonsense. Our philosophy was very much "of the time" with everyone seemingly tapping things or dancing. In listening to the Indian duets the one thing I didn't like was the mimicking of what someone else had played, which smacked of "look what can I do". But it was the sarod player, Sharon Rani, who enabled me to fathom what was going on in this music. I think the most important thing Indian music taught me, besides the rhythm, was the use of the full range of the instrument, plus the leaps this could involve.

Also, about this time, I was greatly influenced by the music of the Balkans, especially Albanian bagpipes.

I copied the breathing technique as well as I could and the idea of an *acciaccatura*[46] grace note (see *Area Three*). Early recordings for Geesin/Essex Music library were of this type, but I haven't heard them for years. I never listened to classical woodwind. Through Sweeney I heard such jazz greats as Eric Dolphy, Pharoah Sanders and Charles Lloyd. John Coltrane was the greatest influence: I had known his work years earlier and liked his modal period. I copied some arpeggio chords from *My Favourite Things* (*Hyde Park Raga*) and the use of harmonics. I went on to discover more magic in this area.

Trills between a true note and a harmonic equivalent gave a sort of shimmering; nuances between the same note with different fingerings – all now

---

[46]   An incidental note one half or one whole tone higher or lower than the principal note, sounded simultaneously to add a dissonance.

have become standard oboe technique (hear the start of *Egyptian Book of the Dead* and *Area Three*). The only jazz oboist I had heard was Yusef Lateef. It was a slightly corny track with snake charmer overtones and a tone to match. This has always been my gripe with oboists – they often sound like strangled chickens. Ives' music was unknown to me and it came as a pleasant surprise to hear *In the Cage* from his set for *Theatre or Chamber Orchestra* (1906), much later – it has remarkable similarities. *Malipiero* is another I like, but I fancy his rustic lack of modernity would be despised by intellectuals.

The early music evolved over a long period of time – memory being crucial. We played to audiences almost every day – they the unknowing guinea pigs accepted any mistakes as "blind alleys". It seems like a dream now, how liberal people were then. At the *Arts Lab* I remember Jim Haynes marveling at our peregrinations, and the more blind alleys the better. I took comfort from Vylat Khan's sitar "collapses", which occurred regularly - that added to the eventual climax of the raga. In a way these uncomfortable parts gave the listener a clearer idea of what we were trying to do. Another person described the music as similar to the late Beethoven Quartets!

With Sweeney setting each piece with an individual speed and rhythm - added to our key/motif - they soon had an identity. Within a "raga" framework we were able to play for two hours at *Les Cousins* repeating the "same" pieces every twenty minutes. I should add that it was in the early hours and everyone was half asleep. This raga idea - meaning that it would increase in speed - gave this a sense of purposeful drive that the 'constant' pieces never achieved (except the *Egyptian Book of the Dead,* which combined both). *Alchemy*, *Ghetto Raga* and *Area Three* are of this type. *Mosaic* used a form of minimum frills akin to African music, which was not fully explored. I was influenced in this by Stravinsky's *Three Pieces for String Quartet*. Unfortunately this piece coming at the start of *Alchemy* was totally untypical of the album.

The *Alchemy* recording went like a dream and was completed in a week. I remember nothing of the production except that a few unnecessary effects were introduced - the worst at the end of *Egyptian Book of the Dead*, sounding like a pyramid's bathroom. *Dragon Lines* had successful overdubs, but I was basically against any mucking about with the music. If I had had my way I would have had a close sound with no presence, but in the end my tone was changed to fit the track - after half-heartedly agreeing to use this "exciting" medium. I can't honestly say that I felt any different playing live outside than in the studio – I was so immersed in my instrument... The breathing made me so high, I can fully understand why wind players are so reluctant to stop.

I lost the ability to play after the last Hyde Park concert, in 1969. I had problems finding somewhere to live, holding down a part-time job, and my reeds were a continuous problem - for which my tone and technique suffered. Whilst playing at *Arts Lab,* someone from Munich television called Moorse heard us and commissioned the music for *Abelard and Heloise*, an animated film, about 45 minutes long. I remember this as having fixed artwork with tele-visual techniques to give movement.

The artist called Fuchs produced Hieronymus Bosh/Fuseli type colour fantasmagoria. It went surprisingly well. The film had distinct episodes to which we had to play - while watching the film. I remember very little about this except that Coff and Ursula, disillusioned, had formed a clique. Not long after they secretly decided to split and I remember there was a great rush to the bank. It rankled with them that nothing musical was discussed, or in what direction the group was to go. To Sweeney this all smacked of insurrection since it was "his" band.

I was quite unable also to contemplate a more structured approach to the music – perhaps even composition! It sounds daft but I related composition to classical, which could only mean betrayal. As I realise now it was one thing to be able to improvise but quite another to improvise a theme. I have always loved lyrical classical music, like Prokofiev's - and I like to think that this shows. Initially it came easily. For others though it blatantly didn't.

Pressure was put on us to produce the second album in 1970, which was a disaster. At one point I had to convince Coff that it was possible to represent "air" as music. This turned out to be the best track, although it involved a major edit: we tagged the beginning onto the end - which was a pity.

Macbeth was done at *Air Studios* playing live to black and white rushes. Often we repeatedly watched gory scenes. Polanski related quite a bit, but was under pressure from the bankers as things dragged on. He had strong views about film music, such as doing the complete opposite of what was on the screen. This was contrasted with "cartoon" type sound for each action in the fight scenes. We spent a long time in the studio with very little material to show for it. The engineers didn't know what the hell was going on (I don't blame them). I was struggling and had to be restrained from attending the last sessions. Buckmaster reminded us of his need to protect his reputation - and there was general jockeying for Polanski's favour. The Sharon Tate murder had happened not long before and I felt that by choosing *Macbeth*. Polanski had hoped to substitute one grisly act by another - so erasing his memory. My playing was very shaky on the record, which I produced – everyone else having done a runner.

The other major event was The *Sun Wheel Ceremony* with the electronic composers from France. Parmegiani had come over previously to record some of our musical sounds so he could take them back, regurgitate and spew out something tasty.

The idea was to play along with this tape at concert. I remember no rehearsal, although I can't believe we walked on cold, with a predictable result - a mess. The French take themselves very seriously and must have been horrified by our *laissez-faire* approach. I think this had originally been set up by EMI but, as usual, nothing came of it. One novel feature at the time was the quadrophonic sound. Imagine trying to play to it.

Regrets? That more music had not been produced without the strict drum beat; ditched the pop tag; moved on sooner.

Denim Bridges
Electric guitar player, singer and composer with the TEB in 1970-1972.
London, April 6th, 2019

How did you meet Glen and Paul and join the band?

I answered an advertisement for 'Musicians to join recording band' (or words to that effect). I believe it was in *Melody Maker*, but it could have been one of the others. I was asked to audition at the band's base in Balham in South London. It must have gone well because I was asked to join.

I knew of the band because I'd been at the *Blind Faith* and *Rolling Stones* concerts in Hyde Park. I was very intrigued with their music as it then existed, but I was even more intrigued by what the band wanted to do with additional musicians and 'going electric'. I think the fact I had a custom-built double-neck electric guitar helped me to be noticed.

What you were doing in that period? Did you play with other bands before meeting the TEB?

I was just playing occasionally in amateur bands and open mics at folk clubs. I wanted to join *The Byrds*.

What equipment did you have when you met the band and how did previous experiences influence the music of the band?

My guitar amplifier was the Vox AC50, an amplifier developed specifically for George Harrison and John Lennon. Where *The Beatles* went, so did I. I had my double-neck guitar custom-built by John Bailey - and made famous by the lie of Glen Sweeney that one neck didn't work. The top neck was 12 strings and the lower 6 strings. I can be seen and heard playing both necks on *The Lost Broadcasts* DVD. I think someone else should answer the second part of your question. I think I was a 'blank page' at that time.

Have you still the legendary double-neck electric guitar Glen mocked?

My double-neck didn't survive the ravages of the New Jersey climate (hot and humid in the summer/freezing and dry in the winter) and, in 2001, the 12-string neck irreparably split along the grain of the wood. So it seems Glen was quite prophetic about one neck not working.

About the composition of new electric TEB music, who were the main musicians to involved? was there a leader?

Each member of the band would offer either fully developed compositions (as was the case for my songs) or partially developed ideas for the band to develop at rehearsals.

What was the modus operandi *of the band for composing?*

Ideas could be musical modes or scales - inspired by music from abroad, or from early forms of music. As the new guy with the electric I was, of course, always pushing for my ideas, with a rock sensibility, to be considered.

About the Macbeth *soundtrack: can you tell us what were your main musical influences?*

For *Macbeth*, as for every aspect of the band's music, we were influenced by many, many composers, musicians and musical forms from exotic parts of the world, and from the ancient past. We applied many of those influences to *Macbeth,* but some scenes in the movie did dictate that we had to be traditional. I took the melody and chords for *Fleance's Song* from a song I had composed before I joined the band. I used just a small part of that song because the stanzas we had been given to work with were very short. I used the line "Oh your two eyes will slay me suddenly" to repeat at the end of the verse as a sort of refrain. Could anything be more contrived? *The Groom's Dance* was based around a riff on the electric 12-string guitar (heavily influenced by *The Byrds*) but with the rhythm of a jig imposed on it. I suppose it's just a matter of opinion for that to be dismissed as 'just medieval'. For the incidental music for the film, of course, we were much freer.

And what about your approach to the tunes for Macbeth?

It is very difficult, if not impossible, to answer that question. Each scene required a different approach. *Lady Macbeth's theme* required at first a 'traditional' melody, which then had to get darker and more threatening as the piece progressed. To that purpose, I suppose, we applied the influences of - for example, Schoenberg - as you suggest. *The Witches Theme* is inspired by a scale of notes fewer than modern western music but typical of eastern or ancient cultures. This might be a real scale or one that we imagined but, hopefully, it should suggest weirdness and evil to the listener. We were sharing and listening to a lot of music all the time. Absorbing those influences just by osmosis would have flavoured what we did for *Macbeth* - and all our other music. I can't be more specific than that.
Did you ever see the movie? What do you think of it?

I watched it again only a few weeks ago. Shakespeare's dialogue, and the acting - by the best of Britain's acting elite - is of the highest calibre. In my humble opinion, there are a few clunky bits but I would rather take from the following story. In the mid-1990s I was at a gathering of friends in Montclair, New Jersey, and we were going to see *Shakespeare in the Park*. One of the people there was a teacher at the local high school who, in the general conversation, said that Polanski's *Macbeth* was the 'go to' version for his pupils. I think there are sequences in that movie that don't have music that would benefit from having it and a few of our bits work less well than I would like.

What was the mood when you played on stage with the band?

I have never suffered from stage fright or any nervousness on stage. I'm aware of what Paul said about skating on thin ice, or words to that effect, and I can relate to it, but I always believed the performance would come together – eventually. Sometimes it would take an interminable amount of time to prompt some members to start to play (as evidenced by *Druid Grocking* on *The Lost Broadcasts* DVD) and to (loosely) quote a band friend, "it always seemed to be grinding to a halt" - but most performances ended in elation. Most times our performances worked well – sometimes not so much. Could we then be described as 'thrill seekers'?

Which gigs do you remember most?

I remember many shows by who we opened for; *The Rolling Stones* at The *Roundhouse*, Cat Stevens at Sheffield University and *Love Sculpture* at Swansea University. The stage experiences I remember most are the ones that were very much out of the norm - like the time Richard Hopkins (from *Blond on Blond*) deputized for the departed Paul Buckmaster. That was a rocking gig. We played at a university in the East Midlands and the next day at Essex University, in Colchester - in the open with Roy Harper. Another 'aberration' was at *The Alhambra*, In Bordeaux, with *Centipede* when Glen said "Thank you very much" and walked off stage after 20 minutes or so of us playing. He claimed he thought we had played a full set. Oops! Unfortunately I also remember one of our road managers behaving rather badly behind the amps at *The Paradiso* in Amsterdam at one of the shows we opened for *Pink Floyd*. Some things just can't be erased from the memory.

Do you remember what happened after Macbeth? *Why everything faded away...?*

Although being engaged to provide the music for *Macbeth* was a great opportunity and a fantastic experience in many ways, it did make the band do a U-turn musically, reverting back to pre-electric Third Ear Band and away from the Electric Ear Band Glen had announced in the press earlier – before getting the *Macbeth* job, I assume. This is my read of what happened: I think Glen and Paul Minns decided that TEB should not go electric after all, but build on the direction TEB went with *Macbeth*. Paul Buckmaster, because of the demands of his arranging work, decided he could not continue in TEB - and his departure was a factor in the bigger picture. Glen had brought in a young chap who played acoustic guitar (I'm embarrassed to tell you, I don't remember his name) to fill Paul's position, but I wasn't convinced that not replacing the electric bass and adding the acoustic guitar was a good decision. I felt the proposed new line-up and the new (old) musical direction wasn't as inspiring to me as when I joined the band - and also wasn't exploiting me as a musician. I was also informed that the recordings we'd made with the electric band would not be released since TEB were out of their contract with EMI. Although I wasn't party to the details, I assume that meant that the *Macbeth* album fulfilled TEB's obligations to EMI. So I left. Or I didn't - since there was nothing to quit by then.

What have you taken from your experience with the Third Ear Band?

When we went into *Air Studios* to record the incidental music for *Macbeth* we used the film-dubbing studio (#4) and improvised as we watched the sequences of film requiring music. That all went quite well but when we came to be in the control room, for example, to edit or mix, we were like the vultures in Disney's *Dumbo* - a little uncertain and undecided. That's when I stepped forward and that's when George Martin noticed me. I also followed through the recording process by attending Shepperton Studios and supervising the laying of the music into the movie. Soon after that I was engaged by *Air Studios* as a recording engineer and later went on to produce records as an independent Producer and Engineer. That is the big take for me from the *Macbeth* experience.

How can you describe the emotion of playing music; that magic (or tragic) interplay on stage?

The feeling I had walking out on stage with The Third Ear Band was always a reflection of the last performance. When we'd really gelled together, and the pieces worked as well as they sometimes could, I very well remember the excitement I felt, and the anticipation of building on what the band had played the show before. When I was in the band, we improvised a lot of our performances; we had 'islands in the potentially stormy sea' (a mode, a figure, a riff) that we could jump on when things got scary.

What is your favourite TEB track? And why?

I would rather use the term piece of music than track because, until the *Elements, 1970-1971* CD became available, the piece was unreleased. *Tellus* had a short life in the recording studio as *Ghoo* but as per *Elements 1970-1971* it was renamed *Eternity in D* by John Peel in a live show out of BBC's Lower Regent Street studios. I'm sure the title would have been provided by Glen, probably under duress. Anyway, the track that is now available is a live version. I don't know why the studio version hasn't turned up. I like this piece because it has strong riffs in the bass and guitar that form a solid foundation for the oboe and violin to improvise over. It's hypnotic. So, did The Third Ear Band invent "Trance'? Maybe.

What are you doing right now, apart from working on the tracks recorded by the TEB for The Dragon Wakes?

I consider myself retired, having ceased performing for retirement homes, condominium associations and beach bars in Florida. That's 2 years ago now. I spend my days working around the homestead on the vegetable garden, the orchard - and generally fixing things. I play occasionally; I played a wedding last year, and I get together with old friends to play a '60s night. Also, I volunteer at a Performing Arts Center - sometimes mixing sound, or just stewarding. That allows me to see and hear a lot of music from a wide variety of bands and solo artists.

VIII

A Chronological Audio and Videography

This audio/videography collects all the records published by Glen Sweeney with his bands – the National Balkan Ensemble, Third Ear Band and Hydrogen Jukebox. It is based on the official UK and Italian records (for the period 1988-1993) with reissues, compilations and rarities included in the notes.

1968

AA.VV. – National-Balkan Ensemble/Comedy Links and Bridges (LP – STANDARD MUSIC LIBRARY ESL 112, UK 1970)
Cosmic Trip. Jason's Trip. Devil Weed.
Three tracks composed and recorded in late 1968 and early 1969 by Glen Sweeney (hand drums), Paul Minns (oboe), Richard Coff (violin) and Ben Cartland (cello) for composer and sound engineer Ron Geesin, who sold the tape to *Essex Music Ltd.* for its sound effects library.

In 2015 the tracks were included in *Necromancers Of The Drifting West*, published by Gonzo Multimedia (CD – Gonzo Multimedia HST311, UK) with liner notes by Luca Chino Ferrari; and in 2019 in the remastered edition of "Alchemy" published by Esoteric Recordings (CD – PECLEC22668) with a booklet edited by Luca Chino Ferrari.

1969

Third Ear Band – *Alchemy* (LP – EMI-HARVEST SHVL 756, UK)
Mosaic. Ghetto Raga. Druid One. Stone Circle. Egyptian Book of the Dead. Area Three. Dragon Lines. Lark Rise.
All tracks composed by Sweeney/Coff/Minns except *Lark Rise* composed by Dave Tomlin and played by Glen Sweeney (tablas, hand drums, wind chimes), Richard Coff (violin, viola), Paul Minns (oboe, recorder), Mel Davis (cello, slide pipes), John Peel (jaw harp), Dave Tomlin (violin on *Lark Rise*). Produced by Peter

Jenner. Engineers: Ken Scott and Peter Mew. Recorded at E.M.I. Studios, St. Johns Wood, London, January-May 1969.

After two reissues in vinyl format by *Harvest* in 1974 and 1980, *Alchemy* was reissued on vinyl and CD by *Drop Out Records* in 1989 (Drop Out/Demon DO 1999, UK); in 2004 by *Gott Discs* (as GOTTCD010) in a double re-mastered CD with *Third Ear Band*, then reissued in 2009 by *Beat Goes On* as BGOCD864. In 2015 Warner Music Japan published a CD edition only in Japan (as SHM-CDS 16334) in the *Progressive Rock Collection Edition Series*.

Through the years *Alchemy* has also been published in vinyl format in other countries: U.S.A. (Capitol-Harvest Records SKAO 376, 1969?); Japan (Odeon EOP 806650, 1972 and Toshiba TOCP-6796, 1991); Germany (Harvest 1C-062 04 066); Scotland (BEI-GI Wax2 Records, 1982); Italy (Akarma-Timeless TIME 732, ITA 2013 – limited edition of 500 copies).

In 1977 *Stone Circle* was included in a various artists compilation, printed by *Harvest Records* titled *Harvest Heritage 20 Greats* (EMI-Harvest SHSM 2020, UK).

In 1984 *Druid One* was included in a *Harvest* compilation titled *The Harvest Story. Art School Dancing. Vol. 1* (LP – Harvest EG2600971, UK) to celebrate the first 15 years of the label, reissued in 2002 in CD format as *Art School Dancing* (EMI-Harvest 756225, UK).

In 1999 *Stone Circle* was included in a various artists 5-CD compilation made to celebrate the EMI-Harvest catalogue titled *Harvest Festival* (EMI-Harvest 7243 5 21198 2 0, UK), also including a short interview with Glen Sweeney and some well-known photos and posters of the band.

In 2019 *Esoteric Recordings* (n° catalogue: PECLEC 22668) published a 2-CD re-mastered and expanded edition of the album with some rare or unreleased tracks: *Cosmic Trip, Jason's Trip* and *Devil Weed* from the very rare *National Balkan Ensemble*'s record and *Raga No. 1* (also titled *Raga in D),* all already included in *Gonzo Multimedia*'s CD *Necromancers of the Drifting West* published in 2015); *Unity* (recorded at EMI Studios in January 1969); *The Sea, Druid* and *Hyde Park Raga* (recorded at EMI Studios in September 1969); *Hyde Park Raga, Druid One*, recorded at BBC Radio One *Top Gear* in July 1969).

CD Booklet written by Luca Chino Ferrari.

In 2019 Cherry Red also published a limited and re-mastered vinyl edition (PECLECLP 2668).

Third Ear Band – *Third Ear Band* (LP – EMI-HARVEST SHVL 773, UK)
Air. Earth. Fire. Water.
All tracks composed and played by Sweeney (hand drums), Richard Coff (violin), Paul Minns (oboe) and Ursula Smith (violin). Produced by Andrew King and the Third Ear Band. Recorded at E.M.I. Studios, St. Johns Wood, London January-May 1970.

After two reissues on vinyl by *Harvest* in 1974 and 1978, this album was reissued on CD and vinyl in 1990 by *Beat Goes On* (as BGO LP89 and BGOCD89), in 2004 by *Gott Discs* (as GOTTCD010) in a double CD with *Alchemy* and, in 2015, by *Warner Music Japan* (as SHM-CDS 16335) in the *Progressive Rock Collection Edition* Series.

In 1970 *Water* was included in the various artists double compilation *Picnic. A Breathe Of Fresh Air"* (2LPs – Harvest SHSS 1/2, UK) celebrating the first year activity of the label.

In 2007 E.M.I. edited also a 3-CD set with the same title (*A Breath of Fresh Air. A Harvest Record Anthology/1969-1974* – EMI-Harvest 0946 388613 2 4) but with a different (enhanced) track selection: Third Ear Band is included here with two tunes – *Druid One* (from *Alchemy*) and *Overture*, from the 1972 *Macbeth* film soundtrack.

Rare editions of *Third Ear Band* were printed in Japan in 1972 on black and red vinyl (as Odeon EOP80511).

In 2018 *Esoteric Recordings* (n° catalogue: PECLEC 32653) published a 3-CD re-mastered and expanded edition of the album with some rare or unreleased tracks recorded between 1970 and 1971: apart from the original album and the soundtrack for *Abelard & Heloise*, there is a BBC *Sounds of '70s'* radio session, recorded on June 18th, 1970 (*The Sea, Dog Evil* and *Water*), a BBC *John Peel Session* radio concert recorded on January 17th, 1971 (*Eternity In D, Water, Druid One*) and some unreleased studio tracks: *Earth, The Sea, Very Fine... Far Away, The Dragon Wakes, Sunrise, Mistress to the Sun, Evening Awakening and In D*)

CD Booklet written by Luca Chino Ferrari.

1972

Third Ear Band – *Music from Macbeth* (LP – EMI-HARVEST SHSP 4019, UK)
Overture. The Beach. Lady Macbeth. Inverness: Macbeth's Return/The Preparation/Fanfare/Duncan's Arrival. The Banquet. Dagger and Death. At the Well/The Princes' Escape/Coronation/Come Sealing Night. Court Dance. Fleance. Groom's Dance. Bear-Baiting. Ambush/Banquo's Ghost. Going to Bed/Blind Man's Buff/Requiescant/Sere And Yellow Leaf. The Cauldron. Prophesies. Wicca Way.

All tracks composed and played by Glen Sweeney (drums), Paul Minns (oboe and recorder), Paul Buckmaster (cello and bass guitar), Simon House (violin and V.C.S.3), Denim Bridges (guitars). Produced by Andrew King and Third Ear Band. Recorded at Air Studios, London between July-August 1971. Engineered by Dave Harris.

Reissued on CD in 1990 by *Beat Goes On* as BGO CD61; in 1999 by Blueprint with the title *Macbeth* CD – Blueprint BP 312CD, UK) with a cover by Carolyn Looker, and in 2015 by *Warner Music Japan* (as SHM-CDS 16336) in the *Progressive Rock Collection Edition* Series.

In 1972 the album was also published in other countries: Italy (Harvest 3C-062 049 66, ITA), Holland (Harvest 501726120617), Japan (Toshiba-Odeon EOP 80512, then reissued by Toshiba as TOCP-7371, 1992).

One of the band's rarest records is the single *Fleance*, taken from this soundtrack, published only in Japan (Odeon EOR10140, 1972). The track was included in "five discs celebrating legendary progressive rock labels" published by E.M.I. in 2013 titled *Prog Rocks!* (EMI Records Ltd. G725 0702, UK).

In 2019 *Esoteric Recordings* (n° catalogue: PECLEC 2656) published a re-mastered and expanded edition of the album with three unreleased tracks, recorded by the band on December 5th, 1970 at *Trident Studios* (London), first version of *Court Dance, Groom's Dance* and *Fleance.* CD Booklet written by Luca Chino Ferrari.

1976

Third Ear Band – *Experiences* (LP – EMI-HARVEST SHSM2007, UK)
Ghetto Raga. Stone Circle. Area III. Earth. Overture/The Beach. Groom's Dance. The Cauldron.

Colin Miles' compilation with tracks from the first three albums. Cover by Lynn Darnton.

A very rare Japanese vinyl edition, realised in 1976, also exists (EMI EMS-80617).

1989

Third Ear Band – *Live Ghosts*
(LP – MATERIALI SONORI MASO 33047, ITA) (CD – MATERIALI SONORI MASO CD 90004, ITA) (CASSETTE – MATERIALI SONORI MASO MC 33047, ITA)
More Mosaic. Ghetto Raga. Druid Three. Live Ghosts.
Recorded live at *Chiostro di S. Agostino* (Bergamo, Italy) on September 8th, 1988 by Glen Sweeney (hand drums), Mick Carter (guitar), Paul Minns (oboe) and Allen Samuel (violin). All selections composed, arranged and produced by Glen Sweeney, Mick Carter and Paul Minns.

Reissued in CD format in 1993 (as MASO CD 90004) with a bonus-track *Necromanticus*, recorded in London in August 1988 by the same line-up.

Third Ear Band – *New Forecasts from the Third Ear Almanac*
(CASSETTE – ADN RECORDS ADN RECO1, ITA)
Egyptian Book of the Dead. Third Ear Raga. Live Ghosts. Witches Dance.
Released only on cassette in a limited edition of 500 copies, this was recorded live at *Teatro Impavidi* (Sarzana, Italy) on January 11th, 1989 by Glen Sweeney (hand drums), Mick Carter (guitar), Lyn Dobson (flute and alto sax) and Ursula Smith (violin). All compositions by Glen Sweeney, Mick Carter and Lyn Dobson.

Reissued in 2015 in CD edition by *Gonzo Multimedia* (HST312CD, UK) with liner notes by Luca Chino Ferrari.

1990

Third Ear Band – *Magic Music* (LP/CD – MATERIALI SONORI, ITA 1990)
(LP – MATERIALI SONORI MASO 33053, ITA) (CD – MATERIALI SONORI MASO CD 90016, ITA)
Behind the Pyramids. Reading the Runes. Solstice Song. Sun Ra Raga. Necromancy. Third Ear Raga.

Produced by the Third Ear Band. Recorded at *Alchemical Studios*, Kent (UK) by Glen Sweeney (hand drums, percussion), Mick Carter (guitar, effects), Lyn Dobson (soprano sax, flute) and Neil Black (electric violin, effects). Engineer Mick Carter. Produced by Third Ear Band.

The CD edition contains as bonus track the live version of *Third Ear Raga* performed at *Sala Piatti* in Gorizia (Italy) on November 24th, 1989 by the same line-up.

In 1995 Japanese label *Nexus* published a CD edition (as KICP 7047).

AA.VV. – *The Greetings Compact vol. 2* (CD – MATERIALI SONORI MASO CD 90014, ITA)
Old Man Kangaroo pt. 1
On this compilation of unreleased and rare tracks Glen Sweeney plays hand drums in *Old Man Kangaroo pt. 1* with Fabio Capanni (from Italian band Nazca) and *Amon Düül*'s Chris Karrer. The track (composed by Capanni) was recorded in Florence (Italy) that year, during the third TEB Italian tour.

1991

Glen Sweeney's Hydrogen Jukebox – *Prophecies* (CD – MATERIALI SONORI MASO CD 90018, ITA)
Kingdom Of The Brave. Life Is An Art. Chrysalis The Man. Voidoid City. Shoe Suede Blues. Ab-ra-ka-dab-ra. Prophecies. To Be Continued.
Hydrogen Jukebox's lost album, recorded at *Dansette Studios*, Kent (UK) in 1978 by Glen Sweeney (drums), Mick Carter (guitar), Brian Diprose (bass) and Jim "Gypsy" Haynes (vocals). Remixed by Mick Carter at *Alchemical Studios*, Kent (UK) in 1991. Song lyrics by Sweeney, music by Carter.

Partially reissued in 1998 in *Songs From The Hydrogen Jukebox*"(CD – Blueprint BP283CD, UK).

AA.VV. – Sonora. The compact (CD – MATERIALI SONORI 2/91, ITA)
Raga Of The Wind.
On this CD, included in the second issue of the Italian magazine *Sonora,* the Third Ear Band (here named *Elektric Third Ear Band*) with Glen Sweeney, Mick Carter, Neil Black and Barry Pilcher play *Raga Of The Wind*. Later this track was re-

recorded with a different title - *Sirocco Song,* with Lyn Dobson on sax instead of Pilcher and included in "Brain Waves".

AA.VV. – All Frontiers (CD – MATERIALI SONORI MASOP CD 90026, ITA)
Live Ghosts.
On this compilation of live tracks recorded at the *All Frontiers* festival in Gorizia (Italy), TEB appears with *Live Ghosts,* taken from the gig at *Sala Piatti* on November 24th, 1989 played by Glen Sweeney, Mick Carter, Lyn Dobson and Neil Black. Years later the track was part of the concert recording published as *Live* by *Voiceprint* (CD – Voiceprint VPR157CD, UK).

1993

Third Ear Band – *Brain Waves* (CD – MATERIALI SONORI MASO CD 90045, ITA)
Sirocco Song. Midnight Drums. Spell to the Voodoo. Dances with the Dolphins. Water into Wine. Alchemical Raga. Psychedelic Trance Dance.
Recorded at *Alchemical Studios,* Kent (UK) by Glen Sweeney (percussion), Mick Carter (zeta midi guitar), Lyn Dobson (vocals, chants, soprano, flute, wind synth and Neil Black (zeta midi violin). All selection composed, arranged and produced by the Third Ear Band. Recorded and mixed by Mick Carter.

A track from the album *Dances With The Dolphins* was included in a *Materiali Sonori* sampler titled *The Materiali Sonori Guide To Intelligent Music vol. 2* published in Italy in 1995 as MASO CD 90068. *Midnight Drums* was included in another *Materiali Sonori* sampler titled *Materiali Sonori* included with the Italian magazine *Olis* (CD – Olis OM0021, ITA 1998).

An unofficial Russian limited edition (published in 1995 by Kahkapa (as TEBCD 06110293) also exists.

This album was reissued on CD by *Gonzo Multimedia* (as HST455CD) in 2017 with one bonus-track recorded in 1991 by *Elektric Third Ear Band* (*Raga of the Winds*) and new liner notes by Luca Chino Ferrari.

1994

Third Ear Band – *Radio Sessions* (CD – VOICEPRINT VPR017CD, UK)
Raga La Luna. Spirits.

Although notes attribute these two tracks (only 21 minutes) to the unlikely line-up: Glen Sweeney (percussion), Mick Carter (guitar), Paul Minns (oboe) and Ursula Smith (violin), this could be a 1988 recording made by the TEB reunion line-up, with Glen Sweeney, Paul Minns, Mick Carter and Allen Samuel during the rehearsals at the London Cambodian Embassy in Summer, 1988.

Mick Carter (8-12-2009): "I don't remember Ursula playing with Paul Minns. While she was in the band it was Lyn on soprano (but I don't remember this recording at all...).

1996

Third Ear Band – *Live* (CD – VOICEPRINT VP157CD, UK)
Hymn to the Sphynx. Sun Ra Raga. Third Ear Raga. Live Ghosts. Pyramid Song. Egyptian Book of the Dead.
Recorded live at *Sala Piatti* in Gorizia (Italy) on November 24th, 1989 by Glen Sweeney, Mick Carter, Lyn Dobson and Neil Black. Some track titles were modified: *Hymn to the Sphynx* is actually *Reading the Runes*, while *Pyramid Song* is *Behind the Pyramids*. Two tracks from this concert had already been issued on the compilation *All Frontiers* (Materiali Sonori MASO CD 90026, ITA 1991) – *Live Ghosts* – and on the CD edition of *Magic Music – Necromanticus* is actually *Egyptian Book of the Dead*.

Solstice Song, in the middle of the concert, has been inexplicably omitted from this edition.

Reissued in 2001 as the second CD of *Hymn To The Sphynx* (2CD – Mooncrest Records CRESTDCD 067 Z, UK) compilation, and in 2002 in a double vinyl record (180 gr.) *Raga Live* (2LPs – Turning Point TPM-02216, ITA) with cover by Carolyn Looker.

1997

Third Ear Band – *Abelard & Heloise* (CD – STAMPA ALTERNATIVA SONIC.005, ITA)
This original soundtrack, recorded by TEB in July 1970 by Sweeney, Smith, Coff and Minns for the German Bremen TV movie *Abelard* (58'35") directed by George Moorse with the screenplay by Ernst Fuchs and Hans Gailling, was

included in Luca Ferrari's *Necromancers of the Drifting west* book published in 1997 by *Stampa Alternativa*, the first authorized biography of TEB.

The soundtrack was reissued by *Blueprint* in 1999 (CD – Blueprint BP 310CD, UK) and by *Voiceprint* in 2014 (CD – Voiceprint VP607 CD, UK) with covers by Carolyn Looker. Years later it was included in 2CDs *Hymn To The Sphynx* (Mooncrest Records CRESTDCD 067 Z, UK 2001).

A remastered version of the soundtrack was included in 2018 2CDs remastered edition of "Third Ear Band" released by Esoteric Recordings as PECLEC 32653.

Third Ear Band – *Magic Music* (CD – BLUEPRINT BP 257CD, UK 1997)
Gog and Magog. Flight of the Coven. Dance of the Elves. Atlantic Rising. Midnight on Mars.
This record, with same title as the original *Materiali Sonori* second release published in 1990 as MASO CD 90016, actually features an excerpt from *Brain Waves*, produced by *Materiali Sonori* in 1990, even if in re-played and re-arranged versions.

Here again, Sweeney shuffles the cards, changing titles and track-list: *Gog and Magog* is *Midnight Drums*; *Flight of the Coven* is *Sirocco Song*; *Dances of Elves* is *Psychedelic Trance Dance*; *Atlantis Rising*, is *Dances with Dolphins*, while *Midnight on Mars* is *Spell of the Voodoo*.

Omitted, but one doesn't understand why, is *Water into Wine*, sung by Dobson, and *Alchemical Raga*.

This *Magic Music* was reissued in 2001 on the first CD of *Hymn to the Sphynx* (2CD – Mooncrest Records CRESTDCD 067 Z, UK 2001).

1998

Third Ear Band – *Songs From The Hydrogen Jukebox* (CD – BLUEPRINT BP283CD, UK 1998)
Kingdom of the Brave. Life is an Art. Chrysalis the Man. Abracadabra. Behind the Pyramids. Prophecies. *Dances with Dolphins. Water into Wine. To be Continued.*
This is a partial reissue of Glen Sweeney's Hydrogen Jukebox: six tracks taken from the original *Materiali Sonori* edition (omitted are *Voidoid City* and *Shoe*

Suede Blues), while three tracks (*Behind The Pyramids, Dances with Dolphins* and *Water into Wine*) are taken from other official Italian records (the first from *Magic Music*, the other two from *Brain Waves...*).

2004

Third Ear Band – *The Magus* (CD – ANGEL AIR SJPCD173, UK)
I The Key. Cosmic Wheel. The Hierophant. The Magus. New Horizon. The Phoenix. Kozmik Wheel.
The fourth lost album, recorded in December 1972 at London *Island Studios* by Glen Sweeney (drums), Paul Minns (oboe, recorder and Hammond), Simon House (VCS3, violin, sitar and piano), Mike Marchant (guitar and vocals), Ron Kort (percussion and doom piano) and Dave Tomlin (bass on *The Magus* and declaiming on *The Phoenix*). Words and music of tracks 1, 2, 3, 4 and 7 composed by Mike Marchant; 5 and 6 words and music by Dave Tomlin; 8 by the Third Ear Band. Produced, engineered, mixed and mastered by Ron Kort. Booklet notes by Steve Barker, Ron Kort, Dave Tomlin, Simon House. This CD was also published in vinyl format by *Akarma* in Italy as AK312 LP.

In 2010 *Cosmic Wheel* was included on a 3-CD anthology of progressive rock titled *Progressive Rock Trilogy*, published in Argentina (Music Brokers MBB7082).

The year after, *I The Key* was included in an *Angel Air* various artists compilation titled *Ventis Secundis, Tene Cursum. This Is Progressive Rock!* (Angel Air SJPCD, UK 2011).

In 2019 a 180 gr vinyl limited edition of the album was released by Tiger Bay Records (TB0006430) with a different cover and liner notes.

2015

Third Ear Band – *Necromancers Of The Drifting West* (CD – GONZO MULTIMEDIA HST311CD, UK)
Cosmic Trip. Jason's Trip. Devil Weed. Raga in D. Raga N° 1. Water. Eternity in D. Druid One.
Compilation of rare tracks recorded by the *National Balkan Ensemble* (a.k.a. Third Ear Band) in late 1968 for *Essex Ltd.* sound effects archive, and the Third

Ear Band in 1968-1971: *Raga n. 1* is an unreleased track from the very first session at the *London Abbey Road* Studios in December 1968, recorded for *Alchemy* by Sweeney, Minns, Coff and Cartland; *Raga N° 1* was recorded at *Abbey Road* Studios in February 1971 by Sweeney, Minns, Buckmaster and Bridges for an announced but never released third album *The Dragon Wakes*. The last three tracks were played live in January 1971 for BBC's *Top Gear* radio programme by the same line-up. Liner notes by Luca Chino Ferrari.

2016

Third Ear Band – *Exorcisms* (CD Gonzo Multimedia HST371CD, UK)
Druid Three. Egyptian Book of The Dead. Live Ghosts. Reading the Runes. Exorcism. Behind the Pyramids. New Age Raga. Witches Dance.

A compilation edited by Luca Chino Ferrari including rehearsals recorded at the London ex-Cambodian Embassy in the summer of 1988 by Glen Sweeney (hand drums), Mick Carter (guitars and effects), Paul Minns (oboe) and Allen Samuel (violin), plus the demos the Third Ear Band recorded in March-May 1989 for *Magic Music* (at the time called *Spirits* or *Magic*). The sessions were recorded at *Alchemical Studios* (Kent) by Glen Sweeney (hand drums), Mick Carter (guitars and effects), Lyn Dobson (flute and alto sax) and Ursula Smith (violin).

2017

Third Ear Band – *Spirits* (CD – GONZO MULTIMEDIA HST428CD, UK)
More Mosaic. Druid. Hyde Park Raga. Egyptian Book of the Dead. Third Ear Raga. Spirits [aka Live Ghosts]. Lark Rise.
All compositions by Glen Sweeney, Mick Carter, Lyn Dobson except *Lark Rise* composed by Dave Tomlin.

Full live concert from *Tuxedo Club* in Piacenza (Italy) played by Glen Sweeney (hand drums, bells, percussion), Mick Carter, (guitar and effects), Lyn Dobson (vocals, bells, flute and alto sax) and Ursula Smith (violin) during the second Italian tour on January 14th, 1989.

Liner notes by Luca Chino Ferrari and Italian film-maker Francesco Paolo Paladino.

Other unreleased recordings:

These unreleased TEB recordings are available on the Web in MP3 format through *Ghettoraga*, the official *esoteric archive* at http://ghettoraga.blogspot.it.

- London, February 11th, 1969 *John Peel Session*: Hyde Park *Raga. Druid.*
- Genova (Italy), January 11th, 1989 *Psycho Club* full live concert.
- Gorizia (Italy), November 24th, 1989 *Sala Piatti* live concert: *Solstice Song.*
- London, December 15th, 1989 *Sir George Robey* pub: full live concert (this recording is also available at the London *British Library* – 96, Euston Road – St. Pancras London NW1 2DB)

Other existing live recordings that have not been yet published:

- Milano (Italy), February 5th, 1990, *Prego Club* full live concert
- Mantua (Italy), April 11th, 1992: *Circolo ARCI Salardi* full live concert
- Rome (Italy), February 4th, 1990: *Classico* full live gig
- Rome (Italy), December 28th, 1991: *Piazza Navona* full live gig

The *Dragon Wakes* recording sessions (Late 1970 - February 1971)
The Third Ear Band (as Electric Third Ear Band*) retired to Sweeney and Minns' in Balham (London) for three weeks to rehearse the pieces for the third album, announced on August 1970 in* Melody Maker *as* The Dragon Wakes. *The line-up consisted of Glen Sweeney (drums), Paul Minns (oboe), Paul Buckmaster (electric bass) and Denim Bridges (electric guitar). Richard Coff (or Simon House) were involved for recording some of the tracks. The record was never published. From these sessions a copy on reel-to-reel of one track was kept for years by Paul Minns -* Raga n.1, *which later appeared on TEB's CD* Necromancers of the Drifting West. *published by* Gonzo Multimedia *in 2015. The other six were kept by Denim Bridges -* Mammatus (Electric Air), Sulis Stirs, Druid One, Hexagonal Wheel, Tellus, The Earth and The Rising Seed) *and these have now been made available for the first time with this book. The band recorded some other pieces at around the same time, probably for the same projected album,*

which are documented in Esoteric Recordings' *3-CD re-mastered edition of* Third Ear Band, *released in 2018.*

Necromancer Suite (October 1989)
A long instrumental suite (about 50') recorded by Sweeney, Carter, Dobson and Black as rehearsal for the *Magic Music* recording sessions. Apparently the tape was lost.

Song of Gaia (1991)
The *Brain Waves* album was originally recorded by the *Elektric Third Ear Band,* consisting of Sweeney, Carter, Black and Pilcher. In 1991, the album was re-recorded with Dobson replacing Pilcher. *Song of Gaia* was a track from the session with Pilcher. Another alternate track recorded with Pilcher was *Raga of the Winds* (then re-titled *Sirocco Song*), which was included on a *Materiali Sonori* sampler accompanying the magazine *Sonora* (issue 2/91), then as a bonus-track on the reissue of *Brain Waves* published by *Gonzo Multimedia* in 2017.

E.M.I./BBC vaults
Thanks to Ken Garner's *The Peel Sessions* book, published by the BBC, in 2001, we know that Third Ear Band played the following sessions:

January 1st, 1969 – *Night Ride*
TEB (Sweeney, Minns, Coff, Cartland) played *The Grove, Stones Circle, Egyptian Book of the Dead, Pierrot*
July 27th, 1969 – *Top Gear*
TEB (Sweeney, Minns, Coff, Smith) played *Hyde Park Raga, Druid, Ghetto Raga.* (Note: this session is available in the Net as a free unofficial download)
June 12th, 1970 – Black
Earth, Downbone Raga, Water (& Festival)
June 20th, 1970 – *Top Gear*
TEB (Sweeney, Minns, Coff, Smith) played *Downbone Raga, Feel Your Head, Hyde Park Raga.*
February 11th, 1972 – *Peel Session*
TEB (Bridges, Pavli, Marchant, House) played *Air* and *I The Key.*

March 21th, 1972 – *Drummond*
TEB played *Groan's Dance, Fleance's Song, Hierophant.*
May 18th, 1973 – *Sequence*
TEB played *I The Key, The Magus, Ten Dimensional Landscape.*

From some other sources (primarily Paul Minns' diary) we know also TEB recorded live for other BBC radio programmes:
May 20th, 1970 – BBC *Sound of Seventies*
June 18th, 1970 – BBC *Sound of Seventies* TEB played *Dog Evil (Mosaic), The Sea (a.k.a. Air) and Water.*
(Note: this session is available through the page: http://ghettoraga.blogspot.com/2010/10/another-old-rare-teb-radio-session.html of *Ghettoraga Archive*)
January 7th, 1971 – BBC *John Peel's Sunday Show.*
TEB (Sweeney, Minns, Bridges, Buckmaster) played *Eternity in D, Druid, Water.*
(Note: this session is available on the TEB's *Necromancers of the Drifting West*, published by *Gonzo Multimedia* in 2015)

In 2012 I did some research to find out which Third Ear Band radio sessions were still in the BBC archive. I asked archive manager Simon Gurney, who said that "the man in charge of the Transcription discs here has checked and can confirm that none exist with the Third Ear Band. You can safely say you have exhausted your search in this regard."

Finally, the following 1970-1971 TV recordings have probably been erased but maybe exist in recordings by fans from that time:

April 24th, 1970 – *Essen TV* programme.
(A 2:38 video excerpt played by Sweeney, Minns, Coff and Smith of "Earth" is available on YouTube channel)
November 18th, 1970 – *Bordeaux* TV programme
November 23th, 1970 – *Paris* TV programme

Video/Filmography
1970

Abaelard, directed by George Moorse (GERMAN TV, 1970)
From the classic medieval love story between Abelard and Heloise, adapted for the screen by Hans Gailing and Ernst Fuchs with music by the Third Ear Band. This short TV film (around 1 hour) was aired on December 6th, 1970 and is available in a DVD-R copy c/o NDR Media – Hugh-Greene-Weg 1 [D] 22529 Hamburg (mitschnittservice@ndr.de).

*Fata Morgana,*directed by Werner Herzog
(Werner Herzog Film, DR 1970)
On the soundtrack is a reduced version of *Ghetto Raga*, taken from *Alchemy*.

1972

Macbeth, directed by Roman Polanski (PLAYBOY PRODUCTION, UK 1971)
The full soundtrack recorded by the band, who also appear as minstrels in a banquet sequence.

1977

Stigma, directed by Lawrence Gordon Clark (BBC, UK 1977)
This short film (31.49) was produced by BBC and broadcast on December 28th, 1977, and then included in a 5xDVD box titled *Ghosts Stories For Christmas* (BBC, UK 2002). On the soundtrack is an excerpt of *Air* by the Third Ear Band.

1979

Geschichte Der Nacht, directed by Clemens Klopfenstein (DR, 1979)
A 61-minute short film directed by avant-garde Swiss film maker Clemens Klopfenstein with an excerpt of 7' of *Fire* by the Thirds on the soundtrack. This intriguing black & white movie inspired by night (the title is *The Story of Night*) is available on the Net at: http://ubu.com/film/klopfenstein_nacht.html

2005

Blind Faith. London Hyde Park 1969 (DVD – SANCTUARY RECORDINGS GROUP, UK 2005)
A fleeting appearance of Glen and Carolyn near the stage while *Blind Faith* are playing *Sea of Joy*. The sharp expression of disgust on Glen's face is the evident proof that his idea of music at the time was totally different from the rock-pop-folk around...

2011

Third Ear Band – The Lost Broadcasts (DVD – GONZO MULTIMEDIA HST069DVD, UK)
In D. Hyde Park. David Grocking.
Live performance in the studio recorded for Radio Bremen's *Beat Club* on September 11th, 1970 by Glen Sweeney (drums), Paul Minns (oboe), Paul Buckmaster (electric bass), Denim Bridges (electric guitar and vocals) and Gaspar Lawal (congas). Insert notes by John Kirkman. The correct title of *David Crocking* is probably *Druid Grocking*.

Other unofficial video recordings
Apart from the official videos, on the official Ghettoraga Youtube Channel at https://www.youtube.com/channel/UCu_9gvPMbfKxpRhtoroxidg some other videos are available:
- short excerpt (1:29) from Hyde Park live concert with *Blind Faith* played on June 7th, 1969 by Sweeney, Minns, Coff and Buckmaster
- 2:38 excerpt from German TV played on April 24th, 1970 by Sweeney, Minns, Coff and Smith (*Earth*)
- full live concert (38:22) on May 28th, 1970 aired at French TV played by Sweeney, Minns, Coff and Smith.
- short sequence (2:57) from a session in *Abbey Road* on February 1971 played by Sweeney, Minns, Buckmaster, Bridges and House.
- live in Piacenza (Italy) at *Circolo Tuxedo*, January 14th, 1989
- excerpts from live concert in Bergamo at *St. Agostino's Cloister*, September 8th, 1988

IX

A Third Ear Band day-by-day Chronology

1966

June

18th – The Royal Albert Hall (London) – *A New Moon of Carnival of Poetry in the Round.*

Considered by some the birth of the English underground, this event involved the most active, alternative poets of that period – Pete Brown, Michael Horowitz, Bob Cobbing, amongst others - and musicians like Cornelius Cardew and John Renbourn. This 'celebration' was a kind of sequel to the first poetry meeting organized a year before, in August 1965 at the *Royal Albert Hall*, with Ginsberg, Corso, Horowitz, Mitchell, Fainlight and others, documented by filmmaker Pete Whitehead in *Wholly Communion*. During this new celebration of the moon, among these "who wish to preserve their freedom by remaining nameless", as it the promotional leaflet had it) was the *Giant Sun Trolley,* a trio of "musical animation" put together by Dave Tomlin on guitar, Glen Sweeney on percussion and Roger Bunn on bass.

Sweeney, coming from his experiences in Skiffle jazz bands (*The Anacondas* and *Sounds Nova*), and a few unsuccessful R&B groups had, until then, mostly strolled from one place to another with the main aim of sparing himself the trouble of working. *Sounds Nova* rehearsed upstairs in a public house in Barons Court called the *Barons Arms*, and later called the *Nashville*. Glen's partner Carolyn read poems by the Beat poets and a primitive lighting system flashed for effect. The band still existed in 1966 when a weekly publication called *International Times* appeared, describing itself as "an underground newspaper".

December

23rd – UFO Club (London) – *UFO presents Night Tripper*. The opening of the Club. Giant Sun Trolley supported The *Pink Floyd*. UFO was founded by John Hopkins (*Hoppy* to friends) and Joe Boyd. [47]

Sweeney and Tomlin played for two or three hours and got a weekly hire for every Thursday night, which continued until the club closed, a year later.

1967

January

13th – UFO Club (London) The Giant Sun Trolley with the Pink Floyd

At the UFO Giant Sun Trolley used to play at dawn. One of the pieces composed by Tomlin in this period was *Eternity in D* and was conceived as in a way to let musicians play the same note for as long as they could, or at least, until the club was empty. In *IT* no. 6 (January 1967), this evening was launched as an "Ultra International Times Event, with The Giant Sun Trolley with Dave Tomlin improvising to Government Propaganda."

Tomlin recalls the origins of Giant Sun Trolley:

"The first gig was at the Marquee. I had a lady playing Bach cantatas and this African, Bongo Louie, playing the bongos. I played soprano saxophone and I'd met this dog that used to come down the *Free School* and I used to practise on him and he would sit in front of me and howl. It was so musical and beautiful, and I had the dog up on the stage and I was playing and the dog was howling and the Bach cantatas and Bongo Louie was bongo-ing. That was my first gig with the *Sun Trolley*. We never knew what we were going to do till we got up there. Some nights I'd play just one note the whole gig. Next week I'd play two notes and wow. Two notes after you'd just been playing one!".

---

[47] An American born organiser, who started working in music for the likes of Muddy Waters, Stan Getz and Sister Rosetta Tharp. That was electric – after which nothing was ever quite the same again. In 1964 he came to the UK to set up an office for Elektra records and set up the UFO Club with John Hopkins two years later, producing the Pink Floyd's first single, *Arnold Layne*, before setting up his own production company *Witchseason*, and producing records by, amongst many, the Incredible String Band, Fairport Convention, Nick Drake, Sandy Denny and John Martyn. He has written a useful book on the period: White Bicycles, *Making music in the 1960s*, which was published in 2006.

20th – UFO Club (London). A replica of the January 13th event.

February

18th – UFO Club (London) Giant Sun Trolley with the *Soft Machine*

March

11th – Whitehall (London) – *The Death Transfiguration of IT*
On March 9th Police closed *International Times* after a raid. A symbolic funeral and rebirth were held on Saturday 11th in Whitehall on the Circle Line - and in Portobello Road. *Giant Sun Trolley* was there with Sweeney playing the drum during the 'funeral' procession...

? – ICA-Institute of Contemporary Arts (London) – *Destruction in Art Symposium*
   A jazz jam session in which Tomlin and Sweeney were part of a 'supergroup' including Mal Dean (trumpet), Rab Spall (violin), Evan Parker and George Khan (saxes), Kevin Ayers (bass), John Stevens, Laurie Allan and Robert Wyatt (drums). Evan Parker remembered: "I'll never forget the moment when Glen Sweeney, during the concert said to me: 'Jazz is dead and we are the gravediggers". It was the only time I played with four drummers. It was funny; a very funny evening".

April

7th – UFO Club (London). Giant Sun Trolley with *Soft Machine*
13th – UFO Club (London)
29th – Alexandra Palace (London) – *the 14-Hour Technicolor Dream*
         One of Giant Sun Trolley's last concerts was at possibly the most iconic event of the English and European underground which involved much of the

best of the English scene of the time.[48] A DVD: *A Technicolor Dream* was released in 2008 by *Eagle Visions* which includes an interview with Dave Tomlin. *IT* wrote, some days before: "Note for all Insomniacs. Forgot to get your Dream ticket? Be cool. Be at Earl's Court Station at 7.30 on Saturday. *The Sun Trolley* and Tony Scott's will unfold to envelop you in music and movement and tickets. At eight, the scene will go underground to Piccadilly. Be there. Join in the swirl. Then to Kings Cross at 8.30 and at 9.00 – it's early bedtime and Dream away to the Palace".

May

2nd – Kensington Gardens (London) Another *Giant Sun Trolley* guerrilla event.

"A Drummer and a Horn player blow to a crowd of sixty to a hundred people for around an hour, until they are stopped by an old Park Fuzz", reported *IT*. [49]

Talking with jazz journalist Duncan Heining in *Jazzwise* magazine (Dec. 2007-Jan. 2008), Tomlin remembered: "After playing with Mike [jazz pianist Mike Taylor], I would play anything. It got very wild. I'd do all sort of things. It didn't matter what I played so long as I didn't stop. I'd just make noises and sounds – Albert Ayler, it was moving into that. We used to do guerrilla music things. Like we'd go to Kensington Gardens. There's a bandstand there and we'd have the instruments in bags, so no-one could see and we'd get them out and see how long we could play before the police or park wardens would turn up. It was a happening which meant you couldn't tell anyone. It had to be spontaneous...". A similar guerrilla event happened in Oxford. This time Tomlin was arrested by police: "In Oxford one time, I was arrested and put in a cell and eventually John 'Hoppy' Hopkins came along. He was the editor of

---

48   A special issue of *IT* was published on 28/04/1967 (vol. 1 issue 12) about it, which is still available at http://www.internationaltimes.it/archive/index.php?year=1967&volume=IT-Volume-1&issue=12.

49   A transcription of the tape recording is available at http://www.internationaltimes.it/archive/index.php?year=1967&volume=IT-Volume1&issue=13&item=IT_1967-05-19_B-IT-Volume-1_Iss-13_007 and a memoir of the event by Dave Tomlin from his book Tales from the Embassy can be found at http://ghettoraga.blogspot.com/2010/03/first-part-of-excerpts-from-tale-from.html

International Times and said: "We're going to do an article about this". The sergeant at the desk, his name was Hilter and Hoppy said to him: "We can do it two ways. Either we can say the Oxford Constabulary were very helpful and treated everybody very nicely. We don't want to mention *Gestapo* do we? And if we mention names typographical errors occur very easily..." So they let me out. Walking back, I thought, shit why am I getting involved with the police? Why do they hate me so much? And I realised it wasn't me, It was my fucking saxophone because there's not a more bolshie instrument on the planet. So, I decided to take up the violin instead." ("Jazzwise" magazine, Dec. 2007-Jan. 2008 interviewed by Duncan Heining)

12th – UFO Club (London). *Giant Sun Trolley* **with Procol Harum and Graham Bond**

13th – *Evening Standard* article about Dave Tomlin with a quotation about the Giant Sun Trolley

14th – Hyde Park (London)

The invitation, typed on coloured tissue-paper said: "The Giant Sun Trolley will devise music at speakers corner on Sunday may 14, '67 from 3 o' clock 'til arrival of opposition, then a procession through Hyde Park." Hidden behind the gate at Speaker's Corner, Sweeney and Tomlin waited for the police, playing their music.

19th – UFO Club (London) Giant Sun Trolley with *Tomorrow, Arthur Brown* **etc.**

26th – UFO Club (London)

"Heroic return of Dave Tomlin & The Giant Sun Trolley with *The People Show* and *The Move*". (*IT* announcement).

June

2nd – UFO Club (London). Hydrogen Jukebox with *Pink Floyd, Mantra, Carol Mann* **and** *Giant Sun Trolley*

9th – UFO Club (London). Giant Sun Trolley with *Procol Harum* **and** *The Smoke*

16th – UFO Club (London) – *All night trip,* **Giant Sun Trolley with** *Soft Machine* **and** *Arthur Brown*

In *IT* issue 15 vol. 1 (March 16th 1967) an article on Dave Tomlin appears with a photo by David Redom – about a process. [50]

24th – *Disc and Music Echo*. Hugh Nolan, writing about the scene at UFO Club, quotes the Hydrogen Jukebox...

July

2nd – Theatre Royal (Stratford, London) – *New Departures*. The Giant Sun Trolley with, amongst others, Davy Graham, Pete Brown and Cornelius Cardew.

August

4th – UFO Club (London)
The Hydrogen Jukebox with Family and Eric Burdon & the New Animals "till dawn"...
9th – Old Place (London)
The Hydrogen Jukebox in *Jazz of Tomorrow*.
? – The Roundhouse (London). Hydrogen Jukebox in concert.

It's the gig that will make them famous, at least for one night, with a mention and, of course a photograph, in the *News of the World*,[51] about their use of amplified scissors to slowly remove a young woman's clothing snip by snip[52]. Now Sweeney moves between *Giant Sun Trolley* and *Hydrogen Jukebox* until the latter break up, acknowledging that it is an unsuccessful project. Even if they only played few concerts *Hydrogen Jukebox*, played

---

[50]   http://www.internationaltimes.it/archive/index.php?year=1967&volume=IT-Volume-1&issue=15&item=IT_1967-06-16_B-IT-Volume-1_Iss-15_002).

[51]   A National Sunday paper founded in 1843 by John Browne Bell who believed crime, sensation and vice would maximise sales. He was right. It was a byword for gutter journalism and had the highest circulation figures. Who better to carry on that tradition than Rupert Murdoch who bought it in 1969 and turned it into a tabloid in 1984 specialising in sex scandals. It was still selling almost 3 million copies a week when it was shut down as a result of illegal phone hacking in search of stories.

[52]   Something of a *News of the World* version of *Fluxus* artist Yoko Ono's *Cut Piece*, premiered in 1964 in which audience members are invited to cut pieces from her clothing. Glen's version lacks the social and moral complexity – but does feature amplified scissors.

regularly at the *Happening 44* club for a few weeks (The *Social Deviants* were the house band there). A little piece titled "Four 4 Four" in *IT* (issue 15, June 16th, 1967) confirms it... Giant Sun Trolley also split at around this time, when Dave Tomlin decided to leave London for a trip and Sweeney had the idea of the Third Ear Band...

15th – All Saint's Hall (London). TEB with *Fleetwood Mac* and *Quintessence*.

This was probably the first TEB gig... "In the late 60s, *All Saints* high church services were also given by David Bowie – during his mime phase, the *Crazy World of Arthur Brown* – doing *Fire*, *The Edgar Broughton Band* – doing *'Out Demons Out'*, *The Third Ear Band* with *Tina's Light Theatre*, and *The People Band*". The Carnival founder Rhaune Laslett recalled an *All Saints* happening involving Jeff Nuttall of the *People Band*: "motorbikes and very scantily dressed girls riding pillion throwing jam covered newspapers and other paint-dripping missiles at the audience".[53]

22nd – Burton Constable Hall (Hull) TEB with *Pretty Things* and *Chicken Shack*
24th – Arts Lab (Leicester) TEB with *The Deviants*, Bridget St. John "and maybe *The Third Ear Band*"

September

20th – Queen Elizabeth Hall (London) – *Crabs & the Crescent Moon* TEB with Bridget St. John and John Peel
21st – Happening 44 (London) – *Environmental Evening*.

Happening 44, founded by Jack Bracelin, was a twice-weekly late-night rock club located in a strip joint at 44 Gerrard Street, Soho.

24th – Middle Earth (London) – *High Tea with* .. TEB with *Graham Bond Organisation* and *Shemiaihs Woorlitza*
28th – The Boat Club (Nottingham) "*Every Sunday night sounds as like... Third Ear Band*"

---

53   Tom Vague at http://www.portobellofilmfestival.com/talkpics/talk-babylon7.html

October

13th – Middle Earth (London) TEB (on the poster as *The Third Ear*) with *Soft Machine, Persephone-Goddess of Dance, Jode Hexogram*, Jeff Dexter and *Utradelic Alchemists*

November

4th – Middle Earth (London) TEB (announced as *The Third Year*), with *The Knack*
14th – Arts Centre (Manchester). Benefit concert with TEB & *Edgar Broughton Band*
30th – Middle Earth (London). TEB and *Soft Machine*

1968

January

12th – Arts Lab (London)

"Haynes, one of the *entrepreneurs* of the London underground culture, had the idea of opening a multidisciplinary venue to present theatre, music, literary events and exhibitions; *The Arts Laboratory* in Drury Lane (Covent Garden), opened on July 1967[54]"

"The Arts Lab was a product of its time", Haynes told Luca Ferrari in 2010. "I was young and full of creative energy and believed that I could do anything. I wanted to make a mixed-media centre that would be full of life. And I succeeded! London was the capital of the world in the mid-60s. I don't remember how I met anyone in the 60s; they just all came to the Arts Lab and I suddenly knew everyone. I loved their concerts. They were magic. Often only with candlelight. We closed the Lab because I ran out of money and the landlord wanted his property back...". Even if there are no traces of it, in the

---

[54]   Read at http://www.jim-haynes.com/life/theatre.htm

same period TEB also played regularly at *Les Cousins*, a folk club in Greek Street, Soho.[55]

February

16th – **Ladbroke Hotel (London)** – *Electric Raga*
21st – **Ladbroke Hotel (London)** – *Electric Raga*
23th – **Ladbroke Hotel (London)** – *Electric Raga*
28th – **Ladbroke Hotel (London)** – *Electric Raga*

March

22nd – **Guildhall (Southampton) – *Blues on Ice* TEB with *John Mayall's Bluesbreakers* and the *Bernie's Music Machine*.**
31st – **Middle Earth (London) – *Albion Awakening* TEB with, among the others, *Fairport Convention, Pete Brown Poetry Band*, Dave Tomlin**

April

19th – *IT* vol. 1 issue 29
In an article titled "UFO is dead – long live UFO!" written by Barry Miles a mention of *Giant Sun Trolley* and Dave Tomlin.

29th – **Odin's Monday Club (London) TEB with Spike Hawkins and K.*I.W.C.***
"The club was originally organised by a manager of K.I.W.C. because there was no club suitable for his group's sound, but it developed into something bigger after talks with 3rd Ear Band and *Tribe of the Sacred Mushroom*. The idea was to provide a small 'family-type' club, specialising in eastern music, poetry and 'experiments'... mantras, chants, audience participations. 'We're trying to change the concept of AUDIENCE and PERFORMERS. We want one group ALL participating, ALL enjoying each other'. The club is, at present, very short of money (performers play free so far) but we are hoping to build up followers and funds" (from *IT* issue 31, May 17th, 1968)

---

55   http://en.wikipedia.org/wiki/Les _Cousins_%28music_club%29

The St. Pancras levitation: just an urban legend?

Sometime in the first months of the year, the St. Pancras railway station levitation occurred. The station was to be moved elsewhere since it was considered a very ugly piece of architecture, hence the levitation.

TEB, of course, supplied the right music for this event and an enthusiastic John Peel was there too. Among the dailies that reported the event was the *Evening Standard*. In a short article *Hippies and the moon can't budge St. Pancras*, they wrote: "One hundred and fifty hippies chanted to the full moon outside St. Pancras railway station last night – in a bid to levitate the railway buildings over the Thames to Bermondsey. Three bemused police officers looked on as the hippies prayed, to the accompaniment of violins, flute and bells. (...) But St. Pancras' Victorian Gothic red bricks stayed put. (...) Why did they choose St. Pancras for the three-mile levitation attempt? A young girl explained: "Because it's so ugly". And why send it to Bermondsey? "Because Bermondsey hasn't got a railway station". The police did not try to intervene. An officer said: "I don't blame them for wanting to remove it. St. Pancras isn't a pretty building".

Asking Dave Tomlin (2010) to confirm TEB's presence he said: "Never heard of the St. Pancras thing but I will ask around" – and then, sometime later: "Glen was a bit of a magician. He could make matchsticks disappear by staring at them. I think he got together with some other magicians and tried to make St Pancras Station disappear. The story is that they succeeded but only for three seconds. After that, they tried to make America disappear but so far no luck...".

May

Albion Magazine – vol. 1, May 1968

Edited by Steve Pank, at that time promoter and driver of the TEB. In its first issue the magazine published probably the first TEB promo ad designed by Glen Sweeney. Later the logo, modified, would be been included like a sticker in the first album.[56]

---

[56]   http://ghettoraga.blogspot.com/2009/12/very-rare-third-ear-band-sticker-from.htm

5th – Odin's Monday Club (London) TEB with Pete Brown and his Drummer and K.*I.W.C.*

19th – Middle Earth (London) – *Magical Sunday Benefit concert* for *Gandalf's Garden* TEB with *Tyrannosaurus Rex*, David Bowie, John Peel and others

22nd – Middle Earth (London) – *Celebration for Albion*. TEB with *Tyrannosaurus Rex, HapsHash & the Coloured Coat, King Ida's Watch Chain* and *The Invisible Union*

June

4th – The Crypt (London). TEB with *Dharma Sounds of Subterranea*

9th – Middle Earth (London) – *The Tribe of the Sacred Mushroom* TEB with *The Tribe* and *King Ida's Watch Chain*

11th – The Crypt (London) – *Cosmolatry* by the *Mandala*, Minstrel Dave Tomlin, *Simon's Sound Poetry*

21st – Avebury (Wiltshire) – *Midsummer reception Committee… to welcome anything which comes*. TEB with *Tribe of Sacred Mushroom* and *King Ida's Watch Chain.*

July

3rd – The Crypt (London) TEB with *Pete Brown & The Battered Ornaments* and Ron Geesin

August

23th – International Times, Vol. 1 n. 38. Glen Sweeney's letter to *IT*.

21st – Arts Lab (London) – *Cosmic Raga*

24th – Safari Tent (London) – *Cosmic Raga*

"In Westbourne Park Road, the Third Ear Band performed 'cosmic ragas' every Thursday at the *Safari Tent Caribbean Store* at number 207 (which also hosted the early '60s Jazz club). Down Lancaster Road, in the Methodist church hall, there was 'music, poetry, theatre every Wednesday' at *The Crypt* folk club, featuring Jeff Nuttall's experimental jazz group, *the People Band,* and the *Third Ear Band*".[57]It was during this period that the TEB's electric instruments were stolen.

September

12th – Safari Tent (London) – *Cosmic Raga*
19th – Safari Tent (London) – *Cosmic Raga*
20th – Queen Elizabeth Hall (London) – *Soundzzz* TEB with Bridget St. John and Sam Hutt
21st – Arts Lab (London)
26th – All Saint's Church Hall (London)

October

3rd – Safari Tent (London)
4th – All Saint's Hall (Powis Gardens, London) – *Four dimensional happening* with TEB, '*Jade Hexagram, Tina's Environment*, poets, revelations'
4th – Arts Lab (London). TEB with Ron Geesin and *The People Band*
10th – Safari Tent (London)
11th – Arts Lab (London)
17th – Safari Tent (London)
19th – Arts Lab (London)
19th – College of Arts (Croydon) – *Concert of poetry and new music* TEB with, amongst others, *The Egar Barry Pilcher Kinetic Ensemble*
20th – Country Club (London) – *Time Out/Free Bank Benefit*. TEB with, amongst others, David Bowie
21st – Arts Lab (London) – *Cosmic Raga*
24th – Safari Tent (London)
25th – Arts Lab (London)
26th – Arts Lab (London)
31st – Safari Tent (London)

---

57   Tom Vague at http://www.portobellofilmfestival.com/talkpics/talk-babylon7.html

November

1st-14th – International Times, Vol. 1 n. 43
Third Ear Band is mentioned for the first time by *IT*.
1st – Arts Lab (London)
2nd – Arts Lab (London)
3rd – Arts Lab (London)
6th – Arts Lab (London)
7th – Safari Tent (London)
7th – All Saint's Hall (London) - *Has the UFO invasion begun – Albion lives*
TEB with *Barclay James Harvest*

      It was at one of the first performances at *All Saint's Hall* that Steve Pank introduced Pete Jenner to the band. Jenner, with his friend Andrew King ran *Blackhill Enterprises*, an agency that some months before had signed the *Pink Floyd, Kevin Ayers, Roy Harper* and others appearing in alternative venues and not yet generally known. TEB became a Blackhill band... "At that time I was very involved in the idea of improvisation and their music – like the instruments they were playing – was different and charming..." (Peter Jenner, 1996).

8th – Arts Lab (London)
9th – Arts Lab (London)
14th – Safari Tent (London)
15th – Arts Lab (London)
16th – Arts Lab (London)
20th – Arts Lab (London)
21st – Safari Tent (London)
22nd – Arts Lab (London)
23th – Arts Lab (London)
27th – Arts Lab (London)
28th – All Saint's Hall (London)
TEB with Pete Drummond, Davy Graham, *Jade Hexagram*, Simon Stable.
28th – Safari Tent (London)
29th – Fishmongers Arms (London) TEB with *Gun*
29th – Arts Lab (London)

30th – Arts Lab (London)
30th – Van Dykes (Plymouth) TEB with Pegasus

December

4th – Arts Lab (London)
5th – Safari Tent (London)
6th – Arts Lab (London)
7th – Arts Lab (London)
8th – Civic Hall (Guilford)
TEB with *Fairport Convention*, Roy Harper, Bridget St. John, *Barclay James Harvest*, Tim Hollier and John Peel

"I was co-promoter of the event (with help from *Blackhill*) and afterwards TEB came back to the cottage I shared with friends and stayed the night, dossing on the floor. Glen endeared himself to one and all in the morning by accosting a passing milkman and then making us all much-needed coffees. Ah, memories!" (Graham Clarke to Ghettoraga Archive, October 4th, 2019)

11th – Arts Lab (London)
12th – Safari Tent (London)
13th – Arts Lab (London)
14th – The Roundhouse (London) – *Middle Earth presents at The Roundhouse*
TEB with *Principal Edward's Magic Theatre, Uriel,* Pandit Trika (sitar master) and *Radha Krishna Temple*. Introduced by John Peel
14th – Arts Lab (London)
15th – All Saint's Hall (London) – *Brave New Departures Revisited*
TEB with, amongst others, Alexis Korner and Cornelius Cardew.

Promoter & *IT* journalist Michael Horowitz wrote about this event in *IT* no. 49 (January 1969): "On 15 December I presented what was supposed to be a benefit show as well as a Xmas party at All Saint's Hall ... an all-day event that might well have graced & packed out the *Roundhouse, Albert Hall, Coliseum* or *Kremlin* or Kensington or Peking palaces or *Hollywood Bowl* or even *Mecca* or Jerusalem's wailing wall - with rhythm, harmony, colour and delight a full and happy house, lit up to sounds from the 3rd Ear Band and Dave Tomlin, Neil Oram, Peter Lemer, Al Kovacs and Cardew, (...) to fellow poets Brown, Pattern,

Carlyle Reedy, (...) – in a rapport with the audience it's not embarrassing to call magical."

18ᵗʰ – Royal Albert Hall (London) – *A Hippy Gathering: An Alchemical Wedding* TEB with John Lennon, Yoko Ono, Steam Hammer, Christopher Lodge and Rip Torn

Organized by Jim Haynes as a benefit concert for the *Arts Lab*, the event featured Lennon and Ono crouched in a sack in the middle of the room with TEB (Glen Sweeney and Carolyn Looker) riding white bicycles around them. The couple's 30-minute conceptual performance was titled *Alchemical Wedding*. The bag was, they explained, to ensure "total communication" with the audience. The following year the concept was reintroduced by the pair as *Bagism*, an attempt to satirize prejudice and stereotyping". (From the Website http://www.beatlesbible.com/). During the performance a protestor ran to the stage, holding a banner about the British government's involvement in the Nigerian civil war. "Do you care, John Lennon? Do you care?" the protestor shouted at the couple".

19ᵗʰ – Safari Tent (London)

20ᵗʰ – Arts Lab (London)

21ˢᵗ – Arts Lab (London)

21ˢᵗ – Mothers Club (Birmingham)
TEB with *Edgar Broughton Band*

26ᵗʰ – Safari Tent (London)

27ᵗʰ – Van Dikes (Plymouth) TEB with *Clouds*

29ᵗʰ -12ᵗʰ January – IT vol. 1 n. 45 (page 16)

In his weekly *IT* survey, John Peel wrote about the TEB: "Recently there was a concert in Guilford in aid for a projected Arts Lab there at which I heard the Third Ear Band for the first time. Most of you probably heard them already but if you have not, then try to do so soon..."

1969

January

1st – **BBC Studios (London)** – Night Ride radio session
1st – **Arts Lab (London)**
2nd – **All Saint's Hall (London)**
TEB with *Edgar Broughton Band*
4th – **Arts Lab (London)**
4th – **Safari Tent (London)** – *Cosmic Raga*
8th – **Arts Lab (London)**
10th – **Arts Lab (London)**
10th – **Safari Tent (London)** – *Cosmic Raga*
11th – **Arts Lab (London)**
11th – **LSE (London) TEB with** *Savoy Brown*
14th – **School Of Art (Winchester)**
16th – **Safari Tent (London)** – *Cosmic Raga*
17th – **Arts Lab (London)**
18th – **Arts Lab (London)**
23rd – **Country Club (London)**
TEB with *Edgar Broughton's Blues Band.*
24th – E.M.I. Studios (London) First recording session, the band recorded two tracks, *Unity* and *Raga no. 1*.
27th – **Harris College (Preston)**
30th – **Stoke-on-Trent**

February

1st – **Magic Village (Manchester)**
6th – **Country Club (London)**
TEB with *Edgar Broughton Band*
7th – **Railway Tavern (London)**
14th – **Manchester College**
17th – **Old Granary (Bristol)**
19th – **Mothers Club (Birmingham)**

TEB with *Edgar Broughton Band*

20th – Country Club (London)

TEB with *Edgar Broughton Band*

23rd – The Roundhouse (London) – *Middle Earth at Roundhouse LSE Benefit Concert*

TEB with *The Who*, Cat Stevens, Pete *Brown & Battered Ornaments* (rescheduled from February 9th)

Simon Stable (*IT* no. 52, 14-03-1969): "Congratulations, Don Stickland, for a very good show at the Roundhouse, a couple of Saturdays ago. Really excellent performances from Principle E's Magic T, Third Ear Band, Mick Hart and Bridget St. John, Circus..."

24th – The Dome (Brighton) – *A Benefit for the Combination*

TEB with *Pink Floyd* and *Pretty Things*.

28th – *IT* vol. 1 issue 51, first *Blackhill* ad in *IT* for the Third Ear Band as *Alchemic TEB*.

March

5th – Mothers Club (Birmingham)

TEB with *Edgar Broughton Band*

6th – Country Club (London)

TEB with *Edgar Broughton Band*

7th – Asgard Club (Stratford)

13th – All Saint's Hall (London) TEB with *Jody Grind*

14th – *I.T.* vol. 1 n. 52 page 13. In a brief article titled "Sound Scene Squashed", TEB road manager Steve Pank talks about the problems of promoting concerts at the *All Saint's Hall*.

21st – Loughton College

Joint, Combination, Third Ear Band, 'Structure poems, stroboplays etc....'

27th – Arts Lab (London)

28th-10th April – *I.T.* no. 53 (page 16) announcement of TEB's first record:

"The alchemically-musical people, The Third Ear Band, whose affiliations with the Druids are even physically real, are visiting Edinburgh and Glasgow on April 16th and 17th. The Scottish sect of Druids are casting a spell over them to protect their bodies from any angry Picts. Their album will be released on the *Harvest* label in May, 'ALCHEMY', is a musical must (?). They are playing a concert at the Purcell Room on April 21st, nice!"

Strangely no reviews were published in the magazine...

April

? – Glastonbury Tor – Concert for the Druids
2nd – Pavilion Ballrooms (Bournemouth) TEB with *The Who* and *The Embers*
(Originally scheduled March 2nd).
3rd – Arts Lab (London)
10th – Arts Lab (London)
11th – *IT* vol. 1 no. 54, page 13 *Purcell Room* concert ad (see April 21st, 1969)
In the same issue (page 16) is a plea for the concert: "Last minute message from Blackhill Enterprise (the well-known entertainment agency) is that, competing with Janis Joplin on April 21st, The Third Ear Band will be appearing at the Purcell Room. Support them!"
16th – The Centaur (Multi-Arts Labyrinth) (Edinburgh) TEB with *Skin and Bare Wires*
17th – Arts Lab (Glasgow).
TEB with *Pete Brown & the Battered Ornaments*
21st – Purcell Room (London) – *Alchemy*
24th – Country Club (London) – *Arts Lab Benefit*
25th – Lancaster University (Lancaster) TEB with *Aynsley Dunbar Retaliation* and Adrian Mitchell
25th – *IT* vol. 1 n. 55 (page 28) *Gandalf's Garden* no. 4 - ad with TEB quotation: in this issue, Muz Murray interviews Glen Sweeney.
26th – Bromley Technical College (Bromley) – *Light and Sound Concert*
TEB with *The Pink Floyd* and *East of Eden*
27th – The Roundhouse (London) – *Dwarf benefit*
TEB with Christopher Logue, *High Tide*, Adrian Mitchell etc.
29th – Hatherton Hall (Walsall) – *Whisky Villa*
During this period TEB recorded some demo tracks.
Three were published as the *National Balkan Ensemble* (probably for copyright reasons). Carolyn Looker: "I find The National Balkan Ensemble a total mystery. All I can think is whoever got hold of these tracks put the name

to them. Before recording *Alchemy*, Glen, Paul, Richard and Ben did some recordings for Ron Geesin, who was going to try to sell the music for background for TV! I don't think anything came of it but maybe these are the tracks anyway, it was done in a small studio on the cheap. I vaguely remember Christopher Logue the poet being there too. Ben's leaving the band was totally his idea, he was very young – about 17! – and didn't want to commit... I think he went off with his girlfriend travelling..." (from a letter to Luca Ferrari – December 2nd, 2005).

May

1st – St. John's College Entertaiments Committee
TEB with *Dada*
18th – Parliament Hill Fields (London) – *Camden Fringe Festival*
TEB with *Procol Harum, Yes, Blossom Toes*, John Fahey, *Soft Machine*
18th – Club Annabelle (Sunderland) – *Annabelle's Workshop*
 ? – *Gandalf's Garden* issue no. 5. "Alchemy and Time Travel" written by editor Muz Murray. This was probably the first review of *Alchemy*.
26th – The Dome (Brighton).
TEB with John Fahey and *Pentangle*
30th – The Roundhouse (London) Harvest Records showcase; introducing its acts to the English public TEB with *Forest, Pete Brown & the Battered Ornaments, Edgar Broughton Band*, Mike Chapman

June

 ? – *Alchemy* released by EMI-Harvest
4th – Mothers Club (Birmingham). E.M.I. Records in conjunction with Blackhill Enterprises launch Harvest artists: TEB with *Edgar Broughton Band, Michael Chapman, Pete Brown & the Battered Ornamants*
7th – Hyde Park (London) – TEB with *Blind Faith, Donovan, Richie Havens, Edgar Broughton Band*
     The first free concert organized by *Blackhill Enterprises*. In front of 100-150.000 people the Third Ear Band opened the concert, playing before *Blind Faith*. Johnny Black from *Mojo* magazine wrote, in *Born under a bad sign*, "June

7, 1969 was a scorcher. By the time *Blind Faith* got to Hyde Park the crowd was 100,000 strong. Jagger and Faithfull were backstage, as were Donovan and Mick Fleetwood, along with former *Traffic* members Jim Capaldi and Chris Wood. "Stigwood stood out like a sore thumb at the gig," recalls Andrew King... For a start, he was the only man there in a suit, a very stylish dark blue job it was. What rather spoiled the image was that the shoulders were absolutely covered in dandruff. The inevitable Third Ear Band took the stage at 2.30pm for their woozy brew of sitars, tablas, strings and oboes, followed by *The Edgar Broughton Band* (also obligatory at outdoor events in 1969). There was a brief foretaste of *Woodstock* from Richie Havens, an unannounced spot by Donovan - inaudible to the majority of the crowd but well-received by the throng at the front - then, with the heady sweet aroma of dope wafting on pale blue clouds from the audience, *Blind Faith* took the stage at 5pm. Kids clambered onto car roofs and shinned up trees for a better look as the opening chords of Buddy Holly's *Well All Right* blasted out"

(http://www.gingerbaker.com/bands/blind-faith.htm).

A lucky witness remembers: "I was there!! Travelled overnight on a bright blue 1940's double-decker bus from Bolton... about 50 of us on board! Hit London 8am... all bowler hats flagging us down thinking we were London Transport (Bright blue and you could smell the dope and patchouli from about half a mile away). D Fell asleep during 3rd Ear Band... woke up and had a walk, saw Donovan busking under a tree... (thought he was a really good impersonator at first, 'til we got close and saw it was really him!)" (Alec Martin from http://www.gingerbaker.com/bands/blind-faith.htm).

11th – Cambridge – *Cambridge Midsummer Pop Festival*
TEB with, amongst others, David Bowie, *Audience, Strawbs*
20th – University of East Anglia (Norwich)
TEB with Bridget St. John
25th – Railway Hotel (Bishop's Stortford)
30th – The Ritz (Bournemouth) TEB with *The Room*

July

5th – Hyde Park (London) – *Rolling Stones Concert* TEB with *Rolling Stones, Family*, Roy Harper, *Battered Ornaments*

Later remembered as the *Brian Jones Memorial Concert*, this was probably the most successful of those organized by *Blackhill* - between 250.000 and 500.000 people attended. TEB opened the concert, followed by *King Crimson*, *Screw* and *Alexis Korner*.

Ray Connolly, in the measured pages of the *Financial Times* (July 7th, 1969), wrote: "Of the four groups to appear, none was particularly outstanding", and defined the TEB's music as "a strange Oriental cacophony, surely designed to lull the audience to sleep".

12th – *Melody Maker*. Chris Welch writes a very good article on the band.

13th – The Roundhouse (London) – *Implosion!*
TEB with *Quintessence, Gypsy, Pink Cheeks*

18th – Marquee Club (London) TEB with *Camel*

24th – Penthouse (Scarborough)

25th – Bay Hotel (Sunderland)

26th – Magic Village (Manchester)

27th – BBC Studios (London) – *Top Gear* radio show

30th – Mothers Club (Birmingham)

At around this time, cellist Ursula Smith joins the group when Paul Buckmaster leaves.

August

15th – All Saints Hall (London) TEB with *Quintessence, Skin Alley* "and
possibly *Fleetwood Mac!*" (*I.T.* ad)

22nd-24th – Arts Centre (Hull) *Humberside Pop Festival* TEB with *The Nice, The Kinks, Edgar Broughton Band, Pretty Things* etc.

24th – Arts Lab (Leicester) TEB with *Jody Grind, Deviants, Bridget St. John* "and maybe" The Third Ear Band

29th – *IT* no. 63 extended TEB interview.

31st – Woodside Bay (Isle of Wight) – *Isle of Wight Festival*
TEB with, amongst others, Bob Dylan, *The Band,* Tom Paxton

31st – Town Hall (Rugby) – *The Rag Ball*
TEB with *Edgar Broughton Band* and *The Deviants*

After the prestigious appearance at the *Isle of Wight* festival, on the evening of the 31st TEB played a gig in Rugby. In a report published in *IT* no. 65

(September 26th), Mick Donovan wrote: "(..started with a local band who didn't impress and weren't very original. Then the Third Ear band and the first signs of audience hang-ups. They played quite well and a surprising number of people seemed into the music, but the majority laughed, or stayed in the bar..."

September

12th – E.M.I. Studios (London) - A recording session at which the band recorded three tracks: *The Sea, Druid and Hyde Park Raga*. Unreleased for years, they were included on a 2-CD re-mastered and expanded edition of *Alchemy* by Esoteric Recordings in 2019.

13th – Rainsbrook – *The Sam Cutler Stage Show*
TEB with *Pink Floyd, Edgar Broughton Band, The Nice, King Crimson, Taste, Free*

14th – TEB photographer Ray Stevenson injured in a car crash

19th – Friars Auditorium – Borough Assembly Hall, Market Square (Aylesbury)
TEB with *Graham Bond Initiation* (advertised but didn't show up).

Introduced on the flyer as the "incredible" Third Ear Band, Sweeney & Co. played two sets to replace Graham Bond, who didn't show up. In the end, a local newspaper reported: "About 350 people did stay to hear the Third Ear Band and their contemplative Indian music invoked a mood of serenity that befitted the situation. Principle instruments used by the four-man group were a cello, clarinet [sic!], violin and bongos [!], and their fusion created a sound most faithful to Indian music that I have heard."

20th – Queen Elizabeth Hall (London) – *The Crab & the Crescent Moon*
TEB with Bridget St. John, John Peel and Sam Hut

The title of the concert was taken "from a dream that Glen had had" (Steve Pank, 2004).

26th – Pavilion Gardens (Buxton) TEB with *Fleetwood Mac, Family, East of Eden, Edgar Broughton Band*

26th-9th October – *IT* vol. 1 n. 65 page 20, Dave Arbus (leader of *East of Eden*) writes a polemical (and clever) letter about the "underground", answering some self-indulgent statements by Robert Fripp. He also mentions the Third Ear Band as an expression of middle-class youth culture.

28th – Redcar Coatham Hotel TEB with *Eclection*

? – *Beat Instrumental* article.

During this period TEB played as the house band every Sunday night at *The Boat Club, in Nottingham.*

October

2nd – University of East Anglia (Norwich)

TEB with *Van der Graaf Generator*

3rd – Ritz (Bournemouth) TEB with *The Room*

10th – Salford University (Salford) – *A Night of Family Entertainment with* TEB with *Family, Killing Floor, The Entire Sioux Nation*

15th – Mothers Club (Birmingham)

16th – Royal Philharmonic Hall (Liverpool)

TEB with *Family* and Bridget St. John

18th – London School of Economics (London)

TEB with *Blossom Toes* and *Eclection*

20th – Star Hotel (Croydon) TEB with *Gracious*

28th – The Magic Village (Manchester)

November

? – Middle Earth North (Edinburgh)

14th – Manchester Arts Centre (Manchester) – Benefit Concert

TEB with, amongst others the *Edgar Broughton Band*

16th – St. George's Hall (York)

TEB with *Fairport Convention*

21st – Brunel University (Uxbridge)

TEB with *Magna Charta*

26th – Mothers Club (Birmingham)

28th – Nag's Head (High Wycombe)

December

14th – The Houldsworth Hall (London)

TEB with John Peel, Bridget St, John, Beau, Mike Hart
15ᵗʰ – Paradiso Club (Amsterdam)

Karl Dallas in the *Melody Maker*, December 20ᵗʰ: "Third Ear Band have an organic sound. And the response they got from their Dutch and Belgian tour seems to indicate that it transcends national frontiers in a way that only music that has grown that way naturally can. (...) In Holland, I saw them working under the toughest possible conditions, and the thing that struck me was the way their music communicated. Not at a cerebral level, but somewhere deeper. Imagine a great aircraft hanger of a hall.. a venue about the size of the Roundhouse. Surround it with freezing fog and put about two or three hundred young Dutch teenagers inside, where the temperature is slightly above the cold outside. Kick off the concert with an announcement that the main attraction can't get there, follow that with a couple of mediocre but noisy native rock bands, one with a singer who's a camp plastic Jagger. Then Third Ear Band take over. Richard Coff's violin and Paul Minns' oboe start a dialogue that develops slowly as they explore the possibility of a simple melodic phrase. Ursula's cello lays a gruff foundation and then the drum starts. (...) I had seen the Third Ear work the same alchemy that afternoon in Amsterdam's *Paradiso*. Again, the place was cold, and the main attraction (the same British group) had blown the gig. Here, in the centre of Amsterdam's hip scene, Third Ear are still not well known and the local freaks have the *blasé* unconcern of people who stand at the centre of things. Again, from this inauspicious material, Third Ear made enthusiasm blossom. It didn't come from the head, from any impressive pyrotechnics or intellectualised concepts. It grew from the heart. Organically."

18ᵗʰ – *I.T.* vol. 1 issue 70 page 3, A poem by Dave Tomlin is published:

Sonnet

If that is that
Then
What is this?
If this is that
Then
What is what

The word is

Is

Did I mean me

When I said that?

Do I mean me

When I say this?

Is I me?

Yes, no, yes, no, yes, no, etc.

27th – Van Dykes (Plymouth)

1970

Al Stewart and Third Ear Band tour

This was the first promotional tour supporting the famous Al Stewart, organized by *Blackhill Enterprises* with the cooperation of *Harvest Records*. The set introduced was based on: *Hyde Park Raga*, *Druid 11*, *Cosmic Raga*, *The Sea* and *The Labyrinth*.

January

3rd – Queen Elizabeth Hall (London)

William Mann : "All four pieces on Saturday (and all eight on the record) were slow in pulse, full of drones and repeated figurations, usually a florid oboe cantillation[58] on the top. Their music is earnest yet carefree, sublimely unconscious of passing time, simple in vocabulary, skilful in ensemble (the violinist's intonation was sometimes suspect), but superficial, almost empty to one who listens attentively. (...) I would call it Un-Pop: English, Scottish and Irish folk dance has taught them something, Indian classical music a little but not enough about phraseology and variety of mood. Some may be consoled, some uplifted, by what they play; I respect

---

[58]   The ritual chanting of prayers and responses.

the intention but not the result". A few lines below, the journalist praised Al Stewart's dull performance...

Anthony Thorncroft writing in the *Financial Times* (January 5th) took the opposite view: "The secret is to close the eyes, let the head nod gently in time with Glen Sweeney's hand drum and enjoy a quiet trance. There is no real harm in falling asleep, for the Third Ear Band sells dreams."

6th – E.M.I. Studios (London). The band records some tracks for a new album.
22nd – Town Hall (Leith)
24th – Town Hall (Birmingham)
30th – North Staffs Polytechnic (Stoke-on-Trent)

February

1st – Colston Hall (Bristol)
4th – Norwich
11th – Fairfield Hall (Croydon)
13th – Guildhall (Southampton)
18th – Century Hall (Manchester)
20th – Crewe Hall (Sheffield)
21st – City Hall (Newcastle)
21st – Brooklands Technical College (Weybridge)
23th – Merry Inn
24th – Bligh's Hotel (Sevenoaks)
26th – Oxford
27th – The Dome (Brighton)
- End of the Al Stewart and Third Ear Band tour.
28th – Bangor University

March

3rd – Ealing Technical College.
5th – Sunderland
9th – Locarno (Bristol) TEB with *Genesis*

? – A piece on the TEB is published in *Zigzag* magazine # 10.

Zigzag was a well-respected rock folk blues publication started by Pete Frame in April 1969. It survived until January 1986.

12th – Stoke City

13th – North Oxfordshire Technical College (Banbury Oxen) TEB with *Arcadium*

14th – The Roundhouse (London) – *Atomic Sunrise* festival with TEB, *Liverpool Scene* and *Kevin Ayers & The Whole World*

16th – E.M.I. Studios (London). The band recorded some tracks for a new album.

19th – Scarborough

20th – Glasgow

22th – The Roundhouse (London) – *Implosion at the Roundhouse* TEB with Kevin Ayers and *Brinsley Schwarz*

26th – Tunbridge Wells

27th – Leicester

28th – Greek Street

29th-30th – Le Bourget airport, Paris – *Music Evolution 70* Festival

A seven-day festival with many groups, including *Pink Floyd, Hawkwind, Pretty Things, Grateful Dead, High Tide*, Al Stewart, Kevin Ayers. The festival was a complete failure and the Third Ear Band couldn't play. *IT* no. 77 (May 7th, 1969) reported: "The French pop festival (...) promised seven days of music, films, happenings, unusual instruments & exotic exhibition. Despite the featured non-stop sounds ... the whole thing collapsed after 3 days of chaos, confusion & conning. Inefficient publicity meant only 5,000 of the expected 100,000 turned up. Just as well, the food ran out. Cops disguised as firemen roamed about the freezing hall, joined by thirty private heavies hired by the organiser, Claude Rousseau. Some English groups were not allowed to play (Third Ear Band, *Cochise*), equipment failed to arrive and most of it fused anyway..."

April

3rd – Cornwall

? – Les Cousins Club (London) TEB with Nick Drake

? – EMI Studios (London) Recording of new album *Third Ear Band*.

20th – Net Television (France). Maybe a TV broadcast at the French *Channel 2* programme titled *Pop Deux* (see May 28th): TEB played *Hyde Park Raga* and an unannounced piece (maybe *Mosaic*).

24th – Essen TV

25th – Paradiso Club (Amsterdam)

26th – Delft (Holland

29th – Whiskey Villa Club (Walsall)

? – Boreham Wood

May

1st – Turnhout (Belgium)

2nd – Hassait (Belgium)

3nd – Glastonbury Tor Druid ceremony

8th – Polytechnic (Leeds)

TEB with *Edgar Broughton Band*

20th – BBC Studios (London). *Sound of Seventies* radio show

23th – Bromley

28th – ORTF (Office Radio Television France) – Channel 2 – *Pop Deux*. TEB played at the inn of Olympia (Paris) *Hyde Park Raga* and *(Mosaic?)*

Broadcast conducted by Patrice Blanc Francard with clips from Kevin Ayers, Bridget St. John and a 17:15 performance by the Third Ear Band - maybe recorded on April 20th (see before).

29th – Twickenham (London)

30th – Liverpool Stadium (Liverpool) TEB with *Edgar Broughton Band* and *Kevin Ayers & the Whole World*

June

? – *Third Ear Band* released by Harvest Records.

The new work got good reviews. *Disc & Music Echo* (June 20th, 1970) defined it as "a carefully made, thoughtful and excellent album", analysing in detail the four tracks: "It opens with a piece on *Air* – mainly featuring strings and very Stravinsky-ish. *Earth* is earth – a jolly, basic 2/4 rhythm with beautiful stereophonic contrapuntal oboe effect from Paul Minns. (...) The band paints a really beautiful musical image of *Fire*, capturing its basic power by the persistent steady percussion, and the flicker of the flames by the vacillating strings and woodwind. With *Water* they use cello and viola for the current while the oboe goes off into little eddies with a flowing, repetitive tune." Richard Williams, appreciatively reported "What they have to do with pop music I don't know, but that's a point of no importance and what matters is that they produce improvisational music of conceptual interest and fascinating content". He concluded: "Difficult music to rationalise about, then, because it simply exists and demands only to be taken on its own terms. If the concept interests you at all, I'm sure you'd enjoy it" ("Melody Maker", June 13th, 1970).

5th – Leicester

6th – Clitheroe Castle (Clitheroe)

TEB with Kevin Ayers and Michael Chapman

7th – Locarno (Bristol)

TEB with *Kevin Ayers & the Whole World, Edgar Broughton Band*

8th – BBC Studios (London) – *Top Gear* radio show

12th – BBC Studios (London) – *Sound of Seventies* radio show

14th – Heppenheim (Germany)

15th – Stuttgart (Germany)

18th – BBC Studios (London) – *Sound of the '70's* radio show

20th – BBC Studios (London) – Top Gear radio show

24th – Royal Festival Hall (London) – *The Sun Wheel Ceremony*

"The Third Ear Band have been working with the top electronic musicians in France, *Group de la Recherche Musicale de l'ORTF*, to create a musical/psychic experience in the concert hall. EMI has developed the concept of periphonic sound and loaned equipment to create a total 'sound surround' within which you can experience the combined effects of the Third Ear and the electronic ideas of Bayle and Parmigiani" (*IT* vol. 1 issue 81, June 18th, 1970). The band played two tracks with Bernard Parmegiani, *Fire* and the unpublished *Freak Dance*.

Chris Charlesworth wrote about the event in *Melody Maker* (July 4th, 1970): "The hall was barely half full. Accompanied at times by electronic machines making weird sounds the Third Ear Band droned through two lengthy pieces which were well accepted by their fans. Their music has no title and is 90 per cent improvisation. It just starts and finishes when the band feel like it. There's a vague anonymity about their music. However, violinist Richard Coff, who hates to make announcements, did mention that one piece was called *Freak Dance*. This contained some haunting oboe work from Paul Minns, and I rather enjoyed it. Their second piece was more ambitious and, I thought, less enjoyable. At one stage I actually saw Richard tapping his foot!"

27th – Kralingen, Rotterdam (Holland) – *Holland Festival 70*
TEB with Al Stewart, *Tyrannosaurus Rex, Family, Byrds, Country Joe and the Fish and etc.*

On the same day *Third Ear Band* appeared in the UK charts at #51 position (leaving on July 4th at #49).

? – *Harvest Records* promotion for *A Breath of Fresh Air* anthology a double anthology to promote the label's first albums. *IT* no. 81 (June 18th-July 2nd, 1970): "Harvest's first sampler – a double album at 29/11d, which can't be bad. And it ain't. Yeah! Good guide to the Harvest range of goodies, and despite of a pair of album tracks (the Shirley and Dolly Collins thing is horrible), it's really good value."

July

2nd-3rd – Munich TV (Munich, Germany) TEB record *Abelard & Heloise* soundtrack

The TV transposition of the famous Medieval story, directed by George Moorse with drawings by painter Herbert Fuchs (who died in 2006), told the dramatic, contrasting love story between Peter Abelard (1070-1142), a French philosopher and theologian with a troubled life, and Heloise, niece of the canon Fulbert who to stymie the passion between tutor and pupil, hired some villains to emasculate him.

4th – Hamburg (Germany)
6th – Ursula Smith and Richard Coff quit the band.

An agreement is signed by group members in which a clearance fee of £ 200 is paid to Smith for the recording of the second album and £300 to Coff for the rights to *Alchemy*, ensuring that they can't claim any rights over the recording other than for the royalties accruing from record sales.

15th – Glastonbury Tor – *Solstice Ceremony*

The band takes part in the ritual celebration of the Summer solstice organized by the London Order of Bards, Ovates and Druids

18th – Hyde Park (London) Free Concert with TEB, *Pink Floyd, Edgar Broughton Band* and *Kevin Ayers*.

24th-26th – Worthing – *Phun City Festival. The Furry Freaks Festival* TEB with *Mungo Jerry, Renaissance, Matthew's Southern Comfort*, Roger Ruskin Spear, *Noir, Formerly Fat Harry*, Michael Chapman... TEB played on 26th.

27th – IT vol. 1 issue 86. *Blackhill* ad for TEB: "Blackhill gives you a little more than an orgasm"...

August

1st – *Melody Maker* announces Smith & Coff split. Coff:

"We have actually been split for about a week now and Ursula and I are forming a new group. There were a lot of reasons for the split and the main one is the new group we want to form. It had a lot to do with musical policy and things like that." The fleeting band, which was named *Cosmic Overdose* won't record anything.

2nd – Cambridge Folk Festival.

The sixth edition of the legendary folk festival promoted on the ground of Cherry Hinton Hall with among others *Pentangle,* Ralph McTell, Bridget St. John and the Third Ear Band with a new line-up including Sweeney, Bridges, Buckmaster and Minns.

8th – *Melody Maker* ad for a third new album, which is never released.

Sweeney and Minns form *Electric Earband* with Paul Buckmaster on bass and Denim Bridges on electric guitar.

4th – London Lyceum (London)

TEB with *Edgar Broughton Band, Kevin Ayers and Formerly Fat Harry*

6th – BBC Studios (London) – *Sunday Concert* radio show

18th – Eindhoven (Holland)

? – Tilbury (England)

19th – Sittard (Holland)

21st – Bremen Radio (Germany) – *Beat Club*

TEB recorded three tracks live in the studio. With the band in the studio, a Nigerian session man called Gasper Lawal played congas.

26th – "Beat Club" German TV
29th – Twickenham (London)

October

1st – Manchester
2nd – Norfolk
10th – Ealing
14th – Assembly Hall (Walthamstow)
21st – Norwich
23th – Glasgow
27th – Scunthorpe
31st – Cambridge

November

5th – Lady Mitchell Hall (Cambridge)

Steve Peacock in *Sounds*[59] (November 7th, 1970): "The greater your discipline, the easier it is to know whether you have succeeded with your music. As Paul Buckmaster put it after the Third Ear Band's concert at the *Lady Mitchell Hall* in Cambridge, going on stage with the Third Ear is like being given a pair of skates and told to go onto an ice-rink and improvise an ice show with three other people. (...) Theirs is an ambitious approach to music, and even though they are in the process of discovering what they can do with the new line-up, it worked out very well for the most of their set and really lifted in a couple of places. (...) From the loose, organic feel of the first piece, to the intensity of the build-up in the last, Third Ear Band created some inspiring music on Saturday."

8th – The Roundhouse (London) – *Implosion*
TEB with *Soft Machine, Brinsley Schwarz* and others

---

[59]   The third largest weekly pop and rock music paper in the UK, published between 1970 and 1991 by two exiles from the *Melody Maker*, initially specialising in 'Progressive rock', then switching to Punk and Heavy Metal as the climate changed.

11th – E.M.I. Studios (London) The band record some tracks for the announced new album.

13th – George Hotel (Walsall)

14th – University of Sheffield (Sheffield)

18th – Bordeaux (France) TV programme recording

23rd – Paris (France). TV programme recording

24th – University of Keele

26th – EMI Studios recordings (London)

27th – Swansea University (London)

TEB with Bridget St.John

28th – Liverpool Stadium (Liverpool)

TEB with *Kevin Ayers, Edgar Broughton Band, Michael Chapman and Formerly Fat Harry*

December

2nd – Scunthorpe Civic Teatre

5th – Brighton Sussex University (Brighton)

TEB with *Black Sabbath, Patto, Dr Strangely Strange*

5th – Trident Studios (London).The band recorded three tracks for a forthcoming planned album.

8th – Sochaux (Swiss)

10th – Grenoble (France)

14th – Shepperton

1971

January

7th – BBC Studios (London) – *John Peel's Sunday Show*

15th – Newcastle

16th – A letter to *Melody Maker* by Paul Buckmaster published about the leadership of the band.

17th – BBC Studios (London) – *John Peel's Sunday Concert* radio show

During the programme, a third electric album (never released) is announced.

20th – Keele

29th – Free Trade Hall (Manchester)

TEB with *Keef Hartley Band*

30th – Colston Hall (Bristol)

February

6th – Southampton University (Southampton)

TEB with *Keef Hartley Band*

? – Recording Sessions (Balham, London). Third Ear Band retire to Sweeney and Minns' flat in Balham for three weeks to rehearse the third album.

12th – E.M.I. Studios (London). The band recorded *Mistress to the Sun* intended as a single for the forthcoming album.

March

6th – University of Sussex (Brighton)

7th – Guildford – *Contemporary Music in Guilford*

TEB with *Kevin Ayers & The Whole World* and *Poppa Ben Hook*

11th – E.M.I. Studios (London). The band recorded more some tracks for the new album.

19th – Warmington

April

2nd–3rd–4th – Amsterdam (Holland)

16th – Ardleigh House (Hornchurch)

23th – Ipswich

May

1st – York

8th – Manchester

9th – University of Essex (Colchester) – *Essex Arts Festival* TEB with *Family* and Roy Harper

26th – Top Rank (Doncaster) TEB with *Egg*

Around this period, TEB was contacted by Roman Polanski at the suggestion of the actress who starred in *Abelard & Heloise.*

4th – E.M.I. Studios (London). The band record *In D* for the new album.

12th – Wakefield

16th – Southsea

17th – Horst Konigstein

23th – Durham

24th – Glastonbury Faire Festival

TEB with *Henry Cow, Fairport Convention, Edgar Broughton Band*
      Doncaster

July

? – Air Recording Studios (London) – *Macbeth* recording sessions.

   The recording sessions started at George Martin's *Air Studios* (London). They work twelve hours a day for six weeks. For this occasion they are joined by violinist Simon House from *High Tide*.

August

15th-23rd – tour in Belgium

24th – Air Recording Studios (London) – *Macbeth* recording session.

27th-29th – Clacton-on-Sea – *Weeley Festival* T

EB with the *Edgar Broughton Band, Colosseum, Faces, Arthur Brown, Quintessence* etc.

September

4th – Hyde Park (London) – *Hyde Park free concert* TEB with Kevin Ayers, Jack Bruce, Roy Harper

The last *Blackhill Enterprises* free concert.

October

? – *Beat Instrumental*" # 102 publish an article on the Third Ear Band written by Steve Turner.

1972

January

? – *Macbeth* album released.

      Free copies are given by *Rolling Stone* to new subscribers. Again opinions in the press were very favourable. Deborah Thomas wrote: "Film track music often falls down when you take the film away. But the score painstakingly created for Roman Polanski's disturbing version of Macbeth stands on its own. A baleful, but strangely beautiful interweaving of modern and medieval music by the Third Ear Band."

23rd – The Roundhouse (London) – *Benefit for U.C.S* TEB with *Matching Mole, Trees*, Keith Christmas and Mike Gibbs
25th – BBC Studios (London) – Studio T1
John Peel Sessions
31st – Plaza Theatre (London) – Roman Polanski's *Macbeth* premiere.

      "Best film of the Year Award", writes the *National Board of Review*, "Polanski's triumph" says the *Daily Express*.
Fergus Cashin in the *Sun*: "It's sexy! It's modern. It's a work of genius. One hell of story! Polanski gives us a movie to queue for. Not be missed. Better than a Western. I love it."

February

5th – Essex University (Colchester) Benefit concert in aid of striking miners with TEB, Mick Abrahams Band, Lol Coxill and others
12th – Town Hall (Birmingham)
15th – Colston Hall (Bristol)
> At around this time Paul Buckmaster quit the band.

March

1st – Chelsea College (London).
TEB with *Soft Machine* and *East of Eden*
3rd – Seymour Hall (London) – *Fun 'an Games*
TEB with *MC5*, *Pink Fairies* and *Magic Michael*
16th – Kingston Polytechnic
18th – Sweeney announces to a new line-up to *Melody Maker*, besides Sweeney and Minns, Simon House on violin and VCS3, Peter Pauli (ex *High Tide*) on bass and Mike Marchant on guitar an voice.
21st – BBC Studios (London) – *Drummond* radio show
> Around this period E.M.I. Harvest terminates its contract with TEB.

April

20th – "IT" vol. 1 n. 128
> *International Times* announces: "Third Ear Band - a group temporarily without a recording contract.. It seems that EMI's "progressive underground label" (or its overlords) doesn't see fit to employ "pot smokers" amongst its roster of artists. Dear me, we don't want people like Syd Barrett to be influenced in any way, do we?"

28th – London School of Economics (LSE).
TEB with *Camel*, Sandy Denny and others

June

3rd – Clitheroe Castle (Clitheroe) – *Clitheroe Festival*.
TEB with *Trees*, Bridget St. John, *MC5*
9th – King Cross Cinema (London)
TEB with Hawkwind

"As a 19-year-old immigrant from Baltimore. Glen Sweeney was very nice to me. I met him backstage at the premier of *Matching Mole*'s *Little Red Record*. He was the first person to start talking to me. I told him that I had seen Third Ear Band at the Kings Cross Cinema that summer supporting *Hawkwind*. I remember Third Ear Band played last that night well into the dawn they were magnificent". (Craig Runyon on the Facebook TEB's page, September 2013).

July

1st – Battersea Pavilion (London) – *War on Want Benefit* TEB with Steve Tilston, Pete Atkin and others
9th – The Roundhouse (London) – *Implosion*.
TEB with *Egg* and *Edgar Broughton Band*
18th – Marquee Club (London) TEB with *Camel*
22nd - Philp Palmer in *Billboard* magazine: "Blackhill, the management and production company, has severed its connections with EMI. "There is now no contractual relationship between us", commented Peter Jenner... Blackhill artists have been released through EMI for nearly four years. The Third Ear Band and Chris Spedding are now free and we owe EMI one more album from Kevin Ayers" claimed Jenner. "Only Roy Harper is still tied to EMI". Blackhill is currently looking for a new production deal although no negotiations have yet been finalized."

September

30th – Battersea Town Hall (London)
TEB with *Matumbi Band*

October

11ᵗʰ – Bumpers (London)
TEB with *Arthur Brown's Kingdom Dome*, Graham Bond etc.

November

16ᵗʰ– TEB signs a record contract with *Island Records.*
      Thanks to Blackhill's manager Peter Jenner, who has placed *The Sharks* with Chris Blackwell, TEB signed a contract with *Island* for a new album, which for the first time will feature formal songs composed and played by Marchant, who got inspiration from the Tarot. The agreement scheduled the following track-list: *Cosmic Wheel, I the Key, Hierophant, Magus, New Horizon and Ten Dimensional Landscape.*
17ᵗʰ – Chelmsford Mid-Essex College

December

16ᵗʰ – *Billboard* magazine Vol. 84 n. 51 (page 48:) "*March Artists*, the agency arm of CBS has secured sole representation of *Blackhill* artists Kevin Ayers, Third Ear Band and Roy Harper."

1973

January

23ʳᵈ – Arts Theatre (Cambridge) – *Multimedia Mixed Festival.*
      TEB performed after *Gentle Giant* with a new line-up: Sweeney on drums, Minns on oboe, Simon House on violin, VCS3 and synth, Mike Marchant on guitar and voice and Dave Tomlin on bass and voice.

February

28th – Royal Albert Hall (London) – *1972 Film Performance Nominations. Awards Presentation Dinner & Dance*.

    TEB gets a nomination for the *Macbeth* soundtrack. The winner was Nino Rota for *The Godfather*.

March

10th – University of Warwick (Coventry) – *Festival*
A three-day festival (9th-11th March) with a lot of bands and events (*Arthur Brown's Kingdom Come, Albion Country Band*, classical music, poetry, theatre and films...).

13th – University of East Anglia (Norwich).
TEB with Clair Hamil

May

18th – BBC Studios (London) – *Pete Drummond'* sequence radio session with Al Stewart
19th – Hampstead Town Hall (London)
TEB with *Global Village Trucking Company*

August

24th-25th – London – *3rd Windsor Free Festival*.
    A festival with a lot of bands, among them *Hawkwind, Pink Fairies, Skin Alley*.

October

26th – Hemel Hempstead Arts Centre (London)
TEB with Kevin Coyne

At around this time, *Blackhill* drops the group.

1976

May

? – *Experiences* released by Harvest Records.

The album, sold at a very special price (£ 1.99!) is launched in the *Harvest Heritage* series with a promo poster.

Back in London with a project to reform the Third Ear Band, Sweeney met Terry Haxton and Gary Heath (probably through a magazine ad). Both had previously played in unsuccessful bands. In the end the new line-up is Sweeney and Minns, with Heath on bass and keyboards and Mick Carter on guitar. They rehearse for some weeks at a Pub in Swiss Cottage (London). But no contract is forthcoming and the band splits again.

1977

June

25th – *New Musical Express* announces Third Ear Band are to reform...

Spring-July

A new attempt to reform the band, this time with ex-*Magic Muscle* Rod Roodway.

Also during the year a new project for the Third Ear Band - thought of as a pop-rock group - involves Sweeney, Minns and Carter. There are a lot of rehearsals (mostly in Minn's flat in Sheperd's Bush) but very few concerts.

1978

June

4ᵗʰ – Roundhouse Downstairs Theatre (London)

Yet another new TEB line-up with Sweeney, Minns, Carter and new musicians Marcus Beale (on Fender violin) and Brian Diprose (bass), the latter a former member of *Ragged Robin* and a session man for folk artists like Anne Briggs and Steve Ashley.

? – Norwich University

During that year Paul Minns quit (not interested in investing energy in a pop-rock project) leading to a new TEB line-up with Sweeney, Carter, Diprose and Jim "Gipsy" Hayes (on vocals). This version also recorded the album *Apocalyptic Anthems* at *Dansette Studios* in Kent under the name *Hydrogen Jukebox*. These tracks, again inspired by the Tarot, had been composed by Sweeney during his 'houseboat period' (1974-1975).

1979

German underground filmmaker Clemens Klopfenstein uses Third Ear Band music for his b/w film "Geschichte der Nacht" (Story of Night): "... a black-and-white record of European cities in the dark (2-5am), from Basle to Belfast. Quiet, and meditative; what emerges most strongly is an eerie sense of city landscapes as deserted film sets, in which the desolate architecture overwhelms any sense of reality. The only reassurance that we are not in some endless machine-Metropolis is the shadow of daytime activity: a juggernaut plunging through a darkened village, a plague of small birds in the predawn light. The whole thing is underscored by a beautiful 'composed' soundtrack, from quietly humming streetlamps to reggae and the rumble of armoured cars in Belfast. A strange and remarkable combination of dream, documentary and science-fiction" (Chris Auty in a programme Note for the *London Film Co-op*).

1984

The Harvest Story vol. 1. Art School Dancing anthology is released.

1987

July

Italian freelance journalist Luca Ferrari, while researching Syd Barrett, interviews Peter Jenner and is given Glen Sweeney's address. He meets the drummer & his wife Carolyn Looker at their home in Shepherd's Bush (London) and tries to convince him to reform TEB.

1988

Summer

After months of hesitation and suspicion Sweeney agrees to reform the band. During that summer, Sweeney (hand drums), Mick Carter (electric guitar and effects), Paul Minns (oboe) and Samuel Allen (a young violinist with academic career and Dave Tomlin's pupil) rehearsed some new pieces at the squatted Cambodian Embassy in London. Meanwhile *The Ear Management,* a sort of agency with the aim to organize band's concerts – mainly in Italy - is founded. They press promotional t-shirts with the TEB concert playbill at Purcell Room in 1970.

September – *The Peanuts* tour

This short tour, so-called by Sweeney because of the tiny fees it attracts, is organized by The Ear Management *(Luca Ferrari) with Gigi Bresciani's* Music On *agency. Third Ear Band are nw Sweeney, Carter, Minns and Allen.*
8th – Chiostro di S. Agostino (Bergamo)

TEB with *Zsaratnok* and *Whippersnapper*
9th – Umbertide (Perugia) – *Rockin' Umbria* festival TEB with *Novalia* and *Peter Principle*

November - Band rehearsals at the Cambodian Embassy.

December

A second Italian tour with four gigs (Gorizia, Bergamo, Genova and Viterbo), organised by *The Ear Management*, is cancelled owing to Sweeney's unexpected personal problems.

1989

January

The Bad News, Baby! Tour.
Three concerts, once again organized by *The Ear Management* and *Music On*, with yet another new line-up: Sweeney, Carter, Lyn Dobson (flute and saxes) and Ursula Smith (violin).
11th – Teatro Impavidi (Sarzana, La Spezia)
12th – Psycho Club (Genova)
13th – Sala Piatti (Bergamo)TEB with Martin Carthy and John Kirkpatrick
14th – Circolo Tuxedo (Piacenza)
This was a day-off gig, just before the band went back to England. Only 50 people in the audience for a very good performance.

March

Live Ghosts is released by *Materiali Sonori* on LP, cassette and CD to enthusiastic reviews. Edwin Pouncey in the *New Musical Express* (August 19th): "New Age fans could do worse than dip into this smoky swamp of drifting sound. No dreamy blue sky gazing anthems here though, instead expect storm clouds, ectoplasmic mirages and as near to an out-of-body experience as you'll get from listening to a mere LP. Let their ghosts haunt your house soon".

March-May

The band, in the tour line-up (Sweeney, Carter, Dobson and Smith), goes into *Alchemical Studios* to record the new album announced as *Magic*. A demo tape is recorded. Nothing is released until 2016, when *Gonzo Multimedia* issue the CD *Exorcisms*. (Gonzo HST371CD).

June

25th – Chiostro di S. Agostino (Bergamo)
Luca Ferrari shows TEB's album *Live Ghosts* at the fifth edition of *Folk Out*, three days of concerts and events promoted by *Gigi Bresciani*.

July

8th – Vinci (Florence)
TEB with *Novalia* and *Nazca*
Because of her job as a teacher, Ursula couldn't stay in the band. Allen Samuel returned to replace her.

October

Neil Black, a young violinist who had played with *UB40*, Joan Armatrading and John Porter joins, replacing Samuel Allen. The new TEB record some rehearsals in London, later titled *Necromancer Suite*.

November TEB at *Alchemical Studios* to record a new album with the final title *Magic Music*.
24th – Borgo Castello (Gorizia) – *Aria, terra, fuoco, acqua...*
25th – Sala Piatti (Bergamo)

In the afternoon the band meet the students of *Centro Didattico Produzione Musica* [Music Production Educational Centre] for a talk on "Research, technique and electroacoustic music instruments".

December

15th – "Sir George Robey" pub (London)

1990

January

Magic Music is released by *Materiali Sonori* on LP and CD.

February

A new tour, organized by *Materiali Sonori* with the cooperation of *The Ear Management* to promote the new album, with Sweeney, Carter, Dobson and Black.
3rd – Teatro Vespasiano (Rieti)
4th – Il Classico (Roma)
5th – Prego Club (Milan)
The gig, broadcast live on the Italian radio programme *RAI Stereonotte* is compromised by problems with the PA system. A nervous Dobson quits the stage, while other band members play on as an acoustic trio.
6th – Auditorium Flog (Florence)
TEB with *Novalia*
That day, just before the gig, Glen Sweeney is invited by Italian avant-garde composer Fabio Capanni (leader of an Italian group called *Nazca*) to record in a studio in Florence with *Amon Duul*'s founder Chris Karrer. A track, titled *Old Man Kangaroo pt. 2* results, later appearing on a *Materiali Sonori* compilation *The Greetings Compact*.
7th – Sgt. Pepper (Genova) – *The concert*
9th – Teatro Municipale (Meda, Venice)

10th – Teatro Petrella (Longiano, Forlì)
Spring

Sweeney Interviewed by Nigel Cross for the English undergrpund magazine *Unhinged*.

May

12th – Dog Club (London)

August

27th – Smallbrook Stadium, Ryde (Isle of Wight) – *Isle of Wight Festival – 20th Anniversary 1970-1990*
TEB with *Edgar Broughton, Audience, Trees*, **DJ Pete Drummond**

September

Glen wrote me a letter proposing to reform The Giant Sun Trolley for a new record: "(... I have a new musical event, it will be the return of the Giant Sun Tolley with the star Dave Tomlin on genar (a musical instrument invented by Dave), I will play drums and Mick will play guitar and effects. Mick will record an LP of this music on digital DAT tape; we will then send you some copies to send to record companies. If we are successful you can get us some dates to promote the LP. I will be busy getting all the promo and photos together for the start, which will take about six months, so we will be ready in March..."

1991

Hydrogen Jukebox's *Prophesies* released by *Materiali Sonori*.

March

Nothing more happened with the new Giant Sun Trolley; Sweeney's new group will be *Elektric Third Ear Band*. They go into *Alchemical Studios* to record a new album. Barry Pilcher replaces Lyn Dobson on sax. Meanwhile, due to disagreements with the band regarding their relationship with the record label, *The Ear Management* winds up.

April

12th – Dog Club (London)
This concert was played as *Elektric TEB* with Barry Pilcher on sax.

May

12th – Il Posto (Verona)
Managed by the *Music On* agency. This concert was cancelled.

August

29th – Sant'Anna Arresi (Carbonia – Sardinia) – *Ai confini tra Sardegna e Jazz*. TEB *Quintet* with Mick Carter, Glen Sweeney and the *Roger Eno Trio*

September

5th – Naples
Lyn Dobson back in the TEB line-up, replacing Pilcher.

December

28th – piazza Navona – Rome

1992

April

A new Italian mini-tour organized by *Music On*. TEB line-up is Sweeney, Carter, Dobson and Black.

Glen tries to involve Luca Ferrari in a new adventure, but Luca is not interested in managing the group anymore. On a postcard Glen writes: "Dear Luca, sorry to hear you are an idealist because playing great music means having a great band and that costs money. My job is getting work for the band and selling records so that more and more people get to hear the band, which makes me an idealist with experience! Anyway, come and hear the band in Bergamo, the first week in April. I will bring you a Jukebox CD. Love and peace, Glen".

11th – Circolo ARCI *Salardi* (Mantova)
12th – Folk Club *Gli Zanni* (Ranica, Bergamo) – *Magiche alchimie*" (*Magic Alchemy*)
With an audience of about fifty people, in a tiny club - the last ever TEB concert.

TEB go back to the studio to record a new album, unsatisfied with the results from the year before. Lyn Dobson on wind instruments and vocals. For the first time TEB record two vocal tracks.

December

Around Christmas, Glen Sweeney has an acute heart-attack and remains in hospital for some weeks.

1993

At the beginning of the year, *Brain Waves* is released by *Materiali Sonori*.

March

Glen Sweeney sends a message to Luca Ferrari, announcing he will stop live concerts and intends to write a novel based on TEB's story. He also proposes to publish records and books by and on the Third Ear Band. He admits not being satisfied with the *Materiali Sonori* agreement and wants to find a new record company to release some remaining tapes.

1994

During the year some new CDs are released by *Voiceprint* and *Blueprint,* with covers designed by Carolyn Looker.

1996

The Italian home-publishing *Stampa Alternativa* releases Luca Ferrari's book on the Third Ear Band *Necromancers of the drifting West*, including a CD of previously unreleased music from *Abelard & Heloise*.

1997

Paul Minns, back in Scotland after the last TEB reunion, commits suicide.

1999

Alchemy is reissued on vinyl by *Drop Out Records*.

October

Carolyn Looker paints a work inspired by her and Glen's story, intended for the cover of a tribute CD proposed by Luca Ferrari, *The Dragon Wakes*. The album is compiled from unreleased studio and radio tracks but is never released.

However, the legendary fourth 'lost' album, recorded in 1972, emerges from the vaults thanks to (the late) sound engineer Ron Cort, and is published by *Angel Air* as *The Magus* in 2004.

2005

August

17th – The Royal Star & Garter Home – Richmond (London).

After a series of heart-attacks and a long sojourn at *The Royal Star & Garter Home*, a residential hospital in Richmond where he recovered from his previous heart attack in spring 1999, Glen Sweeney "dies peacefully".
"(...) It was a beautiful ceremony. Rather than a conventional funeral, Steve Pank read from the *Egyptian Book of the Dead* and tracks from *Alchemy* were played; incense was burning, Glen was in a raffia coffin with sunflowers on top. Everyone said what a wonderful experience it was and some were reminded of being at an early Third Ear Band concert. I'm sure Glen would have approved" (from a postcard sent by Carolyn Looker to Luca Ferrari on September 3rd, 2005).

In the same year Roger Bunn, formerly of Giant Sun Trolley, also passes away.

2007

April

   TEB's original viola player, Ben Cartland, dies. He was living in
Northamptonshire where he played *avantgarde* music with the
Northamptonshire Composers Association. He was writing a book of memoires...

2009

November
13th – Guitarist Mike Marchant passes away.

2011

October

3rd – A DVD of rare TEB television appearances is released by *Gonzo Multimedia*
as *The Lost Broadcasts,* featuring TV videos from the 1970 German programme
Beat Club.

2012

January

   From the miracle of *YouTube* a very rare short clip of the band emerges
playing at Hyde Park on June 7th, 1969.

September

   Another unexpected miracle! On *INAfr* (the Website of French television
http://www.ina.fr/) a rare 27:00 TEB broadcast recorded on May 25th, 1970 at
the *Olympia Theatre* in Paris becomes available. Two tracks (*Hyde Park Raga*

and *Mosaic* played by the legendary quartet of Sweeney, Minns, Smith and Coff.

2013

November

Pianist and multi-instrumentist Mel Davis (who played on *Alchemy*) passes away. Lyn Dobson: "I can say first that Mel was an exceptionally warm, empathetic and caring person, who almost single-handed, started the Free Music movement in the entire world (including the United States!). He also pioneered the self-sufficiency movement in England. I first met him in Luton in my early twenties at Art college, where we played with a young Graham Collier, before all moving to London..."

2014

June

Another unknown short video of TEB from 1971 emerges on the Web, of the band (Sweeney, Minns, Buckmaster, Bridges and House) playing a short version of *Air* at Abbey Road studio.

September

Gonzo Multimedia announces two new records by the TEB, of old material, in cooperation with *Ghettoraga Archive.*

2015

May

English Gonzo Multimedia and *Ghettoraga Archive* publishes *Necromancers of the Drifting West*, a brand new Third Ear Band CD with "Rare gems from the Vaults". The record is edited by Luca Chino Ferrari who writes the booklet detailing the history of the tracks.

June

Luca Chino Ferrari publishes a biography of the English jazz pianist Mike Taylor for *Gonzo Multimedia*, with memories of Dave Tomlin and Steve Pank who played with and knew him in the Sixties.

September

Gonzo and *Ghettoraga* publish *New Forecasts from the Third Ear Almanac*, official reissue of a rare old live cassette recorded in *Sarzana* in January 1989.

2016

February

Gonzo and *Ghettoraga* publish *Exorcism*, an album showcasing recordings from 1988-1989, when the musicians involved were Glen Sweeney, Mick Carter, Ursula Smith, Lyn Dobson and Allen Samuel: three tracks from the Cambodian Embassy rehearsal (Summer 1988) and five from the sessions for *Magic Music* (May-November 1989), with a different line-up from those released on the *Materiali Sonori* album published in 1990.

March

New footage of TEB in 1970 emerges from the Web. Aired by German WDR TV on March 28th, 2016. This brief gem (2:38) may have been recorded by *Essen TV* on April 24th, 1970. It's the last part of *Earth*, played by Sweeney, Minns, Coff and Smith.

2017

September

Brain Waves CD reissued with Carolyn Looker's original cover and booklet notes by Luca Chino Ferrari, with a bonus track recorded in the same year.

November

7th – Paul Buckmaster passes away at his home in Los Angeles.

2018

November

23rd – *Third Ear Band* reissued in a 3-CD re-mastered and expanded edition by *Esoteric Recordings* (PECLE 32653)

2019

January

Music from Macbeth reissued in a re-mastered and expanded edition by *Esoteric Recordings* (PECLEC 2656).

March

29th – *Alchemy* reissued in a re-mastered and expanded edition by *Esoteric Recordings* (PECLEC 22668).

June

31st – *The Magus* reissued by *Tiger Bay* in 12" vinyl format (TB6430).

September

27th – *Alchemy* vinyl 180-gr edition released by *Esoteric Records* (PECLECLP 2668).

FIN

About the Compiler of this Book:

Luca Chino Ferrari is an Italian underground paperback writer who managed the Third Ear Band in the eighties, editing and producing albums for the band. In 1997 he published the first book about the Thirds, *Necromancers of the Drifting West*. Since 2009 he has run *Ghettoraga*, the *Official Third Ear Band Esoteric Archive* (http://ghettoraga.blogspot.it). Following books on cult musicians Syd Barrett, Tim Buckley, Captain Beefheart and Nick Drake, in 2015 he published *Out of Nowhere*, the first biography of jazz pianist Mike Taylor.

Thanks to:

Dave Tomlin, David Loxley, Ursula Smith, Clive Kingsley, Denim Bridges, Paul Buckmaster, Linda Kattan, Ray Stevenson, Brian Meredith, Brian Diprose, Rod Goodway, Morgan Fisher, Dave Harries, Mary Hayes, Martin Davidson, Terry Day, Ray Stevenson, Karen Francis, Barry Plummer, Mike Friggis, Graham Clarke, Martin Cook, Will Hullbert, Mirco Delfino (TEB Italian Facebook channel), Sean Breadin, Muz Murray, Francesco Paladino, Napo Camassa III, Rachael Tyrell, Alessandro Monti, Gigi Bresciani, Jon Limbert and Tim Schwartz.

Special thanks to Carolyn Looker and Steve Pank for suggestions and encouragement, Chris Cutler and everyone at ReR.